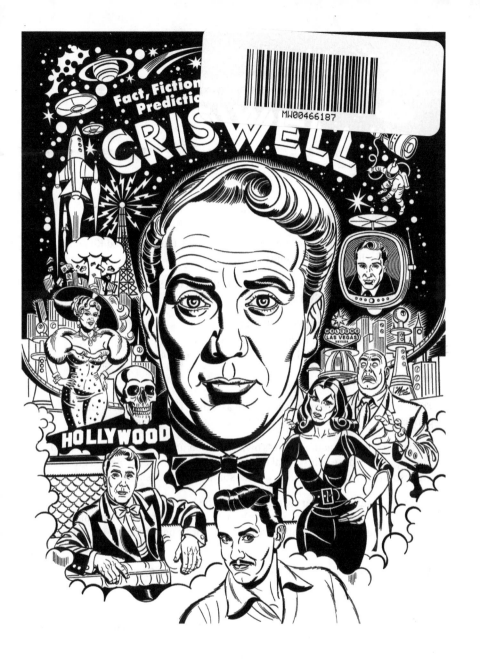

Edwin Lee Canfield

Headpress

A HEADPRESS BOOK

First published by Headpress in 2023, Oxford, United Kingdom
headoffice@headpress.com

**FACT, FICTIONS, AND THE FORBIDDEN PREDICTIONS
OF THE AMAZING CRISWELL**

A CIP catalogue record for this book is available from the British Library

ISBN	978-1-915316-00-4	paperback
ISBN	978-1-915316-01-1	ebook
ISBN	NO-ISBN	hardback (with colour content)

HEADPRESS. POP AND UNPOP CULTURE.

Exclusive NO-ISBN special edition hardbacks and other items of interest are available at **HEADPRESS.COM**

Contents

Dedicated to my father, Edwin Keith Canfield.
The most voracious reader I have known.

Foreword

One morning in the mid-60s my mother and I were apartment-hunting. Newly arrived in Hollywood from New York—and of limited means at the time—our mission was to find suitable quarters for our family of four. It had to be located near to my Dad's work, and my brother's—later to be my—school, Blessed Sacrament. Right on the same block as the latter, at the corner of Selma and Cassil, was an apartment building with four separate flats. The lower left bore a sign—"Apartment to Rent." We rang the doorbell for the upper right. The door opened by a tall, stout woman with wild eyes. This was our first view of Halo Meadows—Mrs. Myrtle Criswell. She and my mother had a long chat, agreed on the rent—and three years of adventure began.

Through the eyes of a child, the Criswells appeared—well, strange. Mrs. Criswell favored bikinis, which displayed her ample figure to some disadvantage. Mr. Criswell—who habitually spoke in the stentorian tone familiar to those who know him only in recordings—remains in my memory in either formal wear, suit and tie, or enormous boxer shorts. Their Sunday brunches gathered their friends on a weekly basis, and as tenants we were expected to appear. Suffice it to say that the guests and goings on were an education neither my brother nor me have forgotten in the decades since!

After we moved to the San Fernando Valley, we had nothing to do with Mr. Criswell and his friends. Decades later, when Tim Burton resurrected them in *Ed Wood*, the four of us were as amused as we were astonished. Through the kindness of *New Yorker* writer John Whalen, I was reunited with Claudia Polifronio in 1999; she had been Criswell's art director on his TV show, and was our favorite neighbor in the building. Hosting a "Criswell Apocalypse Party" at

1

the master's old hangout, Boardner's, to commemorate the date he had predicted the world would end, I was greatly amused to hear Claudia's view of the bizarre events we had lived with. It certainly put that strange time in perspective! Some few years later, together with the author of this book and my friend Tequila Mockingbird, I hosted another party, for Criswell's centennial. I think it fair to say that I feel grateful to have lived for a few years in Criswell's strange world—and just as grateful not to have been a permanent resident.

But I am extremely grateful to Ed Canfield for bringing him to life again and illuminating the dark corners of his biography. For all that conversations at Criswell House might center on ESP, UFOs, Bigfoot, hauntings— a sort of living *Coast to Coast* show, so to speak— Criswell's tale is not one of a Master of the Occult, but of a showman who sought fame any way he could find it. He had the same relationship with the bizarre and the unseen that Walter Winchell had with the news— it was simply another way of achieving the quest for success. If Criswell's story ended sadly, so did Winchell's, for all that the columnist had was a longer and stronger run. In any case, the time we spent living under his roof has definitely been a continual undercurrent in my life, and I am grateful to see him receiving at last an appropriate biography. His story not only sheds light on the era he lived in, but on the eternal quest for fame.

Charles A. Coulombe
Trumau, Austria
May 24, 2021

"Some people foretell the end of time, but the end of time will never be on time."

William "Billy" Childish,
21st century poet

Introduction

Ah, greetings my friend.

We are all interested in the future for that is where you and I are going to spend the rest of our lives, whether we want to or not! And remember my friend, these future events will affect you. The future is in your hands. So let us remember the past, honor the present, and be amused at the future.

Criswell

My fascination and obsession with Criswell began after seeing *Plan 9 From Outer Space* (1957) and the Tim Burton biopic *Ed Wood* (1994), then reading his first book of predictions, *Criswell Predicts From Now to the Year 2000!* (1968) in the year 2000. His mesmerizing and serious delivery of his outrageous prognostications and the fact that his predicted date for the end of the world on August 18, 1999, had passed also drew me under his spell.

My original intent was to write a biopic script or produce a documentary film. I began scouring the then wondrous and new world of the Internet for any mention of Criswell or anyone who had known the man. Online genealogies, newspaper archives, blogs and articles, search engines, and even findagrave.com provided leads to contacting many of Criswell friends and associates such as glamour ghoul Vampira (Maila Nurmi) and Ed Wood actor Paul Marco. I contacted Mr. Marco by phone and he promptly told me in a bitter tone that I had no right to write or produce Criswell's story due to me not actually knowing him and that I needed some kind of special permission. At the end of the call he said, "I'll talk to you later." Sadly, I didn't talk to him later. I was to be in the Los Angeles for work and had planned to meet and interview him. He passed away the day before I arrived.

The more I researched and interviewed contacts, the deeper story of Criswell and his just as eccentric and bizarre wife, known as Halo Meadows, began to surface and reveal an even more fascinating and strange tale.

I attempted to sell the Criswell biopic and documentary project without any takers, but I did receive a very nice rejection letter from HBO. I then decided to make Criswell into a book project which I proposed to publishers a few times over the years without any success. I did get a rejection email from author, editor, and founder of Feral House publishing, Adam Parfrey with some good editorial advice which I ignored at the time.

Over the next twenty years, I would return to the Criswell manuscript when I had time or discovered new information. The worldwide pandemic of 2020 not predicted by Criswell, but certainly foreseen by the scientific and medical communities, provided me the time and ability to focus and return to Criswell's story. Due to the continued proliferation of information on the Internet, I was able to fill in some holes in the story and bring it to a place where I felt it was worthy of publishing and certainly relevant to the current "End Times" feel to the world. I sent out a number of proposals and promptly received a reply from David Kerekes of Headpress publishing with sound editorial advice which I didn't ignore and helped to finally bring the project to an end appropriately.

Criswell also known as "Criswell Predicts!" dubbed himself the "20th Century Nostradamus." He was also called "America's Foremost Prophet" and based on "trend, precedent, pattern of habit, human behavior, and the unalterable law of cycle!" he claimed 87%

accuracy in his predictions. Cris (to his friends,) is known mainly for his opening monologue, narration, and closing comments in Ed Wood's *Plan 9 From Outer Space* (1956), but his career went well beyond that and his persona was a product of the continuing growth and onslaught of mass media during the mid-twentieth century. He hosted his *Criswell Predicts* show on local Los Angeles television, also recorded for broadcast in other markets, penned a syndicated column that was in 300 to 400 newspapers nationwide, hosted radio programs on over eighty-five stations, made numerous guest appearances on network television talk shows such as Jack Paar and Johnny Carson's *Tonight Show* (where he inspired Carson's recurring character "Karnak the Magnificent") and the *Mike Douglas* and *Merv Griffin* shows. He also appeared on *Hollywood Palace* and *Rowan and Martin's Laugh-In* as well as countless Los Angeles television programs. Always productive, he also authored three books of predictions, released a record album of predictions, and appeared in two other Ed Wood films as well.

While there were others dabbling in the realms of psychic prognostication and other forms of clairvoyance at the time, the Amazing Criswell is one of the first pop-celebrity psychics. His ever-present black tuxedo with sequined lapels symbolized the razzle-dazzle Hollywood showmanship that drew his loyal following throughout the mid-to-late 1950s. His place among the assorted cast of characters that were Ed Wood's friends, his lifelong friendship with Mae West, his unusual home life with his eccentric and provocative wife, and his volumes of predictions, most extremely bizarre and inaccurate, further solidified his place amongst Hollywood's mysterious and macabre. Among his close circle of friends, he openly denied any psychic abilities and freely admitted himself to be a fraud. That sentiment was not shared among a number of his friends and associates, many of which continued to believe that he did possess psychic talents.

Criswell's mesmerizing delivery had an appeal all its own. The seeming solemnity of his diction and vocabulary, his unusual appearance—the black evening wear made a deep contrast with his extremely pallid skin and blonde spit curl—effectively compensated for the incredible nature of his predictions. Explaining his abilities in the preface to his first book published in 1968, *Criswell Predicts From Now to the Year 2000!* (hereafter *CPY2K*) he says, "My predictions are not written to win literary attention. I am not sure what they all mean. Some are frighteningly explicit. Others are somewhat vague. All are based on conscious study and sub-conscious realizations." And in the preface of his second book published in 1969, *Your Next Ten Years— Criswell Predicts* (*YN10YCP*), "My parents were shocked at my opinions, which I handed out like samples of soap, for I somehow knew of my gift of deduction.

You start with the facts, and then. . . ."

On Our Stage—In Person

An Accurate Glimpse of the Future

CRISWELL PREDICTS

HE HAS HELPED OTHERS — HE WILL HELP YOU

SPECIAL LADIES ONLY SHOW

SATURDAY MORNING — 10:15 A.M.

CRISWELL Will Deliver His Famous Lecture

"HOW TO SNARE A MAN AND HOLD HIM"

Box Office Will Open at 10:00 A. M. for
Ladies' Matinee

NO MEN ADMITTED SATURDAY MORNING

Criswell Will Appear
ON OUR STAGE
TONIGHT at 7:20 and 10:00

Saturday Ladies Only Matinee — 10:15 A. M.
Saturday Afternoon — 2:40

Ribbon of Time

Many people ask me "Are you fearful of the future, for you know what is going to happen?" Frankly, I am not! The future is merely the continuation of the past abridged by the present. It will never be any later than it is at this moment, and another second has ticked away bringing us all nearer to Eternity.

Criswell

Jeron Charles Criswell King was born on August 18, 1907, in King Station, Indiana, which was south of the town of Princeton in Gibson County located in the Patoka Township. King Station came into existence with the building of the Evansville & Terre Haute railroad about 1851. For a year or more the road's terminal was at the King family farm about a half-mile north of where the station was built. A turntable was used there, and a stagecoach carried passengers on north. The original King family came from Virginia. Jeron's three times great-grandfather Samuel King came from North Carolina to Indiana about 1799 and settled in Gibson County near Fort Branch when it was only a Native American outpost. His son John was a babe in arms at the time. He grew into manhood there and, in 1818, married Sarah Kirkman, an orphan who was reared by Judge Henry Hopkins, the man who gave the land for the site of the city of Princeton.

Mr. and Mrs. John King conceived ten children including Jeron's grandfather John K. King, born October 30, 1833. John K. was raised

to the life of a farmer and followed that occupation throughout his life. When the Civil War began he enlisted in Company A, Eighteenth Regiment Indiana Volunteer Infantry and served as a Private throughout the war. He was in some of the hardest fought battles and was wounded at the battle of Resaca, Georgia. After the war ended he returned to Gibson County and married Helen Hopkins in 1866. He bought his father's farm from the rest of the heirs and continued to operate it until he retired from active life and moved to Princeton in 1897. In 1902, John K. opened the King House hotel at 321 N. West Street. Mr. and Mrs. John K. King had four children, John Herbert, Roy P., Ruth H., and Charles Kimber. The latter, nicknamed Charley, married Anna B. Criswell November 9, 1905, and a little less than two years later the future "Prophet from Indiana" was born.

The Princeton city directory for 1907 showed Anna B. and Charles K. King living at 117 West Pine Street with Charles employed at Agar Company Department store, 210 West State Street.

Criswell opens the preface of *CPY2K*:

I wasn't always Criswell Predicts.
   Once I was baby Criswell!
   And even then I was interested in the future.
   I was born on a Sunday, August 18th when the church bells were ringing, and was the first child on both sides of the family, and basked in the spotlight, which I never gave up. They thought I would be a cardinal or a governor.

Some accounts have baby Criswell born in the back room of the family owned mortuary which is possible since the Criswells were one of the oldest funeral families in America, but not probable.
He continues to recount his youth in *CPY2K*:

I scribbled on the walls, floors, and papers, and did not talk until I was four.
   "Retarded." they said. "Poor Baby Criswell will never talk."
   During an Indiana thunderstorm, I started talking and have not stopped until this day.
   I told my shocked parents that: "The rain will stop!" My very first prediction! And a valid one!
   In our family, the Criswells, the Kings, the Hopkins, the Mulhalls, the Neeleys, the Browns and the Williamses were all proud of Indiana, becoming grocers, newspaper editors, doctors, druggists, politicians, bankers, and undertakers. Schoolteachers competed for God and Glory in the hot Hoosier sun.
   Princeton, Indiana, was in Gibson County, with the Wabash, the White and the Patoka rivers giving the five thou-

sand natives a rich heritage. The Mason-Dixon Line was only twenty-seven miles away across the Ohio River.

I was raised in the King House, the family hotel. I thought any one who lived seven miles away was a foreigner, and was shocked to find out that they did not know who I was. The town certainly knew who I was as I would not let them forget.

On Sunday, I would join the minister in the pulpit. Once I sang a solo without music.

The family could not keep me from getting before an audience, even at a funeral. In the Christmas plays I would stay on stage until I was forcibly removed. I loved political rallies. My Uncle Earl would let me stand by him while he campaigned. Any schoolteacher knew better than to call on me because they could never quiet me. Cousin Alice who taught me history in the eighth grade, never received a simple answer, but an oration.

When the tornado blew down half the town, I proudly conducted tours for the sightseers! Everyone prefaced their conversation by: "Who was there besides Cris?"

April 1953, *Fate* magazine, "Prophecies I Have Heard"

Another amazing character of my boyhood days was a Negro woman, Fannie, who could spread a regular deck of playing cards fanwise and tell your fortune. One afternoon my brother and sister, two cousins and myself, had her "spread the cards" as she called it. She looked up and prophesied, "A great wind will kill 100 people here next spring but we will be safe." It came to pass that a deadly tornado struck Princeton the following March killing 100 people but sparing our street completely.

On March 18, 1925, the Great Tri-State Tornado ripped through Missouri, Illinois, and Indiana. It is widely considered the most powerful and devastating tornado in American history. It traveled 219 miles completely destroying four towns, severely damaging six others, flattening 15,000 homes, injuring 2,000 people, and killing 695. A record for a single tornado. Princeton's loss of life was seventy residents. Jeron would have been seventeen years-of-age at the time of the disaster.

Criswell continues from *CPY2K*:

No club or audience could meet in secret without my somehow finding the way to the platform. I was not really an extrovert just impervious to criticism of any kind.

When they unveiled the Soldier's Monument in the Courthouse Yard, they uncovered me standing there spouting Lincoln's Gettysburg Address.

The Soldier's Monument he refers was dedicated November 12, 1912, but a detailed account of the dedication in Gil R. Stormont's *History of Gibson County Indiana* (1914) had no mention of young Jeron's surprise appearance or speech.

He continues:

I yearned to work on my Uncle Roy King's *Daily Democrat* and he would pay me 25¢ for five personal items. My personal items were exclusive: I would write what people *were going to do!*

I had Vivian Draymeyer attending her sister's funeral in Mt. Carmel when her sister was still alive, but her sister died the next day and it saved me from embarrassment.

And made me stop to ponder the occurrence.

I began to predict things more and more often. I would operate on these "hunches" and found myself able to help solve the problems of others.

Uncle Roy was the editor for the *Daily Democrat* newspaper for several years and well respected in the Gibson County area. He also contributed to Stormont's *History of Gibson County Indiana* with a well-researched and informative chapter on the cholera epidemics that ravaged the area in the mid to late 1800s. A 1910 census lists Criswell's parents and Charles C. as Son and a daughter Clara H. She was born on July 12, 1909, and passed away at the early age of 42 on November 2, 1951, as Clara Helen King Johnston. Criswell's brother, William Robert King was born on March 2, 1911, and served as a Private in World War II and also passed away at an early age on June 22, 1966. Both of Criswell's siblings are interred at the same IOOF cemetery in Princeton. William Robert had a son, Charles "Charlie" William King in 1934, who went on to own the King Family Real Estate and Insurance Company in Princeton and passed away in 2011 concluding the King family lineage. Princeton city directories listed Charles and Anna living at 319 West Chestnut Street in 1914 with Charles listing his employment as an insurance agent. The Kings then moved to 327 North Gibson Street in 1916 where they remained for many years. At this time Farmers & Merchants Mutual Life employed Charles.

From a bio piece by Charles F. Wireman in *Spaceway Science Fiction* magazine April 1955:

Up to the age of ten, Criswell lived in his family's hotel, the King House, in Princeton, and it was there that he learned the great pleasure of knowing people, for guests became his friends, and even today, many years later, he still receives letters from many of them.

April 1953, *Fate,* "Prophecies I Have Heard"

When I was a boy we used to look into the embers of a dying fire to see future events. Some of us became quite proficient. My sister Clara Helen, my brother William, and my cousins John Henry and Marjorie took turns at being seer. Another cousin, Helen Hopkins, always saw a house on a hill overlooking the ocean and today she lives in just such a place. As Mrs. James Warner Bellah she lives in Santa Monica, Calif., overlooking the Pacific.

He continues to reflect on his youth in *YN10YCP*:

I was a freckle-faced, red headed boy looking at life through a picket fence in Indiana, and thought I was something special! In fact, the entire family thought so too. They classified me as a "freak!" And perhaps a freak I have remained!

I had a vaulting imagination, and my searching wet noodle of a mind was hard to control. I was not interested in the present events, but more interested in how they were going to turn out. Everyone knew Mrs. Wentworth Hoggington was very ill, and would die, a fact that did not concern me . . . but which husband would she choose to be buried by for eternity? Annette Jinsey ran away from her husband with a journeyman embalmer and returned two months later, three months pregnant. Who was the actual father, and could Annette be sure? Would Gus Jinsey be happy with Annette, and if she left the next time, who would she go with?

16

I became a prying busybody, horrifying the good citizens of Princeton, by merely asking questions, "How do you think it will turn out?" and if I were not sharply dismissed for impertinence I would tell them how I thought it would all end. Of course, when I was around no adult would even venture a statement about the weather, and I found myself isolated, as what I said proved embarrassing to adult ears. My peculiar point of view and my analytical mind, which gave me unmentionable facts without any slanted propaganda, made me a celebrity with several of the gossips of the town. Grandma Wayne, who, after the birth of her last daughter at 35 took to a wheel chair and 50 years later was being wheeled by great grandchildren, knew more about the town than any one! She would say: "Cris, walk by the Morritons' and see if there is a blue Buick with a crushed right fender parked there!" I would do this errand and she would exclaim, "Frank Gurch is there again! Gus Morriton should know about Amy!" The FBI and CIA would have been proud of me, for I was an apt pupil! Grandma Wayne would ask: "How will this turn out?" I would answer: "Gus is going to come home early for lunch and shoot Frank and Amy!" This deduction proved true.

My parents were shocked at my opinions, which I handed out like samples of soap, for I somehow knew of my gift of deduction. You start with the facts, and then. . . .

My Father, in a rather patronizing manner, told me it would be much better, at least for the present, if I kept my mouth shut and write my *Short History of the Future* as I had so proudly called it. I retired like a hermit to our attic, and wrote pages and pages about the Princetonians and their futures, the results of their present activities. I saw nothing wrong in it, and blamed no one for any future action I had them commit! I did not wish to be an unsung, unheard historian of the future, but insisted that I be permitted to read my short history of the future at the next family dinner. The family thought it would be a dull evening, and the adults were passively polite. I dearly loved an audience and had them from the first. With the talent of an attorney, I had built a case for all those mentioned, and with the finality of a judge I had passed a future sentence. Each item was in three parts (1) background (2) the present and (3) the projected results. I covered all the personalities of Princeton . . . the kindly alcoholic doctor who performed abortions and the ladies he served . . . the widow of a former mayor who was known as "the traveling salesmen's delight" . . . the Minister and the soprano and where they would secretly meet . . . how the butcher would thicken his pork sausage with cornmeal . . . how votes were bought beyond the brickyard pond . . . the never-talked-about drinking lady of the town . . . that artificial hand of an undertaker which he would thoughtlessly leave behind . . . the all night card game the high school athletic coach always ran . . . and the exploits of Miss Nellie who ran the beauty shop and loved to take baths with two men at a time. Names were given along with the times and places plus my forecast of tragedies to come. Had my "Short History of the Future" been published, I would still be serving time for personal libel and many good Hoosiers would have left Princeton for parts unknown. The family sat in stony silence, too shocked for comment. The mind of a twelve year-old boy can be a fearful thing! My Father took the manuscript from my hands and placed it gently on the open flame of the hearth. "Cris, wait until you are over 21 and away from home before you write another History of the Future!"

Criswell's retelling of his youth is no doubt tinged with fantasy, half-truth, exaggeration, and embellishment, if not pure fiction to a great extent. In later years, he claimed he first realized he could predict the future at the age of eight saying, "My family had a funeral home and they used to ask me, 'Well, Crissy, who will be our next customer?' I'd tell them, and in a short time the prediction would come true." He also later stated that his father was a mortician, when in fact he was in the insurance business most of his life. What actually happened, and the "facts" had been lost to time, which allowed him to create his own child prognosticator myth.

April 1953, *Fate,* "Prophecies I Have Heard"

When I was a barefoot boy in Indiana I spent 50¢ one day at the Gibson County Fair—a hard-earned 50¢ that I had got threshing—to 'consult' a gypsy palmist. She looked down into my freckled face, at my torn overalls, my shock of reddish hair, my calloused palm and gave me the following prediction: 'You will leave here when you are 16 and not be the doctor you plan to be.' (I had planned to follow the footsteps of my great-uncle but when I did leave home at 17 to attend the university I changed my mind completely about being a doctor.) I have always remembered the prophecy of the gypsy woman and wherever she is I want her to know that her prediction worked out.

The first mention of Charles C. King in the Princeton city directory is in 1921 listing him as a high school student. 1923 lists him as a clerk at J.C. Penny and 1925 as a student again. He graduated from Princeton High School in 1926 at the age of eighteen.

In the winter 1926 issue of *The Princetonian* yearbook, Charles contributed two poems, "The Maker of Melodies" and "What a Muddle I Have Made of Life." In the first he ponders the path of life using metaphors of music and song.

Excerpt:

The song goes on in a waning note;
Life then loses its zest,
All signs of dreams are swept away
By a despairing flood of unhappiness.

The night comes on
Its cloak is spread,
The melody is waning now,
As the sun slowly leaves the world to darkness.

The curtains are drawn—
The light burns low—
The melody quavers—then stops
That is the answer to life's riddle.
    El' Envoy
Life is a song we all must sing—
A riddle we all must solve,
From early morn till dusk
Then we all must stop.

The Maker of Melodies accompanies each
Through the prologue of the song,
All the way through to the grand finale
And then stops.

We can't keep on living after the sunset
Nor can we live before the dawn;
After all—seems but an hour—
The frail duration of a flower.

And after all
Who is the Maker of Melodies?
Why 'tis God—
For our life is but a song.

"What a Muddle I have Made of Life"
Life is the same from north to south,
You can hear the same things coming
From out of different people's mouths,
"What a muddle I have made of life."

The fruit dealer on the corner,
The debutante of this season;
The milk man on his daily route,
All give the same old reason.

The actress, the lawyer, the merchant,
The sales girl, and the crook,
All stop from their daily toil and say;
"What a muddle I have made of life."

People in every walk of life,
And from every class or type
After they say this sentence
Always think that they are right.

In a way they are,
And in a good way they aren't—
It is a good thing they are not grading
Their life or they would say—Failure.

But if you are a failure, just keep on trying,
Don't ever say this little sentence,
(If you do, you are just as good as gone.)
"What a muddle I have made of life."

—Charles C. King

The spring 1926 issue of *The Princetonian* included the senior class will, which included the leaving of "How I Fascinate the Opposite Sex" from Charles King to Ewing Duncan. It also included "Senior Class Prophecy of 1926" that contains what could be his first printed prediction. "Charles King has become the president of the J.C. Penny Co., and under his supervision the corporation had grown until it sold everything from farm houses to roach powder, on which the roaches were guaranteed to thrive wonderfully." The young Criswell was already shooting for the top and considered himself quite the ladies man. In his senior class picture he is quite handsome, angular, and dapper. A woman that worked with him when he was an eighteen-year-old stock boy at J.C. Penny said the most remarkable thing about him was his ambition.

He sums up his formative years in *CPY2K*:

After High School, I attended the University of Cincinnati, taking Public School Education at the Conservatory of Music, and then tried my hand at teaching which I gave up after one term in Jersey City, New Jersey.

After a pre-med course, further work in a mortuary, which I learned of as a child working in the family owned mortuary, the city morgue and as an ambulance jockey, then I returned to newspaper work and newscasting.

As I predicted more accurately, I became less reticent to predict. I kept score, writing my predictions for my eyes only, then checking to see if they came to pass. My accuracy increased with each year, and I began writing my predictions for others to see and hear.

When he arrived in New Jersey and applied for his teaching license, the clerk accidentally left off his last name of King. Owing to the fact that he could not teach without a license and correcting the mistake could take upwards to six months, he took the name that he would use on his rise to fame and became Charles Criswell. After his short-lived teaching career he returned to Princeton to work on the *Daily Clarion*. The last listing for him in the Princeton city directory is as a clerk in 1935. He later claimed that he was terminated from his first newspaper job when he wrote an obituary prior to the subject's death.

In June 1935, Jeron Criswell rented an apartment at 171 W. 76th Street, New York City. Later in life he claimed he became a freelance writer for confession magazines and that after some of his stories caught the eye of a writer of popular radio soap operas, he began writing for *The Romance of Helen Trent* and *Backstage Wife* radio programs.

On into adulthood, prophecy would continue to be a guiding influence in Criswell's life.

April 1953, *Fate,* "Prophecies I Have Heard"

I attended a Spiritualist church in Cincinnati and the medium told me that I would be lecturing in Carnegie Hall in New York in 10 years. As a shy, stuttering college student I found this quite fantastic but it came to pass— exactly 10 years later! Three years later a nameless tealeaf reader in a Gypsy Tearoom at 43rd and Fifth Avenue, New York, told me that I would spend the following year in Europe. This strangely came to pass.

A fortune-teller in Marseilles foretold a great disaster, which I would witness upon returning to America. I was within 50 feet of the Graf Zeppelin when it exploded.

Actually, the Graf was retired from service, melted down, and recycled into Messerschmitts. The *Hindenburg* was the zeppelin that crashed in Lakehurst, New Jersey in 1937, a minor inaccuracy. There are also no records of him lecturing at Carnegie Hall.

As the Hindenburg was coming down the Hudson River to where it crashed and burned, a thirteen-year-old boy in Poughkeepsie by the name of Edward D. Wood Jr. filmed it. He was so proud that he filmed it before it went up in flames. Many years later on the other side of the country, Cris and Eddie would become close friends and partners in numerous escapades.

Criswell's most cherished interview while doing newspaper work was with H. G. Wells who proved to be a great influence. He considered *Things to Come* (1933), one of the most remarkable books of the Twentieth century for its astute insight into the future. Wells was later quoted on a Criswell promotional flyer for *YN1OY-CP*. "America's Criswell foresees the future clearly."

The legend of Criswell claims he began writing financial news and hosting a radio broadcast on Wall Street. He declared that his economic predictions were 76% correct according to a *Wall Street Journal* article. One evening, a sponsor suddenly pulled their commercials off the air, leaving him with an extra minute of airtime and nothing to fill it. His mellow voice intoned. "I predict. . . " followed by a series of news items he knew would appear on the next day's broadcast. The "I predict" segment became a regular feature of the program and eventually he began to predict events not connected to the financial world. Legend also claims that he predicted a piece of news that did happen, and the radio station was flooded with calls. Some accounts say the prediction concerned a controversy with a local politician, some a natural disaster. It has also been alleged that, needing to pad his broadcasts, he would look at the next days scheduled events and predict that certain things would occur, and his prognostications became a popular feature. His purported reaction to the situation was "What the hell, I've found a gold mine!" Baby Criswell had become Criswell Predicts!

CLAUDIA POLIFRONIO: Cris was a stock analyzer. He got on these programs on the radio, where they would analyze stock because he had a wonderful speaking voice. He would predict which are the good stocks. How the market was going to do. One day, according to the story, he said "I predict" in that way of his and I guess someone said you could do a whole program. So that's how he got into this Criswell Predicts.

Along with newspaper work, radio newscasting, financial forecasting, and lecturing in New York, Jeron began making inroads into the Broadway theatre scene. Records from Broadway at the time show that on July 20, 1936, a play he had written called *Dorian Gray* from *The Picture of Dorian Gray* (1890), by Oscar Wilde, opened at the off-Broadway Comedy Theatre, presented by Groves Quigley for sixteen performances. The July 14, 1936, New York *Daily News* announced the opening of the play. "On Monday, a group of actors which hasn't yet chosen a name will present 'Dorian Gray,' a new three-act adaptation of Oscar Wilde's 'Picture of Dorian Gray,' by Jeron Criswell, at the air-conditioned Comedy Theatre on 41st St. Costumes and settings will be in the Victorian manner and one of the actresses will wear a replica of a gown once belonging to Lily Langtry, who if memory serves, belonged more to the Edwardian era." The article went on to say the play would be produced by Groves Quigley and Edwin O'Hanlon would direct the actors — David Windsor, Robert Carlyle, Oscar Stirling, Vera Hurst, Flora Sheffield, Clement O'Loghlen, Allen Campbell, and Leslie King, several of whom had been seen on Broadway in British plays. The Sybil Vane of the piece would be Winifred Q. Fothergill who had appeared in the Summer theaters at Provincetown and Bar Harbor.

The July 21, *New York Times* ran a review of the play's opening with the headline 'Dorian Gray' Seen at Comedy Theatre; Wilde's Discussion of Soul's Decadence has [an] adaptation by Jeron Criswell. The review was credited to J.K.H.

Excerpts:

Oscar Wilde's celebrated discussion of a soul's decadence came into the Comedy Theatre last night under the abbreviated title of "Dorian Gray" and at the hands of a nameless group and of no particular identity. Mr. Wilde's discussion has done this at least once before—that was in 1928, when, as the records recall to a world that might otherwise forget, it took the form of a play in a prologue and three acts by David Thorne. This time the adaptation is by one Jeron Criswell, and it is in three acts but without any prologue, which placed last night's audience just that much ahead.

However anyone choose to do it, though, the method is going to be pretty much the same. It is going to consist of extracting the epigrams and distributing them like plums in what the wicked Lord Henry Wooten calls a third-rate wedding cake. Some of the epigrams, to be sure, still shine with a hothouse brilliance. More of them are tarnished beyond the repair of adaptation. It became, in fact, a sort of game last evening to listen to them coming from a long way off and then to wait while the luckless actors declaimed them amid a generally heartless silence.

The unfavorable review went on to say that "the luckless actors did not seem to think they were luckless at all." and "They were not merely unembarrassed; they seemed to be having a fine time." The review closed by noting the actors by name and their roles and closed saying, "They all posed enthusiastically, and to no one did it seem to occur that if Wilde had thought there was a play here he would have probably have written it himself. But people never seem to think of those things until it is too late."

Another review that same day by Danton Walker in the New York *Daily News* titled "Dorian Gray' Drama Gay 90's Hangover".

Excerpts:

If the actors who presented "Dorian Gray" at the Comedy Theatre last night had frankly made their offering as a burlesque of the Gay Nineties, they might have awakened this morning with a hit on their hands comparable to "Murder in the Red Barn."

As it is, the three-act drama fashioned by Jeron Criswell from Oscar Wilde's famous years so closely borders on burlesque that it might aptly be titled "Murder in the Old Victorian Drawing Room."

Thinking perhaps that they might need to use the portrait the rest of the week, the leading man failed to stab the canvas last night and died, apparently from natural causes. Thereby adding one more laugh to an evening of unintentional merriment.

Epigrams Tarnished

The epigrams of Sir Henry seemed pretty tarnished as delivered by Oscar Stirling last night. Winifred Fothergill, as Sybil Vane, Dorian's first girlfriend, was too handicapped by an atrocious make-up job to know whether she can act or not. Robert Carlyle, being young, may live down the memory of Basil Hallward and become a good juvenile.

Vera Hurst, wearing some preposterously amusing costumes as the venomous Lady Gladys Femor, was more in the picture, and carried off what humors were to be gleaned from a barren venture. Most of the other actors, happily for them, have appeared in other and better productions.

The *Brooklyn Daily Eagle,* got in on the ridiculing and lambasting of the production with a review by J.S.H. called "New Play."

Although "Dorian Gray" is alleged to be a play in three acts, one needs only to sit through one of them to realize it to be more of a calamity than a play. From the moment the curtain rose the audience was slightly hysterical, but of course this might have been brought on by the sudden view of a particularly hideous, glaring, green set. A very few people tried to be polite, but on the average most everyone was out to make loud, impolite and rather absurd remarks about what was going on on the stage. It really was all very sad and I think any one that had read and enjoyed this fine novel of Mr. Wilde's would feel rather personally insulted if they had to sit through such an amateurish production. Probably the one thing that can be said for this faux pas was that the cast was sincere in all their efforts to really try to make something out of Mr. Criswell's wasted efforts.

I think it would be a good idea for any one who reads this review to promptly forgot it—and a much better idea for every one that had anything at all to do with last night's play to make believe it all never happened. It's just too bad it did.

A brutal review by Lucius Bebe that ran in newspapers across the country and again compared *Dorian Gray* to *Murder in the Red Barn.*

"Weekly New York Letter on Things Theatrical"

This week in Manhattan witnessed the premieres of two plays, neither of which is likely long to survive this chronicling of their twin and dolorous debuts.

Just why someone named Jeron Criswell should have taken it upon himself to make a play out of Oscar Wilde's novel, "The Portrait of Dorian Gray," was not apparent at the Comedy Theatre Tuesday night. As any number of persons remarked at the intermission, Mr. Wilde was a not incompetent playwright himself, and if he had felt that the Dorian Gray theme lent itself to dramatic treatment, it is not too much to suppose that he might have cast the story in this form without Mr. Criswell's gratuitous assistance. The script of Mr. Criswell's alleged drama would have made a dismal reading, consisting as it did of a rosary of familiar and not too wicked epigrams strung on a sleazy story. As one reviewer remarked they could be heard coming from a long way off. But the cast assembled for this precious nonpareil at least had the merit of furnishing forth brief moments of farce which might well be transplanted to Minsky's across the street for interludes between strip tease numbers.

Unquestionably the funniest performance of the season was that of a youth nominated in the cast as David Windsor, whose posturings as the orchidaceous baddy of Mr. Wilde's conception drew almost hysterical applause from the dedans.

Attired in a lavender frock coat and Gloucester-green Ascot, Mr. Windsor's stage version of a fatal and seductive charm resembled nothing in the world so much as Harpo Marx imitating Sally Rand. A low-comedy Lord Henry Wotten, in a collectors item cutaway, frequently adjusted a monocle with infinite elegance, but backward into his eye, as he leered through some pretty fantastic asides designed to insinuate a theme of Byzantine vice into the stage doings. At the last report John Krimaky was angling for "Dorian Gray" and its original cast complete as successor to "Murder in the Old Red Barn" at that temple of beer and Thepis, the American Music Hall.

Despite the overwhelmingly bad reviews, in his hometown Jeron was a Broadway success.

From the July 28, Princeton, Indiana, *Princeton Daily Clarion,* article "Local Man's Play is Approved by Critics":

Mr. and Mrs. Charles K. King, north Gibson Street, have received word that their son Charles C. King of New York City, is having his first play presented. The play opened at the Comedy Theatre on Broadway on July 21 with matinees on Wednesday and Saturday. The three-act play is adapted from Oscar Wilde's sensational novel, "Dorian Gray" by Jeron Criswell, which is King's pen name.

It is staged by Edwin O'Hanlon. King writes that the play is meeting with the approval of the critics. Princeton people will be pleased to learn of a home town boy's success on Broadway.

The *New York Theatrical Index* lists the play's start date as July 20, 1936, then names the cast and describes it as such:

The Entire Play Transpires in the Favorite Room of Dorian Gray, 38 Berkeley Square, Mayfair, London.
ACT I—An Afternoon in June 1890.
ACT II—The Following March, 11 P.M., 1891.
ACT III—Thirty Years Later, Early April, Midnight, 1921.

Closed August 1, 1936, 16 Performances

A practically semi-amateur rehash of Oscar Wilde's well-known novel, which did all any cast or author could do to make the novel seem ineffective. Included in this issue of the *Index* only because its short run terminated on the day that the new season officially started.

The Life and Loves of Dorian Gray written by Cecil Clarke, this time starring Jeron Criswell as Dorian Gray soon after opened at the same theatre for 32 performances. The revamped version of the play was announced on August 11, in the New York *Daily News* "Theatre Notes" by Ruth Hammond.

Annette Schein announces that she will re-open the Comedy Theatre Monday with a revised version of 'Dorian Gray,' this time with music and a new cast. Doris Reed will have the leading feminine role and also sing an aria from 'La Traviata'.

Opening night of the play was announced on August 17, in the *Brooklyn Daily Eagle* "Stage News, In the Wings."

"Murder in the Old Red Barn" celebrates its 20th performance at the American Music Hall tonight . . . Another play about Dorian Gray, Mr. Wilde's imperishable hero, will open at the Comedy Theater tonight. Annette Schein of Brooklyn is the sponsor and the cast includes Jeron Criswell, Dora Reed of Flatbush, Stella Dean Alda and others.

A small ad for *Life and Loves of Dorian Gray* ran in the Brooklyn Daily Eagle on August 29 and called it "Oscar Wilde's Sensational Study of Sex Mad Victorians" at the Comedy Theatre with matinees on Thursday and Saturday.

It was during his Broadway days that Jeron met a woman that would become the future Mrs. Criswell and be a tremendously influential guiding force, financial supporter, and possibly his "beard" throughout the rest of his life.

Myrtle Louise Stonesifer was born in Littlestown, Pennsylvania on May 1, 1905, to Etta Sarah Frances and Dr. Howard Abraham Stonesifer who had married in Adams County in October 1904. Dr. Stonesifer was proprietor of Stonesifer's Drugstore in Littlestown after he purchased it in 1902. Myrtle was a handful when she was young and what could be called "spirited." When she was two-years-old she stood on the pew in the Reformed Church and shouted, "woowoo, woo-woo-woo" during a hymn. Her father whisked her out of the sanctuary and scolded her on the sidewalk. The next Sunday when the preacher started his sermon, she said aloud, "blah-blah, blah-blah-blah." She said in a 1982 newspaper article, "My father whipped me. It was the only time he ever whipped me." He then told her on that sidewalk session that her mother would have sole responsibility for her care and upbringing, he was abdicating his. Her parents were always "after" little Myrtle Louise except, "when I put on plays. Then they left me alone. But, otherwise, they were after me." After graduating from Littlestown High School she went to Wilson College for a year-and-a-half and then transferred to Hood College. She spent her summers at Penn State, Bucknell, and Gettysburg College taking extra courses. After receiving her B.A. degree from Hood College in 1927 she went to the University of Pennsylvania where she earned a master's degree in sociology a year later.

She came back to Littlestown for a year and during that time formed the Littlestown Dramatic Club. She studied piano with Frank Freisinger who "polished her off" in classical music. She then entered the American Academy of Dramatic Arts in New York. Following that she joined Hendrickson's Shakespeare Company touring college campuses in the U.S. She went then to live in the Allerton

House in New York and started writing plays full-time under the name Louise Howard. Her life there inspired her to write *Women's Hotel*. She later alleged that Twentieth Century Fox took the play and cast Linda Darnell in the lead and changed the title to make the film *Hotel for Women* (1939). Elsa Maxwell, the celebrity tattletale columnist, took credit for the script and appeared in the film also known as *Elsa Maxwell's Hotel for Women*. Myrtle would later sue Twentieth Century Fox on the grounds of copyright infringement.

For a short time she had a job at radio station WHMS and then quit "to get my plays going." She wrote *Evasive Joy*, a play about three generations of a family leading up to 1914, and had Audrey Wood, Tennessee Williams' agent try to place the play. She claimed her career on Broadway peaked in 1937 when she was known as "the girl playwright" and wrote *Cloud of Pane*. "It was a sociological kind of thing . . . it kind of fit my master's degree." She had a group that wanted to produce it, but in the eleventh hour, just before the contract was signed, she discovered the group had communist leanings. "I took my play, I thought, *My Father was president of the bank. I can't do this. I've had enough. I'm through with show business.*" She alleged that word got out on Broadway, and she was blackballed and that it was said, "you go with that woman director and you'll be blackballed." Like many things in her life she was almost, but not quite through with drama and she began to manage the Villa Venice nightclub, predecessor to the Copacabana. "It was the classiest night spot on the East Side." she said. She began to produce some of her own plays at the Villa Venice and claimed in the 1982 article that at one time had the Metropolitan Opera star Rosa Ponselle's daughters in her plays. Beginning in January 1937, Louise Howard's activities at the Villa Venice, 14 E. 60th Street, were announced and covered in the local New York newspapers with one of the first declaring "The Villa Venice is experimenting with dramatic sketches as part of its entertainment." In March, a small announcement stated that there would be two tryout performances at the Villa Venice for single-night showings of the play *City Pace* on a Tuesday evening. Then in April, a tryout for one performance only of *City Pace*, "a comedy about an artist's life," by Louise Howard with the curtain at 8:30. A week later it was announced that Louise Howard's comedy *City Pace* would be given a single performance at the Villa Venice under the direction of Orin Jannings. That same week it was reported in the Personals section of the *Adams County Independent*, the Stonesifer local hometown newspaper that, "Dr. And Mrs. H.A. Stonesifer left yesterday for New York City at which place they will visit their daughter, Miss M. Louise Stonesifer."

On June 29, items ran in the local New York newspapers' Stage News and Theatre Notes sections about her play *Live Again*, "a comedy dealing with a small town confronted with some Shakespearean actors." It was for that night only and the author would act in it with an 8:30 curtain. It was also touted as a first production by the "Summer repertory theatre for Summer experiment" organized by Louise Howard and called the Louise Howard Players. In July it was publicized that the Louise Howard Players would tryout *Here's Hoping*, a farce by Dr. O. Lipkind early in August at the Villa Venice. On August 29 it was reported that "Something new in dramatic tryouts" would be presented that Tuesday evening. *Here's Hoping* by G. Lipkind would play at the Villa Venice nightclub with a cast including Louise Howard who had organized the troupe and Marita and Daphne Sylva, daughters of Margarita Sylva, a former opera star. In the 1982 article about Myrtle, she claimed that it had been Metropolitan Opera star, Rosa Ponselle's daughters. In mid-October it was publicized that the former Villa Venice had been remodeled and opened as an intimate theatre with Louise Howard's musical *Whims of 1937*. The following week a short review said that "a young woman named Louise Howard offered an intimate casual entertainment called *Whims of '37*." It reported that the play

34

was produced by unknown players with words and music by Miss Howard and Claude Lapham at a "tiny playhouse which used to be the Villa Venice, original haunt of Rudy Vallee." It also claimed that "the revue played to some 700 persons and from the current look of things, may reach Broadway. The night clubs have already signed Dan Taylor, Bob Merrill and Merritt Smith, and the song publishing firms may take 'Think of Me,' 'Chili Lady,' and 'Luana,' which proved show stoppers."

1937 had been a relatively busy year for Myrtle Louise. Apparently not so much for Jeron, as there were no mentions of any activity from him in the local newspapers. Perhaps 1937 was the year Jeron had been traveling Europe and the Dark Continent as he would later claim as something he had accomplished.

When Myrtle met Jeron, "a double-line Mayflower descendant," she saw the late afternoon sun fall on his Pomeranian dog Trampy. She fell in love with it and told him "I'll be that dog's slave as long as I live on this earth." "Well I go with the dog." he told her. Of her many suitors, including a Vietnamese diplomat, a newspaper editor, and an Indian Chief, Criswell became her leading man, and she renamed the dog Sunshine.

Jeron and Myrtle began a relationship working, collaborating, performing, and living together that would last nearly three decades.

In February 1938, an article titled "Louise Howard Busy" told of *Ladies and How*, a comedy by Jeron Criswell with music by Arthur Jones and lyrics by Louise Howard, going into rehearsal under Miss Howard's direction. Nan Rae and Myra Denver had been added to the cast. This was the first mention of Criswell and Howard collaborating. Later in the month it was announced that *Ladies and How* was due for a regular run at a Broadway house beginning in mid-March after being listed for the preceding week. "It is Jeron Criswell's satire with music by Arthur Jones and lyrics by Louise Howard and William Lord." On March 30 in the "Theatre Notes" section of a paper it was reported that "Louise Howard is hoping to exhibit 'Ladies and How' a satire with music by Jeron Criswell. . . ." On April 22 Myrtle's hometown paper noted in the "Personals" section that "Miss Louise Stonesifer, daughter of Dr. and Mrs. H.A. Stonesifer, appeared over WMCA at their formal opening Thursday evening." WMCA 570 Radio New York, did have an official dedication to their new "ear-tuned" studios with "All the pomp and ceremony of a Broadway opening." April 21, 22, and 23 were set aside for the festivities with Masters of Ceremonies; Postmaster General Farley, former Mayor Walker, Col. John Reed Kilpatrick; president of Madison Square Garden, David Sarnoff, Gov. Earle, Justice Pecora, and others. Miss Stonesifer wasn't mentioned.

Jeron spent the Independence Day holiday with his parents as reported in the July 6 edition of the hometown paper with a piece headlined "Charles King Visiting Parents in Princeton."

"Charles C. King, Jr. of New York City, is visiting his parents, Mr. And Mrs. Charles K. King, in north Gibson Street.

For the past several years, Mr. King has been actively connected with the New York theatre under the name Jeron Criswell. Mr. King has two of his plays produced on Broadway and directing and playing the leading role in them.

He has appeared also with Louise Howard in several New York night clubs, 'The Zebra Club,' 'Swing Club on 52nd Street' and the 'Halliday Club.'

Mr. King will return to New York City in about ten days to make final arrangements for the production of his latest play, "Ladies and How," and to fill an engagement at the International Casino."

Then on July 12 one of Myrtle's local hometown papers reported, with the headline "Filling Chicago Engagement," that she had visited with her parents and aunt, Miss Roman V. Crouse and that "Miss Stonesifer who is known on the stage as Louise Howard, left Monday to fill an engagement in Chicago, Ill. before returning to New York City." A December 30, 1938, "Personals" item in Myrtle's hometown paper reported that her parents were spending several days visiting their daughter, Miss Louise Stonesifer, New York, N.Y.

There are no records or reports in newspapers of the play *Ladies and How* being produced on the stage or having any opening or run, but Myrtle and Jeron continued promoting themselves as Broadway veteran stars, especially in their hometowns. Along with collaborating on their Broadway aspirations, the pair also started their own vanity publishing company called "Howard & Criswell."

In 1939 they published Louise's play *Evasive Joy* as a novel. "A saga of three generations—where lives were wholly governed by fear, criticism, and resentment." It had a foreword and practical explanation on how each character might have lived a harmonious life by Florence Scovel Shinn; then a pair of self-help books, *How to Have Everything You Want for a Zestful Trip Through Life* by Louise Howard "How to be happy, wealthy and wise—know that you're living and make the most of it." and *You Can Have It—anything you want* by Louise Howard and Jeron Criswell "The authoritative handbook for a Successful Career—How to overcome lack, limitation, fear or delay—victoriously!"

On April 7, 1940, a somewhat positive review of the book appeared in the *Fort Worth Star-Telegram* titled "How to Get It."

"How to Have Everything You Want" is a self-help book that ought to end self-help books. A few of the chapter heads are "How to Make a Wealthy Marriage," "Are You a Bachelor Afraid of What a Wife Might Do?" "Where Does Your Money Go?" And many, many more. The strange thing about it is that there's a lot of help in the book.

It offers advice to the glamour-forsaken gal, the fellow who can't pick the stock that's going up, the fellow who wears glasses and stumbles over his feet. As a matter of fact, it covers the majority of human mental ailments.

If you have any complexes, try reading "How to Have Everything You Want." It's funny and helpful.

Neither Criswell nor Howard had any experience in the complexities of marriage but considered themselves expert enough to dispense advice and guidance to anyone hapless enough to mail them one dollar. An advertisement appeared in all of the books for *The Game of Life and How to Play it* by Florence Scovel Shinn. "This remarkable book, written with amazing simplicity, gives definite rules for taking every trick in the Game of Life." Florence was a metaphysics teacher who had drawn illustrations for a number of children's books before World War I then began publishing her own self-help books in 1925 until her death in 1940.

Criswell & Howard also co-authored and published a series of three books on successfully breaking into the Broadway scene despite their combined limited success with that dream of conquering the Gay White Way. The first was *How to Crash Broadway*, "The authoritative handbook for a successful theatrical career" with a foreword by Barrett H. Clark, Executive Director of the Dramatists Play Service Inc.; then *How to Crash Tin-Pan Alley*, "The authoritative handbook for a successful song writing career" by Arthur Jones as told to Louise Howard and Jeron Criswell with a Foreword by Sammy Kaye (Swing and Sway) and lastly *How Your Play Can Crash Broadway* "The authoritative handbook for a successful playwriting career," again with a foreword by Mr. Clark. The books give simply told step-by-step instruction and advice on breaking into the Broadway scene from moving to the big city of New York from the reader's small hometown, through the hardships and struggles with the business side of the scene, to handling your newfound success. They sold for one dollar and could be mail ordered from Howard & Criswell, 12 West 44th Street, New York, N.Y.

In the first book many examples are given of the wildcat schemes and scams to be avoided on the road to success. From unscrupulous producers, directors, agents, managers, and play brokers, to fraudulent Summer Theater groups and Shakespearean Repertory Companies, shady nightclub work, and even radical communist dilettantes. The book can be read as an autobiographical sketch of Howard and Criswell's struggles to become Broadway stars in whatever way they could.

Excerpts from *How to Crash Broadway*:

All this happens every day . . . and it could easily be you.

The theater is a business, and not until you realize it have you begun your climb for fame. The theater is a hard mistress who lavishes wealth and fame on the one hand, while on the other hand causes heartbreak, failure and despair. Repeat to yourself one hundred times, "The theater is a business."

Money is the greatest authority in the theater.

The driving power of the theater is measured by a monetary scale.

The corner-stone of an artistic success is business ability exercised at the right time.

After reading this book telling of hardships, heartbreak, cruel competition, loneliness, despair and negative conditions, does your blood still tingle with the word "Theater?"

Do you wax romantic over the name "Bernhardt?" Can you, at this very moment, hear applause? Can you smell greasepaint? Can you hear the rustle of the falling and rising curtain? Can you thrill at seeing your name on the theater program? Can you feel your voice come back to you in round resonant tones? Can you hear a chuckle start and then roll into a thundering breaker? Curtain calls? Can you mingle with the great and near great without it spoiling you? Can you feel a thousand eyes on you as you lift a candlestick? If you feel this and the heartbreak ahead does not matter— repeat again, "THE THEATER IS A BUSINESS"—and you *can* do it.

We wish you all the luck in the world, and may your life in the theater be easy and everything come your way.

Also included is a kind of Ten Commandments for triumph on Broadway:

A Creed for Theatrical Success

1.
I am not falsely encouraged or discouraged by anyone.

2.
I keep my poise under any condition.

3.
I try at all times to be the individual I want to be.

4.
I daily develop and improve my talent.

5.
I keep my body free from dissipation and my mind clean and alert.

6.

I only associate with people who equal my talents or surpass them.

7.

I make the most of every opportunity.

8.

I am never envious for the same good fortune could easily come to me.

9.

I will always obey my superiors to the best of my ability and be grateful to them.

10.

The success I seek is seeking me for I refuse to recognize failure.

The last section of the book is called *After-Thoughts by Active Personalities on the Broadway Scene* and includes a number of quotes from various actors, playwrights, managers, play brokers, attorneys, etc. . . . One is by Annette Schein who produced the run of *The Life and Loves of Dorian Gray* in which Jeron played the lead. Arthur Jones is quoted on the importance of the proper use of songs in a play. The last quote is by the previously mentioned Florence Scovel Schinn. "Never argue with a hunch!"

The book was reviewed in newspapers across the country in 1939 with mostly neutral comments and a few not so favorable reviews.

From the *Birmingham News*:

If you're bent on a stage career and determined that noth-ing can stop you, then you can afford to read this small volume recounting the pitfalls that lie between you and success. If you're not so determined, the book itself will be pitfall enough to stop you.

With merciless pictures of hopeful youth tramping from frosty agents to frozen stenographers, being gypped out of money by so-called dramatic teachers and paying outrageous sums to be allowed to appear in fourth-rate performances, being fleeced by the registration racket, the small work-for-nothing radio stations, the cross-country troupers and the unsavory propositions-with such pictures the the authors show what happens to stage-struck youngsters who land at the gates of Broadway. They show, too, how some of the more persistent and lucky finally make the grade. But it's a depressing book, depressing because it was written out of experience and aimed at people who will insist on making their own experience.

And from, *The Arizona Republic,* "An Arizona Bookshelf," by Harvey L. Mott:

"How to Crash Broadway,' . . . If you know any more about it when you finish this, a miracle occurred."

It was brutally reviewed in the Allentown, PA, *Sunday Call-Chronicle* "Book Reviews" section:

This is a small book, small in content and in importance. It is authored by a young lady and a young man whose chief claim to the right to issue a set of instructions on the art of "crashing" Broadway seems to be an appearance they made once in the Broadway production of Oscar Wilde's "Life and Loves of Dorian Gray" at the Comedy Theatre, New York City.

The book is a cheaply-bound, poorly written creation which its authors choose to describe as "the authoritative handbook for a successful career," dedicated "to the theatrically ambitious."

The reader will find himself waiting in vain for the magic secret of how to "crash Broadway," while the authors dance around from one subject to another, putting themselves in the place of a disillusioned job-seeker who after much lavish outlay of money finally lands himself a place at "the top" of the entertainment world. We are given a 10-point creed for theatrical success which is impractical and a direct contradiction of the methods which the authors use to get their book character at the top.

Walter Winchell mentioned the book in his *On Broadway* column March 28, 1940. Louise Howard and Jeron Criswell have a gloomy message to stage aspirants in "The Woman." They warn that prospects of breaking into show business are well nigh hopeless. The title of their piece (too whimsical for endurance) is "How to Crash Broadway."

The second book *How to Crash Tin-Pan Alley* follows the same basic formula as the first book but this time the course is fraught with dishonest Song Contest Supervisors, Publisher X, a songwriter called Mr. Top Flight, and a top-drawer nightclub singer called Miss Mauvis Midnight that performs at the "Swinging Bucket." This book can be read as an autobiographical sketch of Arthur Jones' struggle to become a Broadway star in whatever way he could. The book also includes the same "Creed for Success" as the previous book followed by a section called "Marketing and Exploitation Campaign." The preface for this section heartens the reader to promote their self and their song with encouragements and affirmations such as:

Remember: Always act as if it were impossible to fail. There are no obstacles on your pathway except imaginary ones. If need be walk up to this imaginary lion on your pathway and see how quickly he will turn into a friendly Airedale.

You are immune to all petty jealousy, criticism, envy, resentment, fear, discouragement, interference, negative conditions, doubt, worry, lack and delay.

You can be like a rushing tide that sweeps everything before it.

Operate on the supposition that everything works out for the good, and surprisingly you will find that it does.

Let success overtake you overnight.

The last line would become a phrase that Criswell would continue to use throughout the rest of his life in his writings and lectures. Following the preface are "Thirty Steps to Success!" which includes such practical advice as "Get your town's most popular singer to memorize your song, and have it performed at the next large social or civic affair."

"Have your politician contact a local hotel manager who employs an orchestra, and have it play your song, and if possible have your troupe make a guest appearance."

"Daily rehearse your unit, improve them so they appear professional even to people who know them. You are now put of the amateur class. You are now a professional." The last page of the book sums it all up with still more practical advice:

If any point in this final discussion of a proposed career is not clear to you, have your father or some man equally as well versed in the business world explain a few of the finer points to you. It is well that you take into your confidence an older person with a sound business mind for he will prove invaluable to you in your career.

The authors of this book will be delighted to assist you in obtaining publication of your song.

Tin-Pan Alley may be legendary but it still remains a business section like the Loop in Chicago, Fountain Square in Cincinnati, Olive Street in St. Louis, Vine Street in Hollywood, Times Square in New York City or Main Street in your hometown.

TIN-PAN ALLEY is merely a continuation of the street on which you now live.

An extremely neutral review of the book ran in *The Brooklyn Citizen* simply titled "Tin Pan Alley."

Are you itching to crash Tin Pan Alley? Hear your song played coast to coast? Receive magnificent royalties for your masterpiece? Then get 'How to Crash Tin Pan Alley,' by Louis Howard (sic), Jeron Criswell, and Louise Howard. Each step in the process is minutely detailed even to what marriages to make to further yourself in your career.

You can also learn how to crash Broadway with a play, how to get into radio, how to get on the stage and how to have everything you want, the latter the culminating book in a series by Miss Howard.

Tuck these little pamphlets under your arms, son, and you're practically a howling success on the Gay White Way already!

The second mention of Louise in the author listing should have been Arthur Jones.

The third book in the Crash Broadway series, *How Your Play Can Crash Broadway,* is more of a straight-ahead formula with practical advice for writing a successful play and less of the "hometown to stardom" guide of the previous books. It also continues to stress the importance of knowing that Broadway is a business and controlled by money and not art alone. Included in the twenty chapters of the step-by-step process of becoming a playwriting success are: "The 36 Authentic Plots Streamlined for Your Convenience; For your profit, amusement and amazement," "The Practical Way to Write Your Play," "A Tested Recipe that Never Fails," "Hollywood May Consider You, Broadway Wants You," Protecting Your Rights," and "Why Not Make a Business of Playwriting."

Excerpts from chapter 20, "Curtain Line":

Always write with one eye on the box office.

When an aspiring playwright walks with his head in the clouds and his feet solidly treading this earth, he is bound to arrive at his destination.

Be shocking or amusing, but never commonplace.

No adventure—no advance.

If playwriting to you is not just a whim but a deep rooted ambition, it can be achieved. Your constant, active, fearless faith will lead you to your heart's desire.

There are no obstacles on your pathway if you refuse to acknowledge them. There is no tradition in the theater as far as you are concerned. You were not born in the theater, you were born for the theater. Your creative talent is your shining armor which no opposition can penetrate or dent. Either use this talent or lose it altogether.

We wish you all the luck in the world and may your career in playwriting be easy and may everything come your way.

Louise Howard and Jeron Criswell then graciously offer their help saying "You may write to the authors at 12 West 44th Street, New York City, regarding any questions you wish to ask or any problem that may confront you."

The book includes the "Creed for Success" of the previous books and like the preceding book this one also includes the "Marketing and Exploitation Campaign" with the same preface followed this time by only "Twenty Steps to Success!" The practical Broadway veteran advice included: "You have completed your play. You have made a copy for each of your characters plus one for the director and another for the stage manager. Your play has been duly copyrighted. Now you are ready for action." "As soon as you are definitely decided on a member of the cast, see that his or her name is immediately made public through the newspapers. After a person's name has appeared in print, he will not hedge on his obligation." "Keep up a steady stream of publicity in your newspapers and never be modest about your achievement. Be immune to all discouragement and gossip for others are only jealous of your proven ability."

"Before the curtain goes up on your play know how much was taken in and if you cannot get the money to cover your expenses before the curtain be sure that you are reimbursed between act 1 and 2, because you have held yourself responsible for these expenses.

"If each proposed step is not clear to you, the authors will be glad to furnish you with the information you desire." The book concludes on the barely inspirational note of "Broadway is merely a continuation of the street on which you now live."

All three of the books include photographs, mock exploitation flyers, and collages of Jeron, Louise, and Arthur on glossy, slick paper. One photo shows Jeron and Louise standing arm-in-arm in Central Park smiling and gazing into the distance as if anticipating their bright future. The caption for the picture on the facing page reads "The authors, Louise Howard and Jeron Criswell taken on the return from their road tour of the Broadway production, Oscar Wilde's 'Life and Loves of Dorian Gray.'"

Jeron & Louise in NYC from *How Your Play Can Crash Broadway.*

Another photo shows Arthur Jones at the piano with Jeron and Louise leaning on it. The facing page caption reads "The authors, Louise Howard and Jeron Criswell with their composer, Arthur Jones during a night club engagement."

One page is a collage of seven photos that have been stylized to appear as turn of the century Victorian illustrations. The facing page caption reads "Scenes from the Broadway production of Oscar Wilde's 'Life and Loves of Dorian Gray' taken on stage at the Comedy Theater, N. Y. C. Jeron Criswell was starred and heading the supporting cast were Louise Howard and Arthur Jones. The play was adapted by Mr. Criswell and the musical numbers 'I Was Just Around the Corner' and 'Victorian Waltz' were written by Miss Howard and Mr. Jones." A sample exploitation flyer for Louise has three cutout photos of her smiling, gazing into the distance, collaged over a line of musical notes. The text on the flyer reads "Louise Howard of the orchestra known as Louise Howard and Her Gamboleers Originator of Sophisticated—Primitive Music, authoress composer actress." The flyer for Arthur has the same style photo collage and reads "Ar-

Arthur Jones playing piano with Jeron &
Louise from *How to Crash Tin-Pan Alley*.

thur Jones of the orchestra known as Arthur Jones and His Jones
Boys Originator of Jumpy—Bumpy Music, author composer actor." Jeron's flyer also has a three-photo collage showing him writing, gazing into the distance, and looking directly into the camera.
There is also a filmstrip collage of eleven small photos. The text
reads "Jeron Criswell Playwright Motion Picture and Broadway
Producer Actor—Manager" and next to the filmstrip collage "From
the motion picture 'SPAN' starring Louise Howard, Arthur Jones,
Jeron Criswell." *Span*, had been mentioned once in the October 29,
1931, edition of the *Daily News* with Span Productions announcing
a November offering of the play by Jeron Criswell and directed by
Paul Martin. No other records can be found of the play, or the film
being produced.

All three books are long out-of-print and hard to find but are
available at the Los Angeles Public Library along with all three of
Criswell's future books of predictions.

The New York's World Fair, "Building the World of Tomorrow," opened in Flushing Meadows, just east of the great metropolis in April 1939. "The visitor who wants to get the most out of this World's Fair will do best to regard it not as a show of things," wrote H. G. Wells "but let his imagination off the leash of discretion for a bit. Then he may really get a glimpse of the realities of tomorrow that lurk in this jungle of exhibits. It will cease to look like a collection of things for sale and reveal it's real nature as a gathering of live objects, each of which is going to do something to him, possibly something quite startling, before he is very much older."

Being a man obsessed with the future and foreseeing it, Jeron no doubt visited the fair.

The RCA Pavilion, shaped like a radio tube when viewed from above, was the site of the first television broadcasts in the United States. David Sarnoff, president of the Radio Corporation of America made the dedication speech for the opening of the pavilion. The ceremony was televised and watched by several hundred viewers on TV receivers inside the pavilion as well as on receivers installed on the sixty-second floor of Radio City in Manhattan. Ten days later on April 30, 1939, Franklin D. Roosevelt made the first televised Presidential address. The signal was sent by the Telemobile, RCA's mobile television unit, to the Empire State transmitter and rebroadcast. The National Broadcasting Corporation was RCA's broadcasting wing and began regular U.S. broadcasting with the FDR telecast. Visitors to the pavilion could watch the broadcasts on a number of RCA's four available models of televisions that ranged in price from $199.50 to $600. Visitors also stood in line in the garden area behind the pavilion to be televised themselves by the Telemobile unit to the receivers inside the pavilion. This may have been Criswell's first appearance on the new medium that would eventually evolve into a multi-billion dollar global industry and lend to his future fame. Many exhibits at the fair were referred to as "the most popular exhibit of the fair" but none received as much discussion or attention as the Futurama exhibit at the General Motors pavilion. Futurama was a massive 36,000 square-foot scale model of America in 1960, complete with futuristic homes, urban complexes, bridges, dams, surrounding landscape, and most importantly, an advanced highway system which permitted speeds of 100 miles per hour. A film was shown called *To New Horizons* and featured a Technicolor segment of the "Wonder World of 1960." Near the end of the film, over scenes of the bright automobile-fueled future the narrator intones:

> And so we see some suggestion of the things to come. A world, which far from being finished, is hardly yet begun. A world with a future in which all of us are tremendously interested because, that is where we are going to spend the rest of our lives. In a future which can be whatever we purpose to make it.

Slightly altered, the phrase would become a main staple in the Criswell repertoire. He would use it to open his radio and television shows, guest appearances, some of his newspaper columns, and *Plan 9 From Outer Space*. Upon leaving the Futurama exhibit, visitors were given a small blue and white button that simply said, "I Have Seen the Future." Jeron had seen the future and armed with that vision was ready to tell the world of the wonders and disasters of those coming tomorrows.

April 1953, Fate, "Prophecies I Have Heard":

> Loretta, a New York nightclub crystal ball reader, told me. "You will marry a girl whose initials are M.L.S. She will come from a little town in Pennsylvania, will be an actress and you will live in California and will receive 1,000 letters every day!"

I did marry a girl with the initials M.L.S. (Myrtle Louise Stone-sifer) who came from Littlestown, Pa. She is an actress, professionally know as Halo Meadows.

Jeron and Myrtle formed a small troupe for *Dorian Gray* touring it across the country and claiming to play in many college and university auditoriums where they also alleged that their books were used in the English and Drama departments. After the short tour of what they called the "Middle West," they landed in the showbiz promised land, Hollywood, California.

Theme of the
Restless Heart

And I predict that Hollywood is on the verge of the greatest scandal it has ever seen.

The past scandals of the past years mean nothing to the scandal that will soon sweep Hollywood. You and I, who know the very name of Hollywood, will bow our heads in shame at this frightening discovery. To think of it, criminals of this kind lurching in the very limelight of the Hollywood celebrities, the klieg lights, Hollywood Boulevard, Sunset Boulevard, and the opening nights. Who calls themselves American would dare walk in the shadow and the reputation of the great and the near great of Hollywood!

Criswell

Louise Howard and Jeron Criswell announced themselves in Hollywood during the rumblings of the coming U.S. involvement in the war raging across the Atlantic Ocean in early 1940. They boldly proclaimed themselves as, "Broadway Stars . . . Direct from the Comedy Theater, New York City." They premiered *Love Life of Dorian Gray* on May 18, 1940, at the Footlights Theater on Sunset Boulevard and Laurel Avenue. Press for the show called it "Drama and burlesque, melodrama and farce of the Victorian era" and claimed, "In this play Oscar Wilde gives a nostalgic autobiography of his undying affection for Lord Alfred Douglas and the society and times in which he moved." Louise would sing two numbers

Jeron Criswell & Halo Meadows in the Oscar Wilde drama *Sins of Dorian Gray*, promotional photo.

of her own composition in the first and third acts. She would also play dual roles as Lady Gwendolyn Farrol and the misled maiden Sybil Dane. Jeron played the unspoiled youth Dorian Gray. The pair claimed to recreate the roles made famous in the 1890s, by the team of Sarah Bernhardt and Lou Tellegen.

Excerpts from the programme for the production:

Let us turn the clock of time back a mere fifty years to the age you remember with nostalgic reverence. This was the age when Oscar Wilde was the theater and the theater was Oscar Wilde. As Oscar Wilde tells us, "This was the age when the unnecessary things were our only necessities". . . "When everything was priced far above its proper value". . . "When the light things were taken seriously and the serious things lightly". . . "When there were only two classes of people, those who knew absolutely everything and those who knew absolutely nothing". . . "When there was one thing worse than being talked about and that was not being talked about". . . "When men married because they were tired, women because they were curious, and both were disappointed". . . "When they didn't exhaust love, but love exhausted them". . . "When everyone was a peacock in everything but beauty." If you had mentioned Modesty, Economy or Birth Control no one would have the slightest idea of what you were talking about. Let us look back to that century you managed to escape (or did you?) but hush! let us look upon the people created by Oscar Wilde and listen to what they tell us on this first Tuesday in June 1890—

The programme lists "Oscar Wilde's Immortal Cast of Characters" along with the actors portraying those roles followed by an "About the Play" section giving a brief history of how Dorian Gray the novel was adapted from a play manuscript, Wilde's successful theatrical career, and the history of how the playwright's only novel had been brought to the stage previously. "About the Cast" gives an extensive history of Louise's work starting with her productions at her "own theater" in New York City saying, "It was here that Pleasant Dreams and Interesting People, two unit revues that co-starred Howard, Artie Jones, and Criswell, were presented." It goes on telling of her books including the Broadway series and of her musical accomplishments. "To the continental audiences Miss Howard is best remembered for her song, 'I'm Keepin' the Man Who's Keepin' the Man Who's Keepin' Me,' which may be purchased in this country only on private recordings along with her, 'He Thinks He's Hedy Lamarr.' In the field of popular music Miss Howard owns and operates Louise Howard and Her Gamboleers, an orchestra designed for middle western audiences. Since receiving her M.A. from the University of Pennsylvania Miss Howard swings the pendulum of appeal from the lofty to the popular."

About the Cast. . . . Criswell played Oswald in *Ghosts* with Mrs. Fiske on tour after she saw his performance as Young Woodley. The Redpath Chautauqua became interested in

Halo in *Sins of Dorian Gray* does a strip tease gay 90s style, promotional photo.

Mr. Criswell while he was student at the University of Cincinnati and upon his graduation offered him an actor-manager contract. For two summers Mr. Criswell operated the Greenkill Park Theater near Kingston, N.Y. which he lost when Father Divine purchased it for his "Angels" as one of the Heavens. Saratoga and Chautauqua N.Y. have also enjoyed the Drama Festivals directed by Mr. Criswell. While Mr. Criswell was connected with the New York office of Samuel French he became an authority on International Copyrights. He wrote many scripts for the radio day time serials, lectured schools, colleges and universities through the lyceum bureaus. He toured his own productions in Europe and Northern Africa. Mr. Criswell is the great grand-nephew of the late Joseph Jefferson who was the foremost actor-manager of his time, most remembered for his portrayal of Rip Van Winkle. Mr. Criswell has produced *Rip Van Winkle, Joan of Arc,* and *Hamlet* as outdoor spectacles for state fairs and expositions.

The "About the Cast" section continues with a bio of Edward Taylor in the role of "Meadows, a Gray retinue" who was from Lincoln and was educated at the University of Nebraska, Harvard, and in Europe, also playing French speaking roles in productions for royalty in Paris, Greece, and Egypt. He returned to America due to the war, leaving cancelled engagements in Paris and Egypt. Michael Beverley playing "Basil Hallward, the artist" was a chemical engineer from Michigan who joined a drama society and caught the acting bug after being unexpectedly cast in a role that "went dear to his heart so that he could no longer keep his mind on engineering." He then performed at a Shakespearean Drama Festival, Stratford-On-Avon with a role in Othello and then a variety of roles in Chicago and that "he is now as much interested in variety characterization as he ever was in chemical formulas." Edward Kreiling as "Sir Harry Wottan, the noted raconteur" was born in Baltimore and played there with the Vagabond Players, graduated from the American Academy of Dramatic Arts, appeared with the Robin Hood Players in Delaware, and that after Louise liked his portrayal of a fierce town-lyncher in Too Many Heroes on Broadway so much so, that she gave him the role of the Shakespearean actor with young wife problems in her play Live Again.

The last section is on Artie Jones, the composer of "Victorian Waltz," "I Was Just Around the Corner," "It Will Never Work," and "Peers and the Dears" and tells of his work with Howard and Criswell as a writer, co-star, and co-author and that "His musical comedies, revues and nightclub floor shows have attracted the sophisticates of New York, London, and Paris. His song, 'West Point Hop,' was in *The Duke of West Point* (1938) and his 'Arabian Night' was the theme song for the recent revival of *The Son of the Sheik* (1937). Mr. Jones has authored musical albums and children's song folios. His 'Funny Little Bunny' which he sketched from his by the same title has become standard Easter toy. 'Violin in the Dark' and 'I Fell All Over Myself" are his latest recordings."

From *The Picture of Dorian Gray*:

Lord Henry looked at him. Yes, he was certainly wonderfully handsome, with his finely curved scarlet lips, his frank blue eyes, his crisp gold hair. There was something in his face that made one trust him at once. All the candour of youth was there, as well as all youth's passionate purity. One felt that he had kept himself unspotted from the world. No wonder Basil Hallward worshipped him.

CLAUDIA POLIFRONIO: Criswell was very handsome. He had a face like an Apollo. That's why he was up for the part of Dorian Gray [in the Hollywood Movie]. Because if you read Oscar Wilde, Dorian Gray has beautiful, chiseled features, just gorgeous. He [Criswell] was a handsome and very imposing man. Very likable, never grumpy, always up-lifting.

Curtis Harrington was a director of experimental and horror films who worked in film and television for over six decades until his death on May 6, 2007. His debut horror film was the moody and quirky *Night Tide* (1961), starring Dennis Hopper in his first leading role as a sailor obsessed with the idea that a carnival mermaid is a real mermaid and murders at the full moon. Harrington attended a production of *Love Life of Dorian Gray*.

CURTIS HARRINGTON: They gave it a strong homosexual implication. Because there was a scene, I think it's when Dorian Gray kills the painter Basil Hallward, who falls behind a couch and the Dorian Gray character crawls around behind the couch and then he stands up and he says, "Oh my God. His lips are no longer warm." Well, you can get the implication of that easily. That was the line in the play. I just happen to remember that because it was sort of shocking at the time.

May 29, *Hollywood Citizen-News*, "Party Centered Around New Swimming Pool"

Edward Taylor, featured actor in Oscar Wilde's 'Love Life of Dorian Gray' at Footlight Theater, was guest of honor at a birthday party celebration given by his cousin, Roland Boreham, 621 Beverly Dr. Louise Howard and Jeron Criswell, stars of the play, and Michael Beverley and Edward Krelling, supporting players, drove with Mr. Taylor to the party after a recent night performance. Festivities took place around Mr. and Mrs. Boreham's new swimming pool, which had its "official opening" on that occasion.

After a six-week run at the Footlights Theater, Jeron and Louise announced on July 7, 1940, that they were taking a one year lease on the Hollytown Theater at 1743 N. New Hampshire Avenue and opening with *The Gay Hamlet*, the first folio edition as played by Shakespeare in 1542. Other classics of the Howard & Criswell Drama Festival were to include: *Camille the Passion Flower*, the original version as produced in Paris in 1848, with the famous bordello and heaven scenes; *Romeo and Juliet*, the E. H. Southern—Julia Marlow recital version; *Joan of Arc; Hoosier School Master*, the Indiana classic of early America and *Rip Van Winkle*. Louise's own plays, *Women's Hotel, City Pace, Live Again,* and *Clouded Pane,* and Jeron's plays, *Look to Heaven, Angel Breath, Sunrise* and *Span,* and the Howard and Criswell collaboration, *Dancing Ladies,* were all planned for the coming season. On July 14, the duo announced that "unprecedented demand" for *Love Life of Dorian Gray* caused them to change their plans and postpone *Gay Hamlet* until later in the season. Larry Bordan, an actor turned wrecking crew business owner, recalled appearing in a stage production of *Hamlet* with Jeron. "I fought a sword duel on the stage with Criswell in that play and I'll never forget the things that happened." Unfortunately Larry didn't share those "things."

On July 16, in the local Salinas newspaper *The Californian,* it was proclaimed with a headline that "Dorian Gray' to Be Produced in Salinas." The announcement claimed that the plays *Dorian Gray* and *Gay Hamlet* would be brought to Salinas by Jeron Criswell drama festival productions the following month during the annual drama festival and also mentioned the current run of *Dorian Gray* at the Footlights theater in Hollywood. It was declared on July 26 in *The Capital Times,* Madison, Wisconsin, that Howard and Criswell had announced the festival production of the two plays would be held there during the season ahead and in the July 29 edition of the *Sunbury Daily Item,* Sunbury, Pennsylvania, it claimed that *Dorian Gray* would play there "presented by the same cast of characters which appeared in the Comedy Theatre, New York City for a long and successful run." There are no records of these performances.

A 1941 listing in the Los Angeles city directory showed Jeron Criswell as the manager of the Hollytown Theater.

After arriving in Hollywood, the dog Sunshine that Myrtle fell in love with became downcast, so she renamed the dog Victory. "You know, he changed." she said. In the dog's final years he was called Perfect. Myrtle Louise also adopted a new name, Halo Meadows, taking her new first name from a popular hair shampoo she saw in a store. Halo was a "soapless" shampoo claiming at one point in advertisements that it was "America's #1 Selling Shampoo." The uniquely fragrant and pleasant smelling shampoo was marketed with the slogan "Soaping dulls hair, while Halo glorifies it." Radio and television commercial jingles performed by many celebrities and recording artists, including Frank Sinatra, Peggy Lee, and Eddie Cantor declared, "Halo, everybody Halo. Halo is the shampoo that glorifies your hair. So Halo shampoo, Halo"

MAILA NURMI (VAMPIRA): He and Halo tried to lure wealthy investors in their early Hollywood days though they had no money whatsoever. They would serve pigeons and call them capons on thrift shop silver platters.

In 1942 Halo sued Twentieth Century Fox for copyright infringement in a California District Court. She alleged that she originated, devised, and created a dramatic composition under the title *Women's Hotel* and that the composition had been in unpublished manuscript form and that it had been duly copyrighted. She further claimed that Twentieth Century Fox produced and released a motion picture under the title *Hotel for Women,* which contained a substantial reproduction of her title, plot, idea, dramatic situations, and characters of her play, and advertised that the same was adapted from a story by Elsa Maxwell and Kathryn Scola without her consent and in violation of her copyright. The court summarized the story in the play and the story exhibited in the film and stating, "The striking similarities and series of coincidences, and in many instances the very language, cannot honestly be said to be mere chance, but must have been the result of copying." The court also found through testimony that the "Plaintiff operated a theatre in 1937 in New York for the purpose of presenting her original plays and plays of other playwrights. These performances were invitational affairs. The theatre was known as the Villa Venice at 14 East 60th Street, New York City. Her company was known as the Louise Howard players. The plaintiff produced her play, *Women's Hotel* in July 1937 and that Mr. Frank Underwood, defendant's representative in its story department in Radio City, New York, was present at this performance, and advised plaintiff that he liked the play and requested her to submit a script to him for presentation to the defendant. About a week later the plaintiff forwarded copy of the script of play, *Women's Hotel* to Mr. Underwood. Inquiring three or four weeks later of Mr. Underwood, the plaintiff was advised by him that the script was on the coast. About three weeks thereafter, the plaintiff sent her stage manager, Mr. Lord, to Mr. Underwood's office, and the script was returned. In the latter part of 1939, defendant produced, exhibited and distributed a motion picture called, *Hotel for Women* by Elsa Maxwell.

"The Court, the parties to the action, and the attorneys had the advantage of seeing the film 'Hotel for Women' exhibited and the Court is of the opinion that the plaintiff has established infringement by the defendant by copying a substantial and material part of her copyrighted play 'Women's Hotel.' An ordinary observer who had read or seen the plaintiff's play would recognize the infringement in the film produced, distributed and exhibited by the defendants."

The court awarded Myrtle $3,960 in damages along with $1,000 in attorney fees on December 30, 1942. Twentieth Century Fox appealed the case and on February 10, 1944, the Ninth Circuit Court of Appeals, after a thorough review of the case and another reading of the play and viewing of the film stated that, "In each version there are minor scenes characterized by gossipy and envious women who delight in half-veiled remarks; lonely girls; paid escorts, racy conversations; dogs on leashes, and like incidents tending to further warrant the findings and conclusions that the copyrighted play was utilized in a substantial way in the motion picture 'Hotel for Women.' It is true, as appellant argues, that the film and appellee's composition differ in numerous respects. Such dissimilarities result, however, principally from the film's enlarged means to express in a wider latitude incidents necessarily requiring a wider range of settings than a play restricted to the narrow confines of a theatrical stage is able to present. We find no reason to disturb the award of damages or the allowance of attorney's fees."

In 1930 Anthony Norvell moved from his birth state of New York to seek his fame and fortune in Hollywood. The good looking, dapper, and charming "Norvell the great! Hollywood Astrologer" was the confidant of several screen actors and stars and gave readings for his famous friends and clients, such as Ronald Reagan, Tyrone Power, and Clark Gable. He penned astrological predictions for a number of fan magazines and newspapers. His original intent was to be a stage actor and would use his "soothsaying skills" to give readings to actors and other performers when he began to hang around stage doors and theatrical agencies looking for his big break. Some of the more popular Hollywood celebrity fanzines began running advertorials promoting his skills and if the readers sent a dime along with their birthdate and a self-addressed-stamped-envelope, Norvell would read their charts. The popularity of the articles landed Norvell an agent and a transcontinental personal appearance tour on vaudeville in 1939 giving predictions and offering readings from the stage. He collapsed on stage in Lincoln, Nebraska on February 11, 1940, with the February 12, issue of *Variety* joking that he hadn't foreseen that. On January 2, 1941, ads began running occasionally in *Variety* and newspapers announcing that Norvell, "The Man That Rules the Stars" was "Available for private consultations by appointment only."

In mid-1942, Norvell "Mystic Astrologer," began free weekly engagements on Thursdays at 8 p.m. held at the Woman's Club of Hollywood on Hollywood Boulevard with lectures and talks featuring inspirational and cultural entertainment programs on a variety of metaphysical topics like "The Magic Circle," "The Secret of Mystic Release," and "The Shangri-La Within." He would also present world prophecy on the outcome of the war and the destiny of the United States in the post-war period and answer personal questions from the audience astrologically. Newspaper promotions for the events said Norvell had been an astrologer for seventeen years and had been recently elected president of the World Astrology Association, an international organization for the promotion and furtherance of

FREE SHOW CULTURAL ENTERTAINMENT

★ ★

NORVELL MYSTIC ASTROLOGER PRESENTS

THE MAGIC CIRCLE

WOMAN'S CLUB
7078 HOLLYWOOD BLVD.
WED. SEPT 23-24 THUR.
8:00 P.M
GL. 2302
FREE ADMISSION

The Hand of Fate

★

NORVELL'S
WORLD PREDICTIONS
Your Questions Answered
Added Attraction
FOSTER GRUNDY
Classical Dancer In
"DANCE OF THE FURIES"
Public Invited

scientific astrology. Photos accompanying the promotions usually featured Norvell consulting with a famous Hollywood star such as Dorothy Lamour, Jimmy Stewart, or Hedy Lamarr. The October 18 edition of the *LA Times* ran a feature announcing a competition with prizes totaling $10,000 in the "Wheel O' Fortune." Readers were instructed to send in a photograph along with a birthdate and Norvell would pick the most interesting twenty photos which led to the most interesting "readings," winning the contestant one of the daily prizes of ten dollars along with having their photo and "reading" published in the *Times*. The feature said Norvell was one of the world's most widely known astrologers and he claimed his past predictions based on astrological science had proved 85% correct. When asked when the current war would end he said, "The stars show an era of world peace starting June of 1944, and look for the war to end at that time with the democracies on the winning side." The competition that the paper called "not a contest," was of course a promotion to get readers to subscribe to the paper while gathering their mailing information for future inundation with offers of subscriptions to the paper. In the November 5, edition of the *LA Times* a half-page fea-

ture ad ran for Norvell's "Wheel O' Fortune" announcing some of the winners with their photos and "readings."

Below this was a large section of photos of the twenty winners, "Today's Prize Winners of $10 Each—Also Eligible For Grand Prizes Up To $1000" with a short astrological "reading" based on the persons submitted birthdate. One of the winners was Halo Meadows with the photo being one of her headshots from the Broadway days.

> Birth Date—May 6 Taurus is your sign and Venus your ruling planet. You are amazingly versatile and possess more than one talent. This sign rules the voice and generally gives charm, poise and personality in work connected with the public. The year ahead is one of good fortune in connection with your work and a possible trip in the early part of 1943. Finances should be better.

On November 13 a United Press Hollywood byline ran in a number of local papers with the headline "Did They Foretell This?

Film Stars May Lose Their Prophets By Law Banning Astrologers, Psychics." The article told of a model ordinance drafted that day at the request of the county managers office. The recommendation to draw up the proposed model ordinance outlawing seers and fortune-telling in Los Angeles County was made to the Board of Supervisors by the Public Welfare Commission. The Supervisors ordered the model drafted for all municipalities to consider and that legal advisors to the board said the action was directed at nobody in particular among the crystal ball gazers, handwriting and tea leaf readers, and astrologers. The article said that Norvell became the most prosperous of astrologers and psychics having been prophet and counselor to many of Hollywood's most famous film stars, including Marlene Dietrich, and by charging them fabulous fees. The article also gave examples of other astrologers and mystics and the celebrities they served. One was that Bela Lugosi "the movie monster" was guided under the zodiac by Manley P. Hall.

One of the winners in the November 30, "Wheel O' Fortune" was Jeron King Criswell, also featuring a headshot from the Broadway days.

Birth Date—August 18 Your sign is Leo and your ruling planet is the Sun. This sign is artistic and musical and you are fond of creative pursuits. You have the ability to meet the public and are extremely intelligent and forceful in the use of your personality. You make friends easily and should find your greatest happiness and success through influential friends and the artistic and creative world. Work connected with publication, newspapers, advertising and radio are favored for your sign.

Jeron's path was clear. Norvell had spoken!

The December 26 edition of the Los Angeles *Daily News* featured an article with a headshot of a dapper and confident Norvell with the heading of "Metaphysics."

Hollywood's outstanding astrologer and metaphysical teacher, Norvell, will appear nightly starting New Year's night on the stage of the Troupers

NORVELL appears in the Oscar Wilde comedy drama "Sins of Dorian Gray" current at the Troupers theater.

Theater at Las Palmas and Hollywood blvd. in the stage presentation of Oscar Wilde's famous drama, "The Sins of Dorian Gray," it was announced by James Ellis Thompson, producer and director. Norvell will be supported by members of the original New York cast, which includes Jeron Criswell, Halo Meadows and many others.

That same day the *Hollywood Citizen-News* ran another headshot of the handsome lecturer-astrologer announcing he had been cast in the role of Sir Henry Wooten in the play but would continue his series of metaphysical lectures after the opening. It also said that Norvell had appeared in the role at the Greenkill Theater, Duchess County, New York in 1935. Norvell was quoted. "The great message that Oscar Wilde presents to the world through this astounding comedy-drama is something that each person should hear." Headshot promo photos of a demur Halo ran promoting the play and a promo photo of Jeron misspelled his name as Griswell.

The reviews of the play started January 5, 1943, in the *LA Times*, with the bold headline "BURLESQUE OF OSCAR WILDE STARS AS-

HALO MEADOWS plays a wicked woman in the 90's in "Sins of Dorian Gray" continuing at the Troupers.

JERON GRISWELL has the title role in "Sins of Dorian Gray." Opening tonight at Troupers with Norvell starred.

TROLOGER NORVELL" by Katherine Von Bon.

The ultimate irony is perpetrated in Hollywood when Oscar Wilde, the great aesthete and wit of the 19th century, is translated in terms of burlesque. Wilde would in all probability rise from his grave could he witness the proceedings in "The Sins of Dorian Gray," which is showing at the Troupers Theater, starring Norvell, well-known astrologer. Perhaps it is a huge practical joke which Norvell and his associates elect to play upon Hollywood, for there are many young would-be sophisticates from small American towns who never even heard of Oscar Wilde. These actors have chosen to turn the complicated innuendo of Wilde's intellectual mirth into burlesque, perhaps unconsciously, and Miss Halo Meadows clowns through the piece with abandon which is at times piquant to the point of embarrassment.

LAUGH AT ACTORS

The play started with actors flaunting the lush gestures of the Gay Nineties, as they delivered the Wildian repartee. It was quite in the little-theater tradition, with a commendable elegance as to settings and costumes. However with the advent of Miss Meadows, and as the play developed, it turned into a rather outlandish burlesque, which had the audience in stitches. However, it must be admitted that the audience was laughing largely at the actors and their stilted delivery of lines, rather than at the banter.

CAST APPRAISED

Norvell as Lord Henry delivered his lines with a certain style in the first half of the piece and played with commendable poise and reserve. As an old man in the last act he was less convincing. Halo Meadows cavorted in a sort of London Music Hall style as Lady Farrow and won many laughs, though it was plain that she was rather trying to out-Lanchester Elsa Lanchester. Her over acting and gestures were at times on the edge of vulgarity. Ralph Dunhaven as the effeminate Parker proved himself an old-timer through his ability to win laughs. Leonard Walters as Hallward was excellent, though his weeping scenes brought mirth. Jeron Criswell as Dorian Gray seemed rather ill at ease in the role.

Despite the negative reviews, the show went on with announcements of its continuation in the entertainment sections of the local newspapers throughout January. Headlines with announcements such as "Sins of Dorian Gray' Current on Stage at Troupers Theater" touting Norvell, the astrologer, in the lead role and Halo Meadows as the actress appearing in a dual role of Sybil and as Lady Gwendolyn Farrol and proclaiming, "A highlight of the play, according to management, is a striptease number done in the Gay 90's style." Another headline read "Dorian Gray' Run Continues"

"Hilarity reigns nightly at the Troupers Theater, where 'The Sins of Dorian Gray' is showing. Jeron Criswell, Halo Meadows and Norvell, who plays the role of Sir Henry, are featured." A large ad ran headlined with "Norvell in Oscar Wilde's Shocking Drama 'The Sins of Dorian Gray.'"

DUAL ROLE in "Sins of Dorian Gray" is played by Halo Meadows. Production opens Friday at the Troupers theater.

The January 27 edition of a local Hollywood paper featured a photo of Halo. The short caption mentioned her dual role in the play. The play was promoted heavily in the papers through the end of January and into February. "Sins' Inspire Many Chuckles"

Audiences are chuckling at the quaint and nostalgic lines and songs in "The Sins of Dorian Gray," now playing at the Hollywood Troupers Theater. Norvell, star of "Sins," and his leading lady, Halo Meadows, cavort through 50 years of wickedness in this play about Victorian England.

"Dorian Gray' Set Replica of Original"

"Sins of Dorian Gray," now at the Hollywood Troupers Theater, is a replica of the original London production of 1890. The entire staging is complete from the rare Mason-Hamlin parlor organ, authentic Worth of Paris clothing to the naughty songs of that era. Norvell heads the cast and is supported by Jeron Criswell and Halo Meadows.

"Picture People View Troupers Attraction"

The Hollywood Troupers Theater reports that many stars from the film colony have been attending the Oscar Wilde comedy-drama, 'Sins of Dorian Gray' starring Norvell.

On February 20 a short piece ran simply titled "Astrology, Life's Mystic Retreat," "the subject of Norvell, the mystic astrologer, Thursday at 8 p.m. in the Woman's Club of Hollywood. Norvell will at this time give an amazing psychic demonstration." Followed shortly by the February 26 article titled "Failed to foresee this."

Mahlon Norvell had some tall explaining to do yesterday to the Indian Guides of Spookland, Local 606, when he tossed a $3 séance for Mary E. Galton and failed to see that he was going to be arrested in the near future. It turned out she was a policewoman, and she nabbed Hollywood's favorite future gazer under ordinance 4330, which bans fortune-telling, soothsaying and various related activities.

Norvell—whose real name is Anthony Trupo, and who recently went for a stage career in the little theater production of "The Sins of Dorian Gray"—pleaded not guilty to violating the anti-fortune-telling ordinance. His trial date was set for March 25, pending which he was released on $500 bond.

On February 19 Norvell gave a reading to a pretty blonde woman in the parlor of his apartment at 6650 Franklin Avenue, which was decorated with the "usual equipment, such as a velvet drape and crystal ball." She told him her birthdate and he held her hand and while reading her vibrations and told her that she was born under the turbulent sign of Gemini. He also told her that two other planets were influencing her love life and that she had a lost love affair, she would marry twice, was suited to public work, would be offered a new job in the future, get married to an attorney in July of 1944, not have any children, and live to be seventy but never be very happy. The woman then asked Norvell about her mother's health, but he told her he was having difficulty in getting any psychic vibrations from her. The woman then paid Norvell three dollars for the reading. Policewoman Gatlon returned to Norvell's home on February 25 arresting him for violating the city fortune-telling ordinance. The March 4 edition of the *Hollywood Citizen-News* ran a front page article titled "Seer's Nemesis Tells All, Method of Nabbing Soothsayers Revealed." The article explained that Policewoman Mary E. Galton worked as an investigator for the Bunko division of the LA police department and specialized in the arrests of persons suspected of corporate security and real estate frauds, but "knocks over" fortune-tellers as a pastime, resulting in "hundreds of arrests" for violations of the city ordinance prohibiting all forms of fortune-telling. Recounting the Norvell arrest she said, "Norvell was the most belligerent suspect I have ever contacted. Usually, when we make an arrest, the suspect is pretty meek, but not Norvell. He was indignant." The article went on to describe the tactics used by Galton to dupe the fortune-tellers, getting tips from complaints or seeing an advertisement telling of the supernatural powers of the soothsayer, then calling to make an appointment for a reading. When she entered the seers parlor, she would act like the type of woman that would believe everything the fortune-teller had to say and after the reading pay them with marked bills which would be used as evidence in court. She also said that to date, none of the seers had been able to foresee what was in store for them because she had never been spotted. The arrests didn't always come after the first reading and sometimes the policewoman would enlist the help of friends to get a "vision of the future" so there would be no question as to whether or not the seer was accepting payment. The city ordinance banned advertising by fortune-tellers whether they were receiving remuneration or not. Galton said, "Some of the arrested persons have been too ignorant to know that they were violating the law. Yet they feel quite fit to predict futures and give advice. The amount of money which they get from the public—mostly women—over a period of a year is astounding, but that is not the only objection we have. Always there is the possibility that fortune-tellers will resort to blackmail. Frequently they learn secrets which are valuable weapons in the hands of the blackmailer. Often the seers pose as ministers so they can claim exemption from the ordinance, but few can of them can prove that they are *bona fide* church leaders." The remainder of the article told of how licensed fortune-telling in all its forms seemed doomed in LA County and that all the cities in the county had agreed to join in abolishing legalized fortune-telling.

On March 25 the courtroom was filled with about a hundred men and women who professed to be faithful followers of Norvell's teachings. The principal witness for the prosecution was Miss Galton who testified before Municipal Judge Leroy Dawson. Recounting her reading, she added that Norvell said she was by nature "cold and temperamental" while he was holding her hand to sync and receive her "psychic vibrations." Norvell took the stand in his own behalf and in his defense contended that he was acting in his capacity as an ordained minister with the title of Doctor of Divinity and was the head of the Church of Culture, a branch of the International Constitutional Church whose head, Dr. Charles E. Kelso had designated Norvell "Doctor of Astrology" and therefore had not violated the fortune-telling ordinance. He also contended that he was legally entitled to perform marriages and conduct burial or baptismal services although he had never done so. Norvell's attorney, Albert E. Albeck moved for dismissal of the charges, but the judge overruled the motion after Miss Galton's testimony. Albeck tried to argue that astrology was a science and an outgrowth of astronomy, and he denied that his client advertised or engaged in the business of fortune-telling, insisting that Norvell only dealt with astrological horoscopes.

The second day of the trial saw some levity described in an article with a Hollywood (UP) byline titled "Penner's Duck Not Eligible in Trial of 'Seer'." The prosecutor, Deputy City Attorney Lewis Teegarden, tried to prove that Norvell and Joe Penner's ("Wanna buy a duck?" comedian) duck were fellow ministers in the International Constitutional Church since they were both ordained by Dr. Kelso. Norvell's attorneys quickly objected, and the court decided that it had nothing to do with whether or not Norvell was a fortune-teller and Judge Dawson held that "the ordination of the late comedian's duck was not germane to the case at hand."

At the conclusion of the trial on Friday, the judge continued the case until 2 p.m. Monday, March 29 to allow himself time to read the large bulk of exhibits introduced. Norvell was facing a possible sentence of six months in jail or a fine of $500 or both if found guilty.

74

When court reconvened on Monday, the judge found Norvell guilty of the charge, ruling that Norvell had failed to ask the police-woman to become a member of the church and had failed to explain or mention any function of the church to her. He said, "You were acting in a personal capacity, and you were not acting as a minister." The judge then continued sentence until April 2 for probation plea and to allow time for filing a written notice of appeal. Deputy City Attorney Teegarden did not contest the continuance and Norvell indicated he would appeal the conviction. On the sentencing date, he was sentenced to pay a fine of $150 or seventy-five days in jail. His attorney immediately filed a notice of appeal and the judge allowed Norvell to go free under a $100 appeal bond. The decision was upheld by the Appellate Department of the Supreme Court by three Superior Court judges on June 25. Norvell had predicated his defense on the constitutional rights of religious practitioners, but the high court held and said that it did not apply to the case and that Norvell "was engaged in fortune-telling at the time the complaining witness had a 'reading' by him last February 19."

Norvell's conviction and sentencing didn't tarnish his reputation, slow his metaphysical activities, or diminish his profiting from his astrological science. He continued to book engagements touted as "Hollywood's famous philosopher and metaphysician," "the world's greatest astrologist," and "the man who rules the movie stars." In 1953, he and his wife purchased a lavish new home in the prestigious Bel Air area of Los Angeles, followed shortly by the purchase of two apartment buildings. Throughout the 1950s and 1960s he ran ads for Sunday services at his Church of the Religious Mind, continued lecturing, and had a program on KGF radio. He went on to write several books in the 1960s and 1970s on astrology, metaphysics, mind cosmology, and transcendental meditation, along with a couple of oriental diet books and some self-help-motivational tomes as well with titles such as *Think Yourself Rich*, *Mind Cosmology*, *How to Control Your Destiny*, and *Dynamic Laws for Successful Living*. His book *The Occult Secrets of Transmutation* on "how to utilize the higher self to convert through spiritual energy into any material object you desire" was called in a review "psycho physics." He frequently appeared on television as an expert in parapsychology. His most repeated quote is "Plant a kernel of wheat and you reap a pint, plant a pint and you reap a bushel. Always the law works to give you back more than you give." Norvell went to the Great Beyond on July 23, 1990.

The city fortune-telling ordinance would stay on the books for some thirty-five more years until the ban was overturned after numerous pleas and challenges by astrologers, hypnotists, and gypsies who claimed it violated their constitutional right to religious freedom.

By the time the mid-twentieth century came around, southern California was known as being a breeding ground of new esoteric, "oddball" alternative faiths and spiritual movements such Spiritualism, Occultism, Theosophy, New Thought, countless "Temples of Light," UFO cults, and all manner of things metaphysical.

1942 saw Criswell begin to promote himself as a spiritualist and psychic. A newspaper listing for the Spiritualist Science Church promoted Jeron Criswell as a speaker on January 11. In the May 23 evening edition of the *L A Citizen-News* an announcement was titled "Psychic Society Plans Monday Meeting." It publicized that the English Psychic Society would hold all future meetings at the Hollywood Hotel on Mondays at 8 p.m. and would be open to the public. It said the decision followed a meeting the previous night at which the Rev. and Mrs. Jeron King Criswell entertained thirty society members at their Hollywood Argyle apartment and Mrs. Heaton-Barnes, the noted London Medium, was the guest of honor. The May 25 issue of the newspaper ran a small announcement headed "Psychics To Meet" saying that for the first time in 30 years the English Psychic Society would open its doors to the public that night at the Hollywood Hotel where Mrs. Heaton-Barnes, Robert Combs, Jeron

King Criswell, and Lura Gallagher would head the program. On the faith and religious services page of the May 30 edition of the *Hollywood Citizen-News* ran a new, more current headshot of the Rev. Jeron King Criswell, D.D. with the caption saying he was appearing with Mrs. Stella Heaton-Barnes under the auspices of the English Psychic Society in a special series of psychic demonstrations every Monday night at the Hollywood Hotel. Jeron had earned his Doctor of Divinity degree in a very short time.

In June, Jeron began attending events and parties hosted by and for the English Psychic Society as reported in the local papers.

"Party At Malibu Marks Phyllis Priest's Birthday"

Mrs. Audrey Priest entertained the English Psychic Society with a beach party at Malibu in honor of her daughter Phyllis' 17th birthday. Honor guests were Mrs. Heaton-Barnes, Louise Howard, Sally Waltz, Etta Fredrickson, W. T. Benda, and Rev. Jeron King Criswell.

"Garden Party Given At Vista St. Home"

Mrs. Stella Heaton-Barnes delightfully entertained the English Psychic Society recently with an old-fashioned garden party at her home, 1622 N. Vista St. Special guests were Audrey and Phyllis Priest, Sally Waltz, Etta Fredrickson, Louise Howard, W. T. Benda, and Dr. Jeron Criswell.

The July 4 edition of *Evening Citizen-News* ran an ad on the worship page under the prophecy section for the "ENGLISH PSYCHIC SOCIETY" with the details of the meeting and guests: Noted Child Medium-Nancy Dekker; Physical Experiences—Ruth Clark; Direct Questions—Mercia Montagu; Trance Test Questions—Stella Heaton-Barnes; Prophecy For July—Sealed Ballots-Jeron King Criswell

Church of Inner Voice

JERON KING CRISWELL.

The Rev. Jeron King Criswell, America's foremost medium, the new Nostradamus, appears every Sunday, Wednesday, Friday at 8 p. m. at Hollywood hotel for the Church of the Inner Voice.

D.D.; and Louise Howard—Piano Interlude.

In August Jeron celebrated his birthday. A "Penthouse party atop Highbourne Gardens was given by Norvell for 100 guests honoring the Rev. Jeron King Criswell on 35th birth anniversary."

In the Sunday Sermons section of the August 29, 1942, *L A Times,* a listing showed the Church of the Inner Voice at the Hollywood Hotel with Dr. Jeron K. Criswell conducting services at 8 p.m. the next day. The September 5, edition of the *Evening Citizen-News* had a small ad for the Church of the INNER VOICE—Every Sunday, 8 p.m., Hollywood Hotel, The Rev. Dr. Jeron King Criswell, Pastor. All Message Service, Everyone will be reached with a spirit message—FULL ROBED CEREMONY—Louise Howard, Associate; Rev. Maryverne Jones; Dr. Lorenza Oelze. In the obituary section of the Sunday, September 6 *LA Times* with a heading of "To Officiate Services" it states that "Dr. Jeron King Criswell will officiate at the services of the Church of the Inner Voice at the Hollywood Hotel at 8 p.m. today." The September 26 paper also listed the services at the "church" and on the same day, *LA Daily News* on the "Church Services for Sunday" page featured the new headshot of Jeron King Criswell headed with "Church of Inner Voice" and was captioned "The Rev. Jeron King Criswell, America's foremost medium, the new

Nostradamus, appears every Sunday, Wednesday, Friday at 8 p.m. at Hollywood Hotel for the Church of the Inner Voice." A small ad also appeared at the bottom of the page under the Spiritualists section with CRISWELL AMERICA'S FOREMOST MEDIUM in bold type with the details of the "All Message Service" promising "Every one receives a Spirit Message" and a phone number to call Criswell for private consultation. October 3 listed the services with Rev. Louise Howard, Dr. Lorenza Oelze, and Dr. Maryverne Jones as assisting. On the next page of the same edition is a section of bold typed announcements for various religious services grouped by faiths such as Catholic, Episcopal, Presbyterian, Religious Science, Aeonian Institute, Shepard of the Air, Rosicrucian, Assembly of Man, and Church of Light, under Spiritualism is a listing that says "Criswell America's Foremost Prophet (Church of the Inner Voice) in an all message service with Maryverne Jones, Lorenza Oelze, Louise Howard. Each receives a spirit message. Every Sun., Wed., Fri., 8 p.m. Hollywood Hotel-Welcome! For a private reading call Criswell HI-4106." The October 10 edition of the *L A Daily News* ran a small announcement titled "Inner Voice" with details of the services that Pastor Criswell would give "world prophecy and practical visions" assisted by the previously mention members of the "church" with Louise as associate pastor. The next day's conducted service would be a full robed all message service with audience participation. Wednesday would feature Dr. Jones leading the open forum on "Psychic Guidance." Friday, Dr. Oelze would give instruction on "Your Aura" followed by messages. It also claimed Dr. Criswell celebrated twenty years in spiritualism that day. Apparently, Jeron began his studies in Spiritualism at the age of fifteen. The following week a small announcement ran in the *LA Times* for the church with the topic for the week of "The Happy Prince." Next week the topic was "God Has No Dimout" followed the next week by "The Divine Sales Tax."

It was about this time that the Norvell-Criswell-Howard collaboration on *Dorian Gray* began and Jeron and Louise seemed to curtail their "spiritual" work to focus on their stage aspirations for the first three months of 1943.

The March 27, 1943, evening *Hollywood Citizen-News* ran an article announcing that Davis Sturgis, founder of Universalism, would speak on "The Past, Present and Future of Mexico" the next evening at the Universal Forum at the Studio Lounge of the Hollywood-Roosevelt Hotel. There would also be other speakers, special Mexican music and Universal Art, and was open to the public without charge. The article went on to say that the Universal Theater, a unit of Universalism, was planning three productions for the upcoming three months. "I am My Brother's Keeper" by Vincent Godfrey Burns would have the author playing the role of a preacher and Jeron Criswell seen as a fugitive from a chain-gang. In August 1943 the *Hollywood Reporter* ran an article on Val Lewton's *The Ghost Ship* (1943), which stated "Dr. Jeron Criswell, former pastor of the Fifth Avenue Spiritualist Church, NYC, arrives today to serve as technical consultant on THE GHOST SHIP. Criswell is authority on 'psychic phenomena and ESP' and will apply his theories to members of the cast." The October 30, 1944 edition of the *LA Times* in the obituary section with the heading, Harold A. Criswell, stated that "Memorial services were held last night at the Church of the

Inner Voice for the late Pfc. Harold A. Criswell killed in France on Sept. 25, his 30th birthday. The pastor, Dr. J. K. Criswell, his cousin, officiated."

Jeron and Louise were relatively quiet throughout the last two years of World War II with Criswell only promoting occasional free lectures during the first half of 1945, at the Garden Court apartments located at 7021 Hollywood Boulevard near La Brea Avenue on Mondays and Thursdays at 8 p.m. Topics included "The Secret Prophecies of Nostradamus" and "Modern Occultism in the World Today."

The dropping of the atomic bomb on Hiroshima August 6, 1945, effectively ended WWII, unleashing a new fascinating but yet terrifying power onto the world along with new hopes for a better and brighter future for humankind.

In late 1945 Criswell began popping up more in the Spiritualist section of the local newspapers weekly Saturday religious pages. He had started to embrace using just the singular name—certainly something he picked up from Norvell. For the last three months of 1945 the Church of the Inner Voice and Criswell had announcements in the papers as a Spiritualist Church offering Trance Message Service every Monday and Friday at 8 p.m. at the Garden Court apartments.

1946 saw Jeron, Criswell, Dr. J. K. Criswell, Dr. King Criswell, Dr. Criswell, and Rev. Criswell, et al. offering a series of free lectures at the Garden Court apartments covering a number of esoteric subjects but a bit more focused on prophecy including, "World Prophecy," "World Prophecy Under Trance," "How to Psychoanalyze Yourself," "The Prophetic Pyramid of Giza," "Know-

SPIRITUALIST CHURCH

CRISWELL GARDEN COURT APTS.
7021 Hollywood Blvd. HI. 4106
CHURCH OF THE INNER VOICE
Trance Message Service Mon. 8 P. M. and
Fri., 8 P. M.

ing Your Yoga Powers," "The Key to Positive Prayer," "The Psychology of Eventful Living," "Seven Keys to Self Healing," "Healing and Occultism," "The Prophecies of St. Odile, Lord Chesterfield, and Davis," "The Secret of Personal Fearlessness," "God-Magnetism for Success and Happiness," "The Nine Psychological Steps of Marriage," "What the Seers Say About America Between 1947 and 1952," "Coming Events in World History," "Coming World Events in 1947," "Nostradamus Prophecies," "The Secret Prophecies of Nostradamus," "Predictions for 1947," and "Prosperity For You in 1947."

Jeron's father, Charles K. King passed away on March 5, 1946, at his home on Gibson Street after an illness of six and a half-years at the age of seventy-seven. His obituary stated he had been in the insurance business his entire life. He was laid to rest at the International Order of Odd Fellows cemetery located north of Princeton.

During the last months of 1946, small ads ran in local newspapers' church sections using a badly cropped headshot of Jeron from the Broadway days with just "Criswell" in bold type offering "Trance Message Service" by "America's Foremost Prophet" with Lecture & Healing at the Spiritualist Church at the G.C. Apt. Bldg. along with offerings of "Predictions for 1947," "Occult Mastership Class," "Useful Metaphysics," and a telephone number to call for "Divine Healing."

On August 5 an article headline stated "Religious group assists in getting homes for vets." It reported a watermelon party at the home of Dr. P. Rotondi that was enjoyed by 150 members of the Criswell Religious Foundation. "Plans were devised for obtaining more living quarters for returned veterans and their families. Dr. J. K. Criswell has been instrumental in placing more than 100 vaccines at the veterans disposal." And on August 26, "Religious group enjoys summer social" "Members of Criswell Religious Foundation were entertained at a social recently at the home of Dr. Peitro Rotondi. Plans were discussed for sharing homes with returning veterans and their families. Dr. J. K. Criswell, it is announced, has done much work in finding many vaccines for veterans. Guest of honor were Kezzie Jones and Lars Rexford of New York and the Rev. Carl Minugh of Tulsa."

In October the Criswells celebrated their tenth wedding anniversary as divulged in a newspaper's "Just Among Friends" section reporting that "Half a hundred friends and relatives attended a reception given by Dr. and Mrs. J. K. Criswell (Halo Vanessa) (sic) at their home on North Argyle marking their 10th wedding anniversary." and "JUBILEES" with "Dr. And Mrs. J. K. Criswell hosted a reception in their N. Argyle Ave. home on their 10th anniversary." Marriage records for the couple have not been able to be located and if they had held any kind of formal wedding ceremony, it certainly would have been reported in their respective hometown newspapers. At this time they were nearing having been acquainted for ten years having met in late 1937 or early 1938. It has also been claimed that they were married in 1940. Jeron and Myrtle's marriage could be considered as a common law marriage in which the couple lives together for a period of time and holds themselves out to friends, family, and the community as "being married" but without ever going through a formal ceremony or getting a marriage license.

Criswell began conducting séances at the Hollywood Wilshire YMCA located at 1553 North Schrader Boulevard and in Long Beach.

MAILA NURMI (VAMPIRA): The YMCAs at which he did séances were one block from his apartment in Hollywood, and later ones in Long Beach near the Pike. His friend and long-time lover John played the pipe organ at the ones in Long Beach.

Well, there was building near the pier, not directly on the water, but on that main boulevard [Ocean]. There was an old building there that was very tall. [The Blackstone?] Yes, I think so. It had a winding staircase inside the bell tower, and he would conduct séances in the bell tower, but they were, like, private, and limited attendance you know, because it seated only seven or eight people, and so they would have séances. But they had an organ up there. And they did it maybe once a month or so.

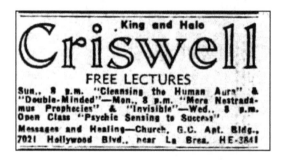

1947 saw a flurry of activity from the Criswells and the blossoming of a new career in a new medium for the medium. The year started with Criswell continuing to run announcements and ads promoting lectures at the Garden Courts apartments ballroom as the "Messages and Healing – Church" with subjects such as "Prophecies About California," "More Nostradamus Prophecies," "Personal Perception in Everyday Living," "Personal Freedom Through Occultism," "The Master Key to Occultism," "The Greatest Human Sin," "The Reward of the Wicked," "Self Deliverance," "Is Soul Travel Pagan," "Inner Wisdom," "Cleansing the Human Aura," "Mystery Behind Human Aura," "Key to Personal Activity," "Success Secrets," "Getting the Most Out of Life," "Double Minded," "True Ghost Stories," "Ten Lost Books of the Prophets," "How to Give Messages," "Psychic Sensing to Success," "Invisible," "How God Forecasts Your

Future," "Man vs. Honesty of God," "Expression," "The Prophetic Pyramid Unveiled," "Outwitting Nervous Tension," "Unexpected Events," "Change of Spirit," "World Prophecy for 1948," "World Conditions in 1948," and offering open classes with Personalized Psychology Tests, Mental-Physical Phenomena ESP, Sacred Rituals for Purification and How to Psychometrize Articles." Cris and Halo teamed-up on lectures and the ads sometimes pictured a photo of Criswell from the Broadway days and some featured a photo of Halo from the Broadway days as well. The ads would either have the names J. K. and Halo or King and Halo Criswell. Some of the ads mentioned Criswell on KFWB (Keep Filming Warner Brothers) radio.

He also founded "The Criswell Religious Foundation (Member Church Federation of America)." Personalized membership cards were issued commissioning the named person as member in good standing and signed by Pastor—Founder Criswell. The card also stated, "In Emergency Call HE 2133." Invitations were printed to the "Criswell Religious Foundation" for Criswell's new series on the occult for September

Ghost Stories Topic

"True Ghost Stories" and "World Conditions in 1948" will be discussed by Dr. King Criswell at 8 p.m. tomorrow and Monday, respectively, at 7021 Hollywood Blvd.

DR. KING CRISWELL and his wife, Halo Criswell, continue their series of Self-Help lectures Sunday, Monday and Wednesday at the Garden Court Apartments, 7021 Hollywood Blvd., near La-Brea. Date of the annual picnic will be Saturday, Aug. 9, at 1 p.m. at Echo Park.

with free lectures on "Mother Shipton and 1948," "Can Hunches Mislead," "Prophecies About Armageddon!," Self Protection in Chaos," "Prophecies About Russia!," "The Reward of the Wicked," and "World Prophecy for October." Criswell private classes were also offered for one dollar each or any six for five dollars. Four classes were listed:

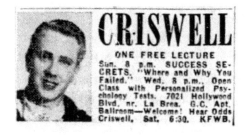

Self-Generation of Power; Psychic Sensing to Success; Using the Psychosomatic Self; and Perfecting the Psychic Hunch. The bottom of the invitation offered, "If troubled call Criswell at HE 3841 for appointment."

November 4 saw Criswell debut his first radio show while teaming-up with co-host Leo Guild on KFWB 980AM at 7:45 p.m. for a fifteen-minute program titled *The Wizard vs. Criswell.* An announcement in the *Hollywood Citizen-News* prior to the debut said, "This should be different: the psychic approach will be pitted against the intellectual on Leo Guild's new series, 'The Wizard vs. Criswell.' The Wizard (Guild) will try to predict election winners, etc., by assiduous study of periodicals, whereas Criswell will get his information via the supernatural." And in *The Valley Times,* North Hollywood, "KFWB has breathed life into and revived Leo Guild's 'Wizard of Odds,' which has now become 'The Wizard vs. Criswell' for a 13-week airing, complete with sponsor." Ads ran for the new program asking, 'What Are Your Odds?' followed by "Hear Wizard of Odds (Leo Guild) vs. Criswell (Jeron Criswell) Tonight 7:45. Prizes for You Listeners! Presented by Wax Seal. KFWB 980 On Your Dial." In the December 16 *Hollywood Citizen-News* on the radio station schedule page, a photo ran of the duo together captioned "MENTAL DUEL—Leo Guild upholds the laws of chance against Jeron Criswell's psychic predictions of things to come, KFWB at 7:45p.m.; 9:15 beginning next week." One of the enlightening subjects the Wizard-Criswell show would cover was "what it thinks is radio's best singing commercial."

MENTAL DUEL—Leo Guild upholds the laws of chance against Jeron Criswell's psychic predictions of things to come, KFWB at 7:45 p.m.; 9:15 beginning next week.

Leo Guild has been called "the greatest hack ever" and "the king of lowbrow literature." He worked as a writer of fiction and non-fiction books, radio and film scripts, and television presentations. He also worked as a Hollywood gossip columnist and film critic, starting his writing career as a public relations man for Warner Brothers and with a column in the *Hollywood Reporter*. This led him to ghostwriting for many Hollywood stars and eventually sleaze and smut exploitation pulp fiction novels. He became known as the "Wizard of Odds" following the popularity of his first book *You Bet Your Life* (1946), with a foreword by Bob Hope. The book was soon reprinted after its initial release with the title changed to *What Are the Odds?* (1949), possibly due to Groucho Marx having a radio program and future television show by the original name and Groucho liked to sue, or at least threaten to do so. In the 1990s, Guild would attempt to sue Bill Cosby for $11 million for using the title *You Bet Your Life* with Guild claiming it was his intellectual property dating back to 1946. The book is filled with oddball "odds" like, "Lipstick is a woman's basic weapon. Odds are 2 to 1 that she'll leave some on you on your first date." Described with what can be called sexist humor, some of the "odds" were accompanied by cartoon illustrations that are seen today as sexually objectifying and belittling to woman. They were similar to *Ripley's Believe it or Not* newspaper panels but with cartoon eye-candy. During the 1950s Guild started ghostwriting book-length autobiographies and puff pieces for fan magazines for a number of Hollywood celebrities and stars. He again worked with Bob Hope penning *Where There's Life There's Bob Hope* (1957), and authoring the blatantly obvious, but half-hearted attempt to keep a gay man closeted for the purposes of publicity, *The Loves of Liberace* (1956), published by Avon books.

The cover of the "Thrilling, Revealing, Authorized—The Fabulous Liberace Story!" features a photo of Liberace kissing Miss Coraleen Jurian, former Queen of the Grand National Livestock Expo, and promises more "intimate photographs" inside. Even though the flamboyant pianist lived with his mother, enjoyed interior design, and designed her room in a "luscious combination of dusty pink and gray," he had allegedly been engaged three times, but was yet unmarried and not ready to settle down saying with a saucy wink, "I guess I am not unlike the sailor with a girl in every port." "Liberace is the perfect specimen of a well-groomed gentleman, he doesn't chew tobacco or drive a truck; but he is as hairy as Rosselini, and who has ever questioned his masculinity? He can move a piano by himself, he chops wood for exercise; and he has always, since he was a very small child, liked to be clean." The book also mentions a date with Betty White.

In the early 1960s Guild's books became racier and more exploitative. Some were "light-hearted fare" such as *Hollywood Screwballs* (1962), "The zaniest, whoopiest, wildest book ever written about Hollywood!" and *Strictly Personal* (1964), illustrated with racy cartoon eye-candy and described as "A hilarious collection of personal ads . . . If you think the things people say to each other in private are wild—wait till you read what they say in public!" One of the more "serious" and exploitative titles was *The Fatty Arbuck-*

le Case (1962), promoted on the book cover as the "Most famous rape case of the century" and "The Hollywood story no one dared publish." One ghostwritten autobiography was *I Am Not Ashamed* (1963), by former starlet Barbara Payton, which luridly details her rise to fame in the "Hollywood Babylon" era via the casting couch, then being ousted from showbiz due to her alleged infamous flings with most of the leading men of Hollywood at the time including Jimmy Cagney, Frank Sinatra, and Gregory Peck. Her very public and "questionable" love life was covered heavily by the paparazzi and gossip columnists presenting her as a Hollywood bad girl. Soon after her exile from the Hollywood establishment, she fell into the world of high-end sex work and became addicted to alcohol and narcotics, finally leading to her being found passed out with her liver failing near a dumpster in a drug store parking lot on Sunset Boulevard. She was sent to her parents in San Diego where she died a couple of months later at the age of thirty-nine.

Ecstasy and Me: My Life as a Woman (1966), was another ghost-written tell-all style autobiography of actress and inventor Hedy Lamarr. She allegedly approved the book before she read it and later said that "most of it is fiction" and condemned the book's contents as "fictional, false, vulgar, scandalous, libelous and obscene."

During the mid-1960s Guild began hacking for Holloway House publishers. Bentley Morris and Ralph Weinstock started Holloway House in the 1950s publishing magazines that emulated *Playboy* with the titles *Adam* and *Sir Knight*. In the 1960s, they flooded the book market with sleaze and smut pulp novels aimed at white males and written by white authors such as Guild. In 1966, Holloway House published *Some Like It Dark "The Intimate Autobiography of a Negro Call Girl"* by Kip Washington, as told to Leo Guild. Sales for the book sky-rocketed which spurred Morris and Weinstock into publishing more blaxploitation type novels. Initially these pulps were intended for their white male audience but eventually moved from black sleaze works geared towards white readers to black pulp fiction, "male-oriented crime, espionage, and action-adventure novels written by black authors for black readers" starting with Iceberg Slim (Robert Beck) and his novels; *Pimp: The Story of My Life* (1967), *Trick Baby* (1967), and *Mama Black Widow* (1969). The books were so popular that Holloway House signed other black authors and David Goines to start *Players*, a black men's magazine partly in the vein of *Playboy*.

Morris and Weinstock certainly manipulated cultural products and exploited the black writers to boost profits which also helped fuel the blaxploitation craze of the early 1970s, but by delving into the black literary underground, where the artists embraced Holloway House, they reworked the communications circuit which allowed black readers and the black authors to effectively reappropriate black pulp fiction for their own uses and for black cultural production. This reappropriation is evident specifically through hip hop music where the artist Ice-T took his moniker directly from Iceberg Slim.

Guild continued hacking for Holloway House for the remainder of the 1960s and through the 1970s with titles such as *The Girl Who Loved Black* (1969), *The Studio* (1969), "the real story of a Hollywood bitch," *Zanuck: Hollywood's Last Tycoon* (1970), *Street of Ho's* (1976), with the representative line "Sheila made him a ham and cheese sandwich and they made love while he ate." *The Senator's Whore* (1976), by Cindy Kallmer, as told to Leo Guild, and *Josephine Baker* (1978), "the first intimate, complete story of the woman who entertained, dazzled and shocked two continents!" Mr. Leo Guild's hacking days ended in 1997.

The Wizard vs. Criswell radio show continued until the end of 1948 at which point the show became titled just *Criswell* and then later *Criswell Predicts*.

Edward D. Wood Jr. arrived in the showbiz promised land in 1948 and began seeking his fame and fortune writing, directing, and producing films like his hero Orson Welles. He worked in the story department at Universal Studios as a night production coordinator for about six months until deciding to go out on his own. During this time, he became friends with legendary horror star Bela Lugosi who was having a hard time finding work in his declining years. Ed's first production in Hollywood was a stage production of his own script called *The Casual Company* based on his experiences in the war. He then shot a Western called *The Streets of Laredo* that was never completed.

Criswell's predictions began appearing in more and more newspapers and periodicals where he was paid two dollars per column. He was beginning to earn a living with his "News of the Future."

CHARLES COULOMBE: He would never say he was a fake (as misrepresented in *Ed Wood.*) He told my father that he had "had the gift, but I lost it when I started taking money for it."

Criswell began getting more attention in print after predicting the 1948 Academy Awards. In a March 1948 column by Hollywood gossip Louella O. Parsons, she said "Criswell who predicted the Academy Award winners and the recent stock crash, comes out with a few new predictions: He says Hitler is still alive and will be found; that Martha Vickers will be the star

Dr. Jeron Criswell King submitting predictions.

of the year; that the stock market will dip again in August; that UNO will be in San Francisco; that strikes around the country will abate in September and that three well-known Hollywood personalities will pass away before September." And from an April 1948 Edith Gwynn, *Hollywood* column. "Criswell, the Hollywood seer, who has attained some fame, is rather red-faced these days, we imagine. From what we gather, his predictions on the Academy Awards winners this year wound up a neat one hundred percent miss!"

An April 28 a Los Angeles UP byline ran reporting on a visit by the Venerable Lokanatha, "Buddhist missionary from Burma." It told of how twelve long-haired women spread their tresses on the sidewalk in front of a lecture club, creating a carpet of human hair for the Buddhist priest to walk across. The shaven pated, yellow-robed Lokanatha stepped out of a shiny automobile seeming embarrassed, but resigned to walk across the feminine locks into the auditorium to speak on "Is Peace Necessary?" Reported as being in charge of the program, Dr. Jeron Criswell explained, "Venerable is not permitted to walk on ordinary pavement. The long tresses form the religious mosaic for his bare feet."

TOM WEAVER: During that time, Dr. Jeron Criswell was the manager of Venerable Lokanatha, a Buddhist monk with psychic abilities whose most famous stunt was his attempt to get in touch with the spirit of Rudolph Valentino in 1947 with the assembled onlookers and press forced to sing "The Sheik of Araby" at Rudi's supposed request! And for the record, Venerable Lokanatha was originally Salvatore Natale Cioffi of Brooklyn. The whole thing certainly has that wacky showbiz quality to it that one associates with Criswell.

The Venerable Lokanatha was an Italian immigrant originally named Cioffi who converted to Buddhism after reading a large volume of Buddhist texts given to him by a co-worker while working as a chemist in Brooklyn. He said later, "I read the book. I became a Buddhist. Self-research is the highest research. From chemistry, the science of analysis, I passed on to Buddhism, the religion of analysis." Cioffi embraced what he saw as the democratic and rational nature of Buddhism, but his interest in the dharma strained his relationship with his devoutly Roman Catholic family who hoped he would focus his religious impulses into becoming a Franciscan monk. In his mid-twenties he traveled from New York to England then India, where he took Buddhist monastic vows in 1925, and became Javana Tikkha. Cioffi then went to his birth country of Italy where he tried to live as a bhikkhu, meditating in solitude and going door to door for alms, but he was repeatedly arrested and deemed a "harmless religious maniac." He then decided to return to India but was blocked from leaving Naples by his family who convinced authorities there to deny him the official pass needed to leave. After several months and a weeklong hunger strike, the family relented

The Venerable Lokanatha walks on carpet of human hair. Acme Newsphotos.

and he left resolved to travel like the Buddha, on foot and with only his robes and begging bowls. The journey took fourteen months covering over 5,000 miles and undergoing numerous hardships including hospitalizations for illness, arrests by French police and Syrian soldiers, and many assaults and robberies. After arriving back in India, he spent the next several years studying and practicing in the Sri Lanka monasteries and holy sites in the Himalayas. While in Rangoon he was reordained as Lokanatha because of his "spiritual radiance" and it was believed he possessed psychic powers and he himself claimed he could read others' thoughts. For the next few years he organized and carried out missionary expeditions throughout Asia until the outbreak of World War II. At that time he was planning a missionary trip to the West but was arrested by the British in India and placed in a prisoner-of-war camp because his Italian background provoked suspicion that he was a Mussolini sympathizer. He pleaded with his family in New York to send proof of his American citizenship, but they insisted he first convert back to Catholicism. He remained a prisoner until the end of the war for a grueling six years which nearly killed him. Due to the horrors of war and the threat of nuclear destruction, he was convinced that humanity needed Buddhism more than ever before. He was appointed to be the Dhamma-Ambassador and initially wanted to begin his mass conversion in Europe but then set his target on the United States. Lokanatha started his "Lightning Preaching Tour" visiting several Asian countries then traveling to Northern California and finally landing in Los Angeles. There he stayed with the well-known socialites Gypsy and Jerry Buys at their Beverly Hills estate formerly owned by Rudolph Valentino. His time in Los Angeles turned into a bit of a farce as his rich, eccentric hosts convinced him to participate in a séance to contact the spirit of Valentino with thirty other mystics and mediums. Jerry Buys also organized the "hair-walking" as a publicity stunt and photo-op. The Venerable completed his tour of America and was pleased with its results saying it was "a great success" and that it had "quite a number of converts." He continued spreading the word of dharma and converting the masses until his death in 1965 at the age of sixty-nine. The Venerable Lokanatha is one of the most significant Buddhists of the twentieth century and his missionary efforts helped shape the practice and demographics of Buddhism into the twenty-first century.

Criswell Speaks debuted in August 1948 airing at 8 p.m. on KMGM 98.7 FM, owned by Metro-Goldwyn-Mayer. Due to FM radio having virtually no listeners in the early 1950s, MGM handed the radio license back to the FCC in 1953. A record store called Crawford's of Beverly Hills was awarded the license a short time later as KCBH which eventually became KJOI and is now KYSR.

An article titled "Get Your '49 News Early, Seer Sees All!!" by Aline Mosby with a (UP) Hollywood byline appeared in October 1948. "Today you can read the headlines that Hollywood is predicted to make in 1949, which ought to save you the trouble of pouring over 365 newspapers next year. This timesaving service comes courtesy of the seer of the cinema city, Jeron Criswell." The article calls him "Mr. C." and tells that he lectures and writes about the future, "from the price of string beans to the next guy to sit on the White House balcony (he says Dewey)." It goes on to say that he predicted what Hollywood headline-makers would be up to the next year and that movie bigwigs often consult with him about the future. "Prediction No. 1: Mitchum's marijuana is a warm-up to a dope scandal that will sear 100 Hollywood names in '49! He further foresees Rita Hayworth with another spouse. And a new California marriage law will turn packs of stars into bigamists." "More future headlines: Famous actor lands in court on paternity charge. Character actor kills self. Head of big studio dies. Crooner and actress divorce. On Hollywood's working side, Criswell predicts movie business will flop toward the end of next year because a $50 television set will flood the market. Theatre tickets thus will nose-dive, he says." The article closed with some of his predictions from the previous year. "For 1948 he predicted in a magazine a star's suicide near a holiday (Carole Landis' July 5, death), an explosion with fatalities in or near a studio (Hillcrest Country club blowup), and the deaths of two stars in a May plane crash (Earl Carroll and Beryl Wallace crashed June 17.)"

In November the *Gettysburg Times* reported in the Littlestown column that Halo's Father and Mother had just returned from a trip of nearly six weeks to the Pacific Coast and spent most of the time visiting their son-in-law and daughter, Mr. And Mrs. Jeron Criswell, Hollywood, California.

In early 1948 Raymond Palmer, a science fiction writer and the editor of *Amazing Stories* started the pulp magazine titled *Fate*, specializing in "True Reports of the Strange and Unknown." Included in the magazine's inaugural edition was an article by Kenneth Arnold called "The Truth About Flying Saucers." Arnold recounted his 1947 encounter with a flying saucer which marked the beginning of the modern UFO era. Criswell prognosticated the future with a six-page article titled "Criswell Predicts for 1949" in the winter issue of *Fate*. In the editorial section the magazine's readers are introduced to "the famous Hollywood predictor, Jeron King Criswell" and it was stated that he would appear in the magazine "each month with predictions for the coming month, or with special prognostications that may apply."

The column continues:

One interesting comment he makes to us in a letter is that he has a regular radio broadcast called "Criswell Predicts" in which he foretells the future. However, on the radio, no word related to mystic, psychic, or spiritual may be mentioned. May the editors of FATE make a point radio should have—that it makes no difference what kind of car the mailman drives, just so the mail is delivered? We are simply not impressed by such words—we want facts. If Mr. Criswell can predict the future, what does it matter where he gets his ability? We will believe him because he's right, not because we're *impressed* with a word!

The article has a short introductory bio about "the favorite prophet of business men, government officials, politicians (Dewey should have used him), movie stars and just people." In the article Criswell claims that in 1445, Leonardo da Vinci predicted "the exact date of the dropping of the first atom bomb!" with the following quote, "In 500 years, man shall make an instrument, shall drop it from a man-made bird, it will stun the earth and cause all to drop dead from it's very breath, shall devastate buildings and entire cities—with its pink umbrella of a cloud."
Criswell then faces the question of the atom bomb.

Now let us face the question of the atom bomb. My definite prediction is that the bomb will be used in 1949! It will be used in Asia, first on a practice scale, then they will really mean it! Russia has the atom bomb, for nothing can remain a secret as long as two people share the same knowledge! By late spring, the bomb will have been used!

He then gazes at the atom in its more useful aspect.

The atom (merely the release of stored energy) will do much for our 20th century civilization—and in 1949 it will be used for locomotion, heat, and light. A full report will be given the nation on atomic progress in the month of March. The most astounding use of the atom will be for the control and cure of the cancer, TB. and polio, by the purging of cell by cell. This medical discovery will be made public by late August 1949.

He then looks into the condition of the USA.

Let us look into the conditions of our own country and things that will come to pass in 1949! The United States of America has emerged from this past useless war the strongest nation in history! Rome, Greece, the British Empire, Russia or any combination of past powers could not equal America in 1949! America is facing a year of struggle—political, economic, racial and international.

He goes on to predict that the federal government will release certain powers that will revert to the individual states including rent control, crop price fixing and educational standards.

For this freedom granted the states, the divorce laws, the marriage laws, the burial laws and the inheritance laws will all be federalized; that is, the one law will apply to every American! Here are some federal laws and how they will affect you: You will see no more signboards along the roadside, for the traffic toll of deaths will increase until a law will be passed prohibiting all roadside advertising! There will be tight federal censorship control over motion pictures and the subjects shown on your local screen. Comic books will be made more suitable for children. Radio will be cleaned of all phony contests, ism-messages and programs not considered in good taste. The news out of 1949, is that you will be able to enjoy television in your home on a $50 set—or rent one at the price of $5 a month, the cost of your telephone rental! There will be television in natural color by 1950!

Criswell then presages for the international scene with a paragraph dedicated to each of the major countries of the world including Great Britain, Spain, Italy, Poland, and of course Russia. By the time 1949 was over he predicted seeing the following inventions.

A pen that writes with perfumed ink . . . ladies' hats with propellers in the crown like Junior's . . . a machine that will give you a sun-tan in one minute . . . a skin-bleaching machine that will bleach freckles in one minute and make your skin pearly white . . . a new drug that will make you fat, and a newer one that will thin you down . . . a box of black stationary with white ink . . . powdered tea . . . a new cornbread mix . . . a new cereal: whole wheat grains soaked in honey. . . . The foregoing has been a general outline of the events that have cast their shadow over the horizon for 1949. From month to month you will be notified of any changes, any new trends in this so-called 20th century civilization in 1949!

He did not appear monthly in the magazine as stated in the editor's column. An article ran in the July 1949 issue which in the introduction verifies the accuracy of some of his predictions in the previous issue. He appeared in the pages of *Fate* two more times in the early 1950s.

Criswell's involvement with the UFO phenomenon went beyond just his predictions and columns in the science fiction and paranormal pulps. He attended meetings with UFO contactees such as Orfeo Angelucci who had been contacted by beings from outer space since 1946. The meetings were first held at the Los Felix Club House and became very popular as people wanted to know more about the visitors from space. Criswell and Max Miller of "Flying Saucers International" suggested they move to the Hollywood Hotel music room to accommodate more of the curious. The Sunday afternoon meetings became so popular that they decided to host the "world's first flying saucer convention" the weekend of August

16-18, 1953. Criswell orchestrated the event and was the principal program moderator. The convention was well attended, and speakers included a who's who list of contactees and Ufologists including; George Van Tassel, Frank Scully, Arthur Luis Joquel II, George Adamski, Truman Betherum, John Otto from Chicago, Harding Walsh and a mysterious Dr. X who spoke long and eloquently on the saucers then left immediately after speaking.

George Van Tassel moved his family to Giant Rock, the world's largest single boulder and Native American holy ground, in the Mojave Desert near Landers, California in 1947 and opened Giant Rock Airport. In 1953 he began weekly meditation sessions in rooms underneath the Rock. Soon after he began being contacted by extra-terrestrials from Venus who landed at Giant Rock and invited George onto their ship. Onboard they gave him the technique for rejuvenating living cell tissues and plans to build a dome shaped structure called the Integratron to perform the rejuvenation. He began building the Integratron in 1954 and held the first Space Convention at Giant Rock on the weekend of April 4 to raise money for his project. Speakers included Orfeo Angelucci, Truman Bethurum, Daniel Fry, and George Hunt Williamson. Speaking from the platform built against the Rock, they took turns describing their contacts with physical and ethereal beings. The conventions were held annually and attended by thousands until 1970 when attendance began to dwindle, and bikers crashed the convention and set fire to a car. George Van Tassel died in 1978 under suspicious circumstances with the Integratron ninety-percent complete. Criswell attended the conventions, lecturing and giving his predictions. He predicted that Giant Rock would be the place where World War III would begin.

William F. Hamilton III attended the conventions as well and visited Criswell at his Hollywood home. Bill has worked in the information technology field for decades and studied psychology, physics, and engineering in college. He's pursued interests in science, mathematics, aeronautics, computers, and parapsychology as well as studying the UFO phenomenon since 1953. He worked as a Senior Programmer-Analyst at UCLA and was Executive Director of Astrosciences Network whose mission statement reads:

> Our mission is to establish a self-sustaining, continuing research program to advance our space program, space exploration, space free enterprise, and space settlement through scientific and peaceful means, to work toward peaceful solutions to humanity's problems, and to educate the public through all recognized forms of media. To promote an ecologically viable planet earth with sustainability for all of its life forms. To establish the verified existence of extraterrestrial life, extraterrestrial intelligent life and contact and communicate with same in order to gather knowledge of, about, and from extraterrestrial entities with the goal of forming peaceful and mutually beneficial alliances."

BILL HAMILTON: My impression was he was a very personable man who had found a niche in televising screwball prophecies. Once he predicted on *Criswell Predicts* that giant grasshoppers were going to swarm over the Empire State Building and hit every brick, what a hoot! I guess he was just another form of entertainment.

As predicted, an explosion of television sets into the American marketplace did occur in 1949, paving the way for Criswell to enter a new form of media that was still in its tentative stages. He began making guest appearances on local Los Angeles television talk shows such as *City at Night*. During the end of the war decade of the 1940s and the new beginnings promised by the 1950s, the future was bright as the flash of an atomic bomb and everyone was "tremendously interested" in what the wonder world of the future would hold. Many turned to the "Journalist of the Future, Criswell!" and he was prepared to tell them.

On December 9, 1949, an article with an accompanying photo of Criswell in the Long Beach, California, *Press-Telegram* newspaper announced that he would begin writing a daily column in the paper with the headline "World Events Forecaster to Write Column in P.T." "A MAN whose forecasts on future developments in national and international affairs, Hollywood happenings and trends of the times have been 85% correct over the years, will begin writing a daily column for the *Press-Telegram*, starting next Monday. The article claims that Criswell doesn't claim to be a seer or prophet but had "scored some spectacular bull's-eyes with his predictions and long has been a favorite in Hollywood, both among the stars of the films and the motion picture executives as well." It then recounts his predictions of the previous year of the suicide of Carole Landis and the deaths of Earl Carroll and Beryl Wallace in a plane crash and that he also foretold that Ronald Reagan-Jane Wyman would divorce and the marriage fiasco of Robert Walker. "Here are some predictions he makes for the immediate future: John L. Lewis will obtain a seven-hour day for the miners; sex crimes will be made federal offenses and President Truman will embark on the biggest spending spree the world ever has known." The article concludes saying that the Criswell column would appear on the newspapers' theater page six times a week and that he would answer letters in a special column once weekly and "Once weekly he will predict 'What People Will Do.' Other columns will be devoted to the trend of the times; what people will like in the theater; a column for 'Women Only'; headlines of the future and once weekly the column will be devoted about Hollywood's future."

On December 12, 1949, "Criswell Predicts" began running in the Long Beach, CA *Press-Telegram* with the headline "U.S. Recognition Soon of Red China Is Forecast." In the column he expands on the predictions from the announcement article and goes on to predict "One of our famous burlesque queens, now on the point of death, will prove to be a female impersonator . . . Sex crimes will be a federal offense, and all persons convicted of such crimes will be required to register and carry identification with them all the time. Many nationally known personalities are very much against this coming law for personal reasons, and will fight this ruling openly! Dean Acheson will soon announce that U.S. will recognize Red China! . . . Your superstition will drive the $2 bill out of circulation in 1950." Readers were invited to send questions to Criswell for "analysis and predictions" saying "Criswell has established a phenomenal record for accuracy on his predictions about everything from international politics to individual love problems." with the disclaimer, "He will not attempt to answer questions pertaining to legal or physical matters in which advice of an attorney or physician is needed." and "Criswell makes no claim of being a seer or mystic. He foresees though a knowledge of trends, precedents, patterns of habit, human behavior, the law of cycles, psychological reaction and basic percentages."

December 18, 1949:

Q: Will we ever have anything? Will my husband always drink and gamble? Will we pay for this place or lose it?—M.V.M.

A: I sense that your husband will have a setback in health, which will cause him to reform. Through some inheritance, you will be able to pay for the place. Your children will soon leave home to make their own way and this will be much better for you, as they do not appreciate anything that you have done for them.

Q: Will my husband buy the farm he is wanting?—Wondering, Long Beach.

A: Your husband already purchased the farm, but he did not tell you.

Q: How will this trouble end? He makes me so miserable with his jealousy and his unjust accusations. If we sold and moved, would conditions change? If we separate, what will I do and where shall I go?—Very Worried, Seal Beach.

A: The long arm of fate will intervene before too long, so just sit tight.

January 4, 1950:

FOR WOMEN ONLY: One of you women will give birth to the one-hundred-and-fifty-millionth citizen of the United States before January is over!

More girl babies will be born in 1950, than in 1949!

Make-up styles for 1950 include the new Holly-Red color for your lips and nails. The lips will be drawn to a cupid's bow, the rouge worn high and heavy, the eyes widened and the hair worn in the heavy bangs of the Buster Brown era. Your flat-heeled shoes will make you walk fast and free.

Psychologically, woman will come into a new independence in 1950 . . . and the styles certainly show that trend!

You women in 1950 will control 78% of all the wealth of this nation, be the definite balance of power at the polls, control 81 cents out of every dollar over the counter of our stores by spending it yourself . . . plus receiving more alimony than ever before!

1950 was a very busy year for the newfound prophet. His popularity grew from his column in the *Long Beach Press-Telegram*, and he began making personal appearances at local movie theaters billed as "Criswell Predicts" where he would answer questions submitted by the audience. On February 22 he opened at the News-Palace Theater with a two-week program of five shows a day. His first performance

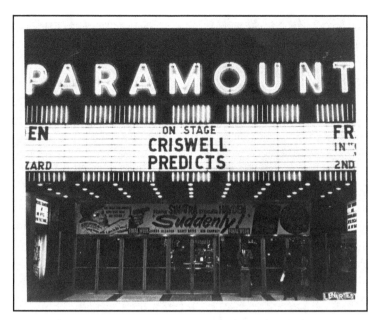

On stage Criswell Predicts. Courtesy of Jason Insalaco.

was at 11 a.m. By 10 a.m. the waiting line extended down the block. Fifteen minutes before the theatre was scheduled to open, 300 people, mostly women, were waiting outside in the chilly fog. Occasionally, he would do special early matinee shows for women only, giving the first 300 in line autographed photos of the newfound celebrity. "A young man from Hollywood who looks like a motion picture star but in reality is a close confidant of many stars." In an article covering the opening event, Criswell said the three main subjects that dominate the questions asked of him by letter and at theatre engagements concern love, money, and health, in that order. He gets three questions from women to every two from men. He attributed his success at predicting to what he called "a mathematical knack for judging trends . . . and the law of averages." He said he could answer more successfully when he is completely objective, and his emotions

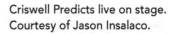
Criswell Predicts live on stage.
Courtesy of Jason Insalaco.

are not involved. He said he discovered his talent or "knack" when he was a youngster carrying papers for his Uncle Roy, publisher of the *Princeton Daily Democrat.* "People on my route began asking me questions, and I nearly always could answer them." He also claimed that he had worked in New York radio writing soap operas, that his column was in thirty papers, and that he spent ten to fifteen hours a day answering questions mailed to him. The article also describes his physical appearance. "He is a tall man, nearly six feet, with wavy hair, piercing blue eyes and a friendly handshake. He speaks quickly and decisively."

Predictions he gave from the News-Palace Theater stage included a worldwide prediction: "Stalin will die in 1950." A fashion prediction: "You women will wear the 'little boy' look. Don't say you will not—because you will. You will wear short jackets. Windsor ties, middy blouses and skirts." On marriage and divorce: "Soon marriage and divorce laws will be nationwide. Then you will not have to go to Reno for a divorce. Divorce and alimony laws will be liberalized. You will get more alimony." In his column the day after the opening he said, "I regret deeply that some of my mail was delayed. During the time I was away filming some television shorts, my questions and answers to you readers of the Press-Telegram were lost in the mail but now have been located. Now that I am in Long Beach appearing daily at the News-Palace, I'll work direct from an office here to speed your replies. Incidentally, I thank you folks a lot for the big reception given me on my opening day."

In March Criswell began an engagement at the Strand Theater followed by the Lakewood and the Atlantic Theaters with afternoon and evening shows including a special Friday afternoon matinee for women only. The newspaper reported that Criswell's opening at the Strand set a new attendance record with triple the normal totals for a Thursday according to the theater manager. An

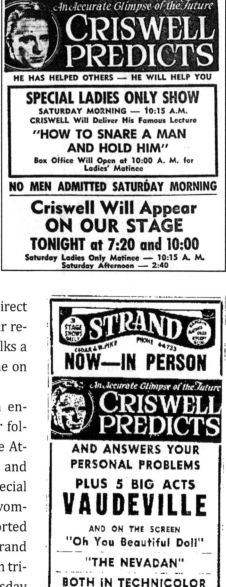

article announcing one opening said that Criswell was returning to Long Beach after leaving the previous week for Monterey to film some television shorts that would soon be released nationally. At another personal appearance he gave interviews to women shoppers visiting the cosmetics counter of Walkers Department Store, stating in an ad, "No extra charge for consultation with this noted personal guidance expert, when you purchase REALLIE---the new cosmetic revelation." He made appearances as a guest speaker at local business and advertising club meetings. At one such meeting, he said that Long Beach was the friendliest coastal city in southern California and that 10,000 new jobs would come to the area in the next year. He also predicted a woman Vice-President elected in 1952. At another he told the members to, "always think a smile. Let that smile, that pleasurable comfort, get into your writing." Some of the luncheons were held in the Sky Room of the Wilton Hotel. Press for one of the ad club conferences, said Criswell would, "...make predictions concerning the advertising business. Following the luncheon he will talk to the wives of the delegates." Criswell was quite the ladies' man.

March 24, 1950, About Hollywood:

Ginger Rogers and her mother, Lelia Rogers, will appear together as mother and daughter in a Broadway play. Red Skelton will be a bellhop in his next picture. One more Marx

Brothers picture will be planned in which the blondes chase the brothers instead of vice-versa! The life of Sid Grauman will be filmed with Spencer Tracy in the title role.

One Hollywood star, now on a personal appearance tour with his latest picture, is becoming a violent alcoholic, and you will probably read of his "collapse" any day.

James Warner Bellah, who scripted such hits as "Dancing Lady" and "She Wore a Yellow Ribbon" will soon unveil his latest filmic work which will win an award in 1950.

Movie magazines will become more and more sensational in order to meet the competition from the feature stories and articles now appearing in newspapers.

You will be shocked at the latest example of poor taste by coupling two features together whose combined titles mean off-color things! The next good-will gesture of Hollywood will be the sending of its great and near-great to entertain the victims of World War II who are still in our crowded hospitals.

That same month the *Long Beach Press-Telegram* announced in the column "TOO MANY LETTERS" saying, "Because Jeron King Criswell has been literally swamped by the volume of questions sent by the readers of the *Press-Telegram*, no additional questions will be accepted until the letters now on hand are answered. Giving individual attention to the thousands of letters received has been a big task—too big to keep pace with. So until the present backlog of communications has been processed, no further letters are invited. Hold all questions until those already received have been answered." Occasionally the *Press-Telegram* would run a story about Criswell and the thousands of letters he was receiving and accompany the article with a photo of him surrounded by the mail.

HIS MAIL IS HEAVY—Jeron King Criswell, whose daily column in the Press-Telegram is drawing wide reader response, is shown as he called in the news room yesterday and looked over some of his mail. Besides a daily column of predictions, Criswell answers questions mailed him by the readers. "I employ not mystical means," he explains, "but forecast through trend, precedent, pattern of habit, human behavior, the law of cycles, psychological reaction and basic percentage." He is known for his high record of accurate predictions over the years.—(Press-Telegram Photo.)

Success and fame were now finally coming to Criswell in the pivotal year of 1950, which saw him also begin to make more appearances on local television programs.

In 1951 he began running ads to sell pamphlets of his predictions and self-help guides. The ad had the catchy headline of "A PERSONAL NOTE TO YOU FROM CRISWELL, Internationally Known Lecturer, Author and Prophetic Columnist."

The note read, "My Dear Friend: Thank you for your interest in my predictions. I have made it possible for you to secure and profit by all my lectures, heretofore only available to those attending my lectures in person. I will also send you a complete personal analysis of your problem and answer your questions FREE with the purchase of any of the following dynamic and reveling transcripts. Remember, no problem can exist without a solution. I know that I can help you. Your Sincere Advisor, CRISWELL."

The transcripts were listed and described:

CRISWELL PREDICTS TO 1999 (Sealed). These are the off-the-record prophetic views of the coming years up to the date A.D. 2000. They are sensational, shocking and astounding. Forewarned is forearmed. We are all interested in the future for that is the place were (sic) we will spend the rest of our lives! Criswell pulls no punches and plainly revels what to expect. Criswell remains a consistent 87% in all his predictions to date!

SUCCESS WITHOUT STRUGGLE, the full secrets that have aided many over the rocky road of every day living to a full rich life!

MIRACLE DIET FOR MAGNETISM, the proper mental attitude, plus a diet that will help you to make the most of your opportunities and assure a more complete enjoyment of living.

THE SEVEN SECRETS OF CHARM, my most famous lecture FOR WOMEN ONLY, plus the Seven Secrets of feminine popularity and power.

HAPPINESS THRU THOUGHT CONTROL, an up-to-date and sensational method of attaining the things you want, and finding inner peace and happiness thru the simple method of thought control.

HOW NUMERALS INFLUENCE YOUR LIFE, the accepted power of numerology, the undisputed science of numbers, and how you can use this secret, to further your success by knowing the most favorite time for action!

HOW TO INTERPRET YOUR DREAMS CORRECTLY, the age old and accurate method used by the Romans, Greeks, Egyptians and our modern day Psychologists and Psychiatrists. This includes a full table of interpretations and a key to all dreams. With this knowledge you can become a dream analyst for others.

THE TEN STEPS TO HYPNOTISM, for the first time, Medical Hypnotism has been placed in a language that can be understood by everyone, and this latent talent in you can be used for fun and to achieve the things you want in life from others.

THE SECRET SCIENCE OF BEING LUCKY, a full outline of practical superstition plus the 20th century use of charms, omens, portents and magical words which have aided great men to become greater and more powerful.

HOW TO CONDUCT A SUCCESSFUL SÉANCE IN YOUR OWN HOME: This is the famous lecture that I delivered before the skeptical English Psychic Society which convinced even the most violent disbelievers of the unseen powers that operate in our normal world. You can safely experiment with the table-tipping, ouija board operating, the spirit message circle in your own living room. This will convince you and others of the spiritual power we all possess.

The coupon below the descriptions states that the lectures cost one dollar each and includes an area for the purchaser to write their question for their full analysis of their present problem.

A PERSONAL NOTE TO YOU

From
CRISWELL

Internationally Known Lecturer, Author and Prophetic Columnist

My Dear Friend:

Thank you for your interest in my predictions. I have made it possible for you to secure and profit by all my lectures, heretofore only available to those attending my lectures in person. I will also send you a complete personal analysis of your problem and answer your questions FREE with the purchase of any of the following dynamic and revealing transcripts.

Remember, no problem can exist without a solution. I know that I can help you..

Your Sincere Advisor

CRISWELL.

Jeron King Criswell

March 1951, *Fate,* "An Accurate Glimpse of the Future, Criswell Predicts"

For over ten years, Jeron King Criswell, the Indiana Prophet, has peered into the future. His forecasts have been 87% accurate. His syndicated column appears in 44 daily newspapers; his transcribed radio program over many stations, and his television appearances bring an avalanche of mail. During the single month of June 1950, Criswell received 830,000 fan letters. At present he is on a lecture tour of 30 states. Here are his predictions for 1951. Read them and judge for yourself. 1951 will be the connecting link of the two 50-year periods, which make up our 20th century. This conjunction will be fraught with fire, fear and trembling!

Nudism will have its fling next year, as many more nudist camps will open. Several states that now prohibit these health clubs will relent.

What will be the fate of Communism in America? It will be driven underground and destroyed. It is true that America will move toward a socialized state, but it will be in a God-like manner, not a Godless one! Concentration camps will be erected and native Americans who are proven Communists will be forced to work for their livelihood in some type of manufacturing that will aid our nation.

When can we expect to profit from peacetime atomic energy? . . . Next year, in 1952, new doors will be opened thru which we shall glimpse he wonders of atomic power.

Our homes will be heated, lighted, cooled and made more livable, our vehicles will be propelled by jet-atomic power, our food will be scientifically vitalized, our physical ailments will disappear as if by magic.

"Commie" fear was prevalent, and the Cold War was heating up, but the future was brighter than ever. Nudism would figure into his visions of the future numerous times throughout his career. Sex and fear always sell.

Criswell's new success prompted Myrtle's parents to visit Hollywood more often. Dr. and Mrs. Howard A. Stonesifer would make the trip by airplane from Washington, D.C. as mentioned in their local newspaper.

On the evening of December 12 Criswell hosted the Christmas Full Moon Festival held at the Villa Riviera, Chapel in the Sky.

In 1952 Criswell took his radio show to 1020AM KFVD (Venice Dance), broadcasting Monday through Friday at 1:30 p.m. On March 20, Criswell Day was declared in Long Beach. KFVD and the P.J. WILLIAMS VITAMIN CO. "Makers of Master Formula 303 V.T." hosted the event. Criswell broadcast his show live from the Marine Room at the Wilton Hotel at 8 p.m. in conjunction with the Model Guild presenting a fashion show.

CRISWELL PREDICTS
HEAR CRISWELL DAILY
KFVD 1020 ON DIAL
Daily Mon. Thru Fri., 1:30
Now Meet Him in Person
THE P. J. WILLIAMS VITAMIN CO.,
Makers of Master Formula 303 V. T.
Presents Criswell Day in Long Beach
Wilton Hotel, Marine Room
Tonight, March 20, 8 P. M.
Be Our Guest, Bring Your Friends
NO CHARGE, MANY GIFTS
Radio Broadcast, Fashion Show
Many Stars

In May Criswell appeared at a picnic and political rally hosted by Republican congressional hopeful Craig Hosmer. Hosmer was a USC Law School graduate that served in the Navy and was the attorney for the Atomic Energy Commission at Los Alamos before returning to Long Beach and a private practice. He was elected to congress for 1953 and served until 1974. From 1975 to 1979 he was president of the American Nuclear Energy Council. He was a resident of Washington D.C. until his death aboard a cruise ship bound for Mexico on October 11, 1982, exactly one week after Criswell's death.

Throughout 1952, Criswell continued to make personal appearances at local clubs such as the National League of American Penwomen, speaking at a luncheon at the Hollywood Knickerbocker, and he started to get more guest appearances on KLAC television programs billing him as the "American prophet." One such guest appearance in November was with one of Liberace's beards, Betty White.

In August of 1952 a sketch plan and rendering were drawn and designed by architect William Alexander for the proposed Criswell Religious Foundation with a Hollywood site. The design is a basic sleek mid-century square with flat roof shape and full length glass along one wall and the Foyer. The floorpan shows a large Lecture Hall with Dais and a small Office beside it. A long rectangular space was designated for Club Dining and Conference Room with a small Bar and Kitchen area.

Like a lot of Criswell's endeavors, the Criswell Religious Foundation Building never went beyond the drawing board. The two basic sketches are housed in the William Levy Alexander papers collection at the Art, Design & Architecture Museum, University of California, Santa Barbara.

As Criswell was continuing to hone his mass-media prophet persona, he rented the top front penthouse, with rooftop garden, of the Highland Towers apartments at Franklin and Highland Boulevards in the Hollywood Hills under the name Dr. Jeron King Criswell. The building was designed for young, single film players during the 1920s and was one-time home to Mary Martin and young son Larry Hagman, and Thelma Todd. Criswell would use the apartment for private cocktail parties and entertaining guests such as Liberace and Ed Wood. Lyle Talbot, another Ed Wood collaborator, lived in the building at the same time as Criswell and was bewildered by him. From his daughter Margaret Talbot's book, *The Entertainer: Movies, Magic, and My Father's Twentieth Century* (2012):

You had to be pretty seriously weird to register as weird with my father. He'd grown up around carny people, acted with and been directed by every kind of personality you can think of, and basically lived his life in the company of exhibitionists. If you were a nice person (big bonus points if you listened to his stories), then your eccentricities were safe with him. Criswell was one of the few fellow performers I ever heard him describe as 'a very strange person.' (Hell, he didn't even describe Ed Wood that way.) Criswell lived in the Highland Towers at the same time that Lyle and the family did, and when they ran into him in the elevator, he'd speak to them in the same stentorian tones in which he'd predicted the future enslavement of men by women (not at all a bad thing, in his view) and fix them with that nearly translucent blue gaze (were those contacts?) from beneath that frothy platinum coiffure. Either the guy never broke character or he truly believed in his psychic powers. Both explanations puzzled my father, a performer who was almost never in character when he didn't have to be—that is, when he wasn't actually working—and who'd known too many charlatans in his day to set much store by psychic powers.

Lita Bowman, a disc jockey at nearby KMPC radio on Sunset, had her own music program called Bolero Time. She moved into the Highland Towers and the apartment just below Criswell. She was a single mother of a young boy and girl and also worked at the Hollywood American Legion Post just across the street. Lita and Cris were friends until the late 1950s. She was often a guest in his home and attended séances and other spiritualist happenings with him. She doesn't recall ever meeting Halo or seeing her at the penthouse. She did meet Ed Wood and all the gang and was included in one of Ed's productions in a scene where she enters a subway platform out of breath and leans against a man and says, "Thanks for being a leaning post." Eddie directed her to do the line like Mae West.

LITA BOWMAN: Everyone, it seems, was interested in Criswell. The believers and non-believers. Intellectuals and groupies. Even children, were attracted to him. My children thought he was GOD himself. He looked Teutonic, had a soothing voice and lived on the rooftop. Everything in the penthouse was white and cushiony, so the kids figured, it had to be heaven. They would take the elevator up and Criswell returned them down.

Many years later the son left the following posting on Criswell's virtual grave web page, "My sister and I were only 5 and 8 years old when we lived one floor below your penthouse on Highland Ave. I remember when we wandered up to your garden and you were so nice to us and offered us tea, which you so graciously poured us. Afterwards, you gently took us by the hand and led us back home. Our single mom was your friend after that for many years. God bless you, Criswell!!—Christian"

Occasionally on their visits Cris would allow the children to play with his immaculate, white, silky fine hair, and as you can imagine, he was very particular about his hairdo.

George William Jorgensen was a Danish-American army veteran who went to Demark in 1950 and returned to the U.S. December 1, 1952, as Christine Jorgensen after a sexual reassignment operation and hormone therapy and was the first publicized transsexual, which caused a media sensation. In 1953 Ed Wood was hired by George Weiss to write and direct a film based on the story of Christine Jorgensen. It was filmed at Larchmont Studios under the working titles of *Behind Locked Doors, Transvestite*, and *I Changed My Sex*. Eddie got his friend Bela Lugosi to star in the picture for $1,000 as a puppet master/godlike character that decides the fate of the characters in the film. It turned out to be the autobiographical story of Eddie's transvestism and fetish for angora sweaters. The film opened as *Glen or Glenda* (1953). *Christine Jorgensen Presents Denmark* premiered at the Orpheum Theater in L.A. on May 8, 1953. It was a travelogue film that didn't do well because people wanted actually to see her and not a movie. Paul Marco attended the premiere and had the opportunity to meet Christine. They became lifelong friends and Paul would eventually introduce her to Criswell.

A January 20, 1953 newspaper article related that Criswell's outstanding hit prediction for the previous year was the death of King George and his worst miss was the marriage of Eleanor Roosevelt. It went on to relate the following predictions for 1953, "a tragic air crash that would take the lives of ten notables, a most powerful drug that would sober up alcoholics and keep them sober, flying saucers would be admitted by the defense department as cold actualities, American scientists would send a jet rocket to the moon from a landing platform in space, a San Francisco doctor would produce a cure for cancer, and nudism would become more popular."

April 1953, *Fate,* "Prophecies I Have Heard"

Jeron King Criswell is nationally known through his column, 'Criswell Predicts,' which appears in over 400 newspapers daily, as well as on radio and television. Mr. Criswell also makes an annual lecture tour of over 50 dates. A student of prophecy for twenty-five years, he says, 'Some people go to football games, movies, or nightclubs, but when I have time off, which is rare, I like to go to a fortune-teller. I have learned much, even to place greater faith in myself.' He has kept an accurate diary of the many predictions which have been given to him all over the world and has carefully checked up on them over the years. He reports, 'I find a very high batting average in favor of these predictions. Even those which did not turn out exactly as forecast, nevertheless, did have a great factual element in them which showed the trend—and even a partial result!' We have persuaded Mr. Criswell to reveal the contents of his diary for the first time and to let our readers know the outcome of some of these predictions.

Sydney Omarr, known as the astrologer's astrologer, cast my horoscope for 1952 and told me to the very day of three important events: a new radio series, the start of a lecture tour, and a new contract for television! Only a short time ago Rev. Beulah Englund, 1900 West Sixth Street, Los Angeles, called me on the telephone and told me I would write an article for a national magazine within the next week. This article is proof of her prediction!

Omarr was known as another "astrologer to the stars." His horoscope column appeared in over 200 newspapers. He made numerous guest appearances on television talk shows, had his own show for a short time, and penned a number of books. One was written with astrological foundations on his good friend and author Henry Miller. Omar passed away in January 2003.

Los Angeles television legend Tom Hatten began working in the early days of television at KTLA Channel 5 and wore many hats at the station including a sailor's hat to host the afternoon kid's program *The Popeye Show*. He remained very active for more than half a century as an actor, television and radio personality, writer, and producer.

TOM HATTEN: Sydney Omarr had a Sunday night show, and the reason he had it, I don't even think it was legal because you weren't supposed to be able to have people that predicted things like Kenny Kingston and Mr. Omarr, who was very famous. Omarr was in papers all over the world. You weren't supposed to be able to do those shows without permission from the government or something, but our station didn't, who cared ya know, nobody was watching it. Seven-thirty on Sunday night everybody's watching "What's My Line" on channel two. He used to bring in the most interesting guests. Old character people that loved him and were friends of his and appeared on the show as favor to him.

Criswell's predictions for 1954 appeared in articles by writers of local newspapers across the country in December 1953, and January 1954. The articles would start by telling of his correct predictions for the previous year. He predicted that March 5 would be a fateful day for Stalin (he died on that day) and that July 27 would see the end of the Korean War (armistice was signed on that day). His predictions for the New Year were then quoted: "1954 will be the pivotal year of the 20th Century. You will be amazed as we actually contact another planet . . . The Democratic party will offer the nomination for President to Senator McCarthy to offset the result of McCarthy's fearless expose of Communism in the Roosevelt-Truman regime." He goes on to predict suburban growth, a buyers' market, Jack Cortez making Las Vegas the Monte Carlo of America, a federal sales tax, an eight-lane superhighway from San Francisco to New York, five of the world's greatest leaders passing by April 11, and important tragic dates to remember; March 27, August 5, and October 18. For women he envisioned a home face lifting, Venus hairstyling, Princess sandals, and sky-high skirts. He also predicted that "5,000 more neighborhood movie houses will close due to the inroads of TV . . . Paid TV will fail and investors will lose millions on the project."

Maila Nurmi, better known to the world as glamour ghoul and television horror-host Vampira, met Criswell while she was at the height of her television career hosting horror movies each Saturday night at eleven on KABC-TV channel 7. She would wander through a hallway of fog and cobwebs to greet her viewers with a blood curdling scream and then orating in a dark, husky tone, "Good evening. I am . . . Vampira. I hope you all had the good fortune to have had a terrible week." In between commercials from her skull-encrusted couch she would make double entendre necrophilia jokes, recite bizarre poems, sing strange jingles, and hunt for her pet spider Rollo around her tombstone coffee table. Her horror hostess persona was so popular that she was nominated for an Emmy in 1954 as "Most Outstanding Female Personality." *Life* magazine did a four-page spread on her and she was featured in *Newsweek* as well. Maila would fast for two days prior to the show so she could cinch her waist with a belt and achieve her claimed measurements of 38-17-36. After the show, starving and still in full costume, she would go to the open 24 hours Hollywood Ranch Market for a chili dog. James Dean had a donut at the market the morning of his final drive.

MAILA NURMI (VAMPIRA): They had a hotdog stand affixed to it. So when I finished my show across the street at Channel 9, I'd be famished, because for two days before the show I don't eat or else I wouldn't fit into my corset. So then I'd be famished, as soon as the show was over, "Food, gimme food!" Like a bulimic, screaming. And the nearest food was the hotdogs across the street. So I ran over in full costume to grab a chili dog in a hurry. It was midnight and the streets were deserted, and there I was in a strange out-of-the-time dress with a train, and there was a gentleman in a tuxedo. A very distinguished gentleman in a tuxedo, and he said, "How do you do?" So he extended his hand to me at the hotdog stand and he said, "I am Criswell. You're Miss Vampira?" I said, "Yes, how do you do?" And he said, "Oh, I have a friend who wants to meet you. I'm pleased to meet you, but I wish you could meet her. Perhaps I should tell you who it is. It's Miss West, Mae West." And I said, "Well, she's already met me." He said, "She watches the show and likes it." But actually, she didn't want to meet me. She didn't like women in her life. She liked the idea of meeting me, but. . . .

So when I had been in the Mae West show in New York on Broadway, "Catherine is (sic) Great," we had five handmaidens to carry her train. At the out of town tryouts, you have a full company, and then during the opening in New York you still had a full company until the reviewers leave. And then you cut down and you fire some people. And so they fired a girl, a girl who was drunk all the time. And we all commiserated with her. But the next day they said, "Oh no, there's been a mistake," and they said drunk girl could stay, and they said to me, "You're the one who has to go." It was because I wiggled. I didn't wiggle on stage, and if I had you couldn't have seen it because we wore platform shoulders and big velvet draperies. You couldn't see our bodies. So she felt threatened by me. I was just double jointed; I couldn't help it.

She used to send food over to Criswell . . . by her driver. She liked to cook interesting little things that she was making. It was good. She'd cook cabbage rolls, Russian food, and Asian food. So she'd send food over to him, and then he'd call me and say, "Well, Mae has sent some food over." And I'd go over and eat. Well, she didn't join in with that.

I did not ever visit Miss West with Criswell as she did not allow women under any circumstances.

VERNE LANGDON: Maila remarked in *The Plan 9 Companion* (1992), she says of herself and Criswell and Tor, "We were the Hollywood bottom fish." And, my God, that's really what she thought of herself and them, where in fact they were icons. She copied her character from Charles Adams' Morticia but she made it her own with her own voluptuousness and beauty and wonderful hairstyles, that was not Morticia's. She was a combination of Adams' drawing and her own and was a tremendous attraction on television. People tuned in to see her more than they tuned in to see the old movies. And she spawned a whole era of horror hosts. When Universal released *Dracula* (1931), *Frankenstein* (1931), *The Wolf Man* (1941), and so on to television, all of these guys like Zacherly, followed in her footsteps. So Maila was first, and she was a bigger icon than she has any idea. And history will show, a hundred years from now or two hundred years from now, when everything sifts down, as it does over the period of time, only certain things remain in the history books, and you can bet she'll be one of them.

She'd ride down Hollywood Boulevard in an old jalopy screaming at the top of her lungs and people would just go bonkers over her.

In 1953 Criswell purchased a month's worth of five minute slots on KCOP-TV (formerly KLAC-TV Lucky Channel 13) to promote his "Criswell Family Formula" vitamins. Classified ads ran in the *LA Times* seeking salesmen. "How would you like all the leads you can handle? How would you like to sell one of the finest food supplements? Can you sell? If so, you have an opport. to become part of the fastest growing co. selling food supplements. 100 sales earns you $500 per mo. 100 sales + 5 distributors under you earns you $1600. Come to the Criswell Room. Hollywood Hotel. Highland & Hollywood. Mon. 22nd of

Help Wtd., Men, Women   113
——————————————
✔ CRISWELL
        PREDICTS
An incredible future for you!
CRISWELL'S FAMILY FORMU-
LA needs men & women able to
handle salespeople in all areas.
We have salespeople waiting
for leadership. Also salespeople needed to call on our customers in all areas to repeat
our TV sales.

THIS is a FIRST-TIME OFFER!

A wonderful career awaits those
able to see this opportunity!
Training given. TV support &
leads. Send brief resume.
Box 135, Hollywood 28, Cal.

Feb., 7 p.m." Classified ads seeking distributors and salespeople for "Criswell Family Formula" food supplements would run until the shows' eventual cancellation.

TONIGHT AT 10:30 P.M. ON CHANNEL 13
"CRISWELL PREDICTS"

KCOP   *SEE THE 20TH CENTURY NOSTRADAMUS — MON. THRU FRI.*

The *Criswell Predicts* television program started its run in April 1954. It was broadcast Monday through Friday nights at 10:30 and was fifteen minutes in length. Late in 1955 it was moved to the 10:45 slot.

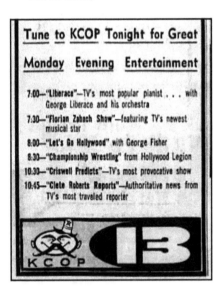

VERNON KOENIG: Criswell's TV ratings were mediocre. His audience consisted largely of older senior citizens. The programs were broadcast live in Los Angeles and kinescoped for syndication in other TV markets. I went to several of his broadcasts. The studio looked like an old, converted chicken coup with everything painted flat black. The stage consisted of an elevated platform with a mahogany desk and chair. There were three cameras used. One was positioned in front of the desk, another focused on a display of Criswell Family Formula products with some gorgeous alabaster statues on a black felt tablecloth, and the third was used for the announcer, Bob Shields (years later, the judge on *Divorce Court*). The program director would start

124

counting backwards from ten to zero and Criswell's theme song, "Pomp and Circumstance" would begin to play. Remember, this was LIVE. Criswell would enter from the right side (as seen on TV) in his sequin tuxedo, place both hands on the desk while still standing, leer into the camera and say, "Good evening my dear friends..." and immediately go into his monologue. He was good at delivering a very serious looking appearance.

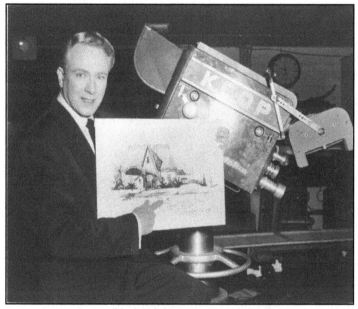

Criswell behind the scenes at KCOP-TV.

As the *Criswell Predicts* television show increased Criswell's audience and mass-media appeal, the critics were watching as well. In a June 8, 1954 column titled "Tele-Vues," writer Terry Vernon said. "SPINNING THE DIAL—Three months ago it was announced in news stories that JOHNNY RAY, the famous crying singer, would become an evangelist. Tonight CRISWELL PREDICTS that JOHNNY

RAY will become an evangelist. This earth-rocking 'news' is about as good a prediction as CRISWELL could ever come up with since it has already been made known throughout the world. KCOP (13) carries 'CRISWELL PREDICTS' to fill the time at 10:30 p.m. for some reason." On August 3 Vernon wrote, "Corrine Griffith, will appear on 'Criswell Predicts' to discuss her campaign to repeal the Federal Income Tax law, but we fear even Criswell can't predict the success of this one for many a year to come."

It is likely that Cris and Eddie Wood met during the filming of the television program with Eddie directing as evidenced by the show and the opening of *Plan 9* being exactly the same, including the "Criswell Predicts" onscreen title. Author, Joe Blevins said, "Since *Plan 9* is almost inevitably the first of Eddie's films that most people see, it's fair to say that Criswell is the gatekeeper to the strange, surreal kingdom of Edward D. Wood, Jr. or at the very least, he's the *maître d'*, complete with a fancy tuxedo." The roster of directors for the program includes such B-movie legends: as Lee Sholen, *Catalina Caper* (1967), *The Doomsday Machine* (1972), and William "One-Shot" Beaudine, *Jesse James Meets Frankenstein's Daughter* (1966), *Bela Lugosi Meets a Brooklyn Gorilla* (1952).

After doing the television show and still wearing his pancake make-up so everyone would know he just came from the TV studio, Cris along with Buddy Hyde (the

Criswell and Singer Eddie Fisher. Father of Carrie Fisher.

show's producer) and other members of the crew would head to the Brown Derby restaurant for a cocktail and to go over the show. They began what was called the Brown Derby Friday Night Club. It grew to 125–150 people for over ten years. Ed Wood and his entourage of actors were regulars.

Ed Wood, Jr., *Hollywood Rat Race*

You'll see actors and actresses of renown at the Brown Derby in Hollywood, if you're there at the proper time. (Criswell and I even talked to the Three Stooges and Pat Butram the last time we were there.)

VERNON KOENIG: I can remember sitting with Criswell at the Brown Derby (along with many other people). He usually drank one or two Beefeater Martinis, was very sociable and adored his fans. If anyone came up to the table, he would always stand up and give them a warm greeting. He had a way of making people very comfortable in his presence. I never heard him ever use any vulgar language. In short, he was "Criswell" both on stage as well as off stage.

MAILA NURMI (VAMPIRA): Brown Derby Fridays were in the late 50s and 60s on Vine Street four blocks away. Ed and his gang were invited, not I of course. They met at the Brown Derby every Friday night. He would pick up the tab.

In the 1974 bestselling "tell-all" book, *The Life and Curious Death of Marilyn Monroe* by Robert Slatzer, the author claims to have been secretly married to Marilyn, had a lifelong friendship with the star, and that evidence he possessed (in a mysteriously missing Red Diary) proved that the Kennedys had her killed due to her affairs with JFK and RFK. It was shown shortly after the release of the "Bizarre and disturbing...touching and convincing." book that there was no evidence that what Slatzer, also known as "the Toad," claimed was true. Slatzer was a book critic and used his press pass to gain access to the set of *Niagara* (1953), where he was photographed with Miss Monroe on the only time that they had ever met or would ever meet again. In the chapter "Psychics, Seers, Psalms, and Palms," Slatzer claims that he introduced Marilyn to Criswell at the Brown Derby in 1950. He "recalled" the time saying that he saw Criswell waving to him across the bar then he joined the "couple" for a drink and when Marilyn realized who Criswell was, she inundated him with questions saying later, "I was really impressed by his truthfulness and his prediction about me came true." Slatzer claims that Criswell was impressed with her desire to succeed and her positive thoughts of succeeding against the odds at a time that she was already twenty-four years old and had barely begun her career and that he had said to her, "You're getting a late start but you'll finish ahead of all the others. I predict you will become not only a successful actress but the most famous blonde in the world." Slatzer goes on to claim that twenty years after that encounter, Criswell related to him of when in the mid-1950s he was attending a private art exhibit at the home of actor Edward G. Robinson when Marilyn pushed her way through the crowd to him asking if he remembered her, saying, "You were right. It happened." At first Criswell couldn't quite recall what he had said to her, so she reminded him of the Brown Derby encounter which then caused him to remember them meeting and him then telling Slatzer that she had impressed him the most of all the girls he had met due to her drive to become somebody. Criswell recalled, "She had positive attitude toward stardom. Her mind was made up. She had only positive thoughts and never thought negatively. That alone compelled me to make my prediction. She knew that she was going to succeed, and after talking with her that day in the Derby, I felt I had made a pretty safe prediction." Slatzer goes on to claim that Criswell remembered Marilyn long before he had introduced them to each other at the Derby, saying that during Criswell's youth in Princeton his father was a mortician and was the "first call" man whose duty is to pick up dead bodies. A young Criswell went to Frisco, Indiana and worked at a mortuary owned by Bob Yeager who with his son, later bought Westwood Memorial Park located in the Westwood Village area of Los Angeles where Criswell frequently visited and often saw Marilyn placing flowers on the grave of a relative. Criswell concluded, "Of course that was a long time ago." Marilyn is interred at what is now known as Pierce Brothers Westwood Village Memorial Park and Mortuary because it was the resting place of her mother's friend and an aunt that had cared for Marilyn as a child. After the book's publication, Criswell backed the book and Slatzer's claim to its veracity in his column saying, "I predict at last there has been a breakthrough in Robert F. Slatzer's, 'The Life and Curious Death of Marilyn Monroe,' of the true kind. This is just not another Hollywood biography. This full and complete record of Marilyn's personal life was really the history of Hollywood from 1948 to 1963, and the tragic aftermath that followed. Robert Slatzer's full and complete breakthrough shatters many legendary incidents which have been manufactured by her so-called 'intimates' and 'her friends.' I have known Slatzer since my arrival in Hollywood, and his recounting our past ventures from his office high atop the Taft building at Hollywood and Vine, I remember so clearly my contacts with Marilyn Monroe through the years. I predict that this biography will remain one of the most important records of Hollywood." And he forebode that "I predict Hollywood Boulevard will become haunted again by the wraith of Marilyn Monroe. Many report seeing her in the vicinity of the Chinese theater during the afternoons. A full account of these hauntings now appears in Robert Slatzer's . . . most complete and truthful of the Monroe biographies." He then predicted that *Marilyn the Magnificent* based on Robert Slatzer's . . . "will use actual locations in

Hollywood and New York." and "The *Marilyn the Magnificent*... will go into production in February. I have been signed to play myself as I knew Marilyn and her tragic life very well from the first interview I had with her at the Brown Derby."

Slatzer's book should be and is considered total fiction. He authored another book *The Marilyn Files* (1992), continuing to perpetrate his "story" of his involvement with her and the conspiracy theory of her being killed by the Kennedy family. His books, along with many others including Norman Mailer's *Marilyn* (1973), which claims she was murdered by FBI and CIA agents due to her involvement with Robert F. Kennedy, help maintain and fuel the cover-up and conspiracy theories surrounding her death and adds to the myth and tragic legend of the "Blonde Bombshell" called Marilyn Monroe, while securing her place in history as a major pop-culture icon.

It was during the Brown Derby days that Cris and Eddie became good friends and drinking buddies, going out to popular night spots such as the Trocadero, Macombo, Parisian, Allah's Gardens, Ciro's, Boardner's, and Musso & Franks's. Eddie's drink was Imperial whiskey neat, and Cris drank double Beefeater martinis, extra dry. They would also go up the Sunset Strip to see Herb Jeffries who had been a star of early black cowboy movies in the late-thirties such as *Harlem on the Prairie* (1937), and was known as "The Bronze Buckaroo." Jeffries went on to become a popular solo jazz vocalist after a stint with the Duke Ellington band as lead vocalist. Herb also married the famous exotic dancer Tempest Storm in the late 1950s They divorced in 1969. Eddie was involved in promoting the movie *Calypso Joe* (1957) which starred Jeffries and featured Angie Dickinson.

Criswell also began making appearances at Eddie's fundraising cocktail parties to finance whatever was his latest film project. Money for *Bride of the Atom* (1955), *Graverobbers From Outer Space* (1956), and *Revenge of the Dead* (1958), was raised in this way with other Wood regulars also appearing.

Criswell predicted on his television show that an actor by the name of Paul Marco would go far in the motion picture business. A showbiz friend had introduced him to Marco. Paul was born and raised in Los Angeles and had always wanted to be an actor. He worked as a child actor in the Meglin Kiddies troupe and graduated from Hollywood High School then served in the Navy during WWII. He returned to Hollywood and his quest for stardom after the war, appearing in local theater productions, which led to his film debut in *Sweet and Lowdown* (1944). Reports differ on how Marco met Wood. Some claim Criswell introduced the pair, but in fact it was Paul's agent and manager Marge Usher that introduced them. Eddie was so taken with Paul that he wrote the part of Kelton the Cop into his latest project *Bride of the Atom.* Eddie decided to rewrite the part of the older, more imposing desk sergeant into a younger man in order to cast Paul in the role. Paul became a regular member of the Wood troupe of actors as well a close lifelong friend to both Eddie and Cris.

Bride of the Atom, released as *Bride of the Monster* (1955), would be Bela Lugosi's final speaking role as the mad scientist, Dr. Eric Vornoff. Shortly after production on the film ended, Bela checked himself into rehab for methadone addiction. Ed decided to make the film's sneak preview a benefit for the ailing actor. Invitations were sent out and it was advertised as a benefit for Lugosi, but when the affair was held at the Paramount Theater on Hollywood Boulevard, unfortunately no one came except for the Wood entourage including Vampira.

In the August 6, 1954, issue of *TV-Radio Life* magazine appeared an article called "Who is Criswell?" by Jack Holland.

The following are excerpts:

Just how much on the level is Criswell? What is his back-ground? Is he another TV "character" or is he really a man who can foresee future events? And what are his predictions for the future of TV?

Criswell, his first name is never used, is a debonair gentleman who predicts coming events on KCOP. He has been tabbed a fake, he has been called one of TV's most interesting new personalities, and he has received wide recognition for many of his forecasts. So what is he really like? Just what is he?

It seemed best to let his answers to questions thrown at him during an interview decide the issue. You can be the judge of this man who is certainly offering something different to TV.

What do you think of those who have tabbed you as a phony?
Criswell: "You cannot doubt the prophet—you can only disbelieve him. Each and every forecast I make is well-founded on incidents which will cast definite shadows —and all coming events cast shadows. I base my predictions on trend, precedent, pattern of habit, on human behavior, and the unalterable laws of cycle."

What is your background?
Criswell: "I was raised in a family owned hotel and my first jobs were errand boy for the hotel guests and newspaper carrier for the two newspapers my uncle owned— 'The Daily Democrat' and 'The Clarion News.' I was always able to keenly and unemotionally analyze problems and look into problems of the future. I learned that the best student of the future is the best student of the past—and if you know the past and can be unemotional you can predict the future. Every word uttered on my program and every word written in my syndicated columns can be pegged on some estab-

lished fact or incident. At one time I had a job in public relations for a financial firm. I gave talks and found I was being widely quoted, especially on my forecasts of financial conditions"

What is your forecast for the political future of this country?
Criswell: "I won't predict who will be the next president, although in 1946, I predicted that Eisenhower would be elected in 1952, by a landslide and I have a printed column to bear this out. I feel the trend now is for conservatism. People again want to be practical and this is reflected in a great surge of home ownership and suburban development. Even food is more practical since we are getting back to old-fashioned three meals a day routine—and all good, substantial meals."

What is the future for TV?
Criswell: "I predicted over three years ago that the sponsors would demand a great deal for their money and that many of the high budget shows would be found most impractical and that the public taste would change to simple formulas and to one-man shows with low budgets but with wide appeal. Within five years everything on TV will be on film and shows will be instantly filmed and developed through a new Swiss invention that will revolutionize motion picture making as we know it today. There will be great strides in color TV."

Do you see many new stars hitting TV?
Criswell: "TV is not a place for youngsters and no teen-ager or even one under thirty-five will be able to crack the top crust. Years of experience are necessary for TV success. TV belongs now—and will belong even more so in the future— to the experienced personality."

Criswell was forty-seven-years-old and definitely considered himself "the experienced personality" and a TV success.

His syndicated newspaper column was now in newspapers nationwide and was titled, *An Accurate Glimpse of the Future CRISWELL PREDICTS*. The column covered national and international politics, celebrities, fashion, natural disasters, and everything else under the sun with titled segments; What People Will Do, Women Who Will Make News, Coming Hush Hush Events, Watch Out for This Fraud, Just for You Girls, What You Will Do in 1999, Your Headlines of the Future, A Very Famous Prediction, and For People and Places.

The *Anderson, South Carolina Daily Mail* began running Criswell's predictions column and invited readers to write and ask his advice on personal matters.

July 26, 1954:

Criswell estimates that 87 per cent of his predictions come true.

Follow his interesting column in THE DAILY MAIL, which presents this service solely for entertainment purposes. He will answer your question—write him in care of THE DAILY MAIL, sign your full name, but only initials or your code number will appear. Send no stamps or money. Answers appear in rotation as received and as space permits. Your letters go to Criswell unopened!

Predictions Of What People Will Do

Ptomaine poisoning will soon be a thing of the past due to a coming discovery by our Scientists who will perfect a way to prepare food which will outlaw this deadly killer. A harmless preservative will be added and this will insure (sic) public safety. Three out of 5 deaths occur and result in a round-a-bout way from stomach upsets due to tainted foods. Yes, in six years we will live longer and happier thanks to the coming advancement of Science! . . . Tyrone Power will win the Academy Award Oscar for the best performance of 1954, in the forthcoming "The Long Gray Line" which is a 50 year history of West Point from 1903 to 1953. Harry Carey, Jr. will also win the supporting role Award for his portrayal of President Eisenhower as a Cadet!

Criswell Answers Anderson Questions

Puzzled: This boy is quite fickle and you are very young to be thinking of marriage at this time. You should date other boys, and you will meet someone who is financially secure and more settled who will make you a worthy husband.

Lucille S: I am very sorry but I can only answer you through the columns of The Daily Mail. You should seek the man who shows the greatest willingness to be a good father for your children.

Rosa LR 324: I suggest you take your mother to a large local clinic for further medical diagnosis and treatment, for they will be able to aid her considerably.

G: I feel this money has been misplaced and will one day be recovered.

The 1954 Academy Awards were dominated by Elia Kazan's *On the Waterfront* (1954), with twelve nominations and eight wins including Best Picture and Marlon Brando's first Oscar for Best Actor as the confused ex-prizefighter and roughneck longshoreman Terry Malloy. The Best Supporting Actor Oscar went to Edmond O'Brien for his portrayal of a slimy and nervous Hollywood publicist/press agent named

Oscar Muldoon in Joseph Mankiewicz's trashy melodrama *The Barefoot Contessa* (1954). *The Long Gray Line* (1955) was not nominated for any Academy Awards and was not released until 1955.

August 15, 1954:

What You Will Do in 1999:
By looking 45 years into the future you will find that all traces of modesty as we know it today will have disappeared, and nudity will be the accepted condition. There will be nude public bathing beaches like Europe has today and all sports arenas will feature nude racing, sports, basketball, football, track with both men and women entrants! The sexes will not be on the same level, for the women will control and own the world by that time and men will be tolerated merely for the continuation of the race. Yes, in 1999, men will bear the names of the women they marry, and woman will never give up her name for a man's. Stand by and see!

August 22, 1954:

What You Will Do in 1999:
Here is what I predict you will be doing 45 years from today— in 1999: You will arise in controlled temperature, have your first breakfast snack of one pill which will be orange juice, ham and eggs, buttered toast with jam and coffee, all contained in one tiny capsule. There will be no overweight, no sickness, no stomach disorders, for this will all be controlled through enforced diet. You will work only three hours a day at an assigned job and have the rest for relaxation. You will not permit anything to worry you, due to enforced scientific thinking, you will be free as an individual, and content with your lot! Speed the day!

This prediction is for four days after Criswell would later predict to be the end of the world.

August 29, 1954:

Women Who Will Make News:
Halo Meadows will open a huge dance palace overlooking the Pacific at Malibu which will feature buffet dining at the water's edge and will be completely constructed of glass!

Just For You Girls:
William Hibbler will soon place a most remarkable reducing item on the market—rubber panties! They fit snugly to the figure, are air tight and will give the body a steam bath, which will reduce, thin and firm the figure. Many movie stars who were verging on the heavy side have found that this reducing garment can thin them without dieting. I predict that more men will buy this item than women!

What You Will Do In 1999:
Here is what I predict you will be doing exactly 45 years from today in 1999:

Diamonds will have lost their commercial value and will be used as freely for dress decorations at that time, as we use rhinestones today! The great coal mining centers will be closed down completely due to the use of solar heating and a newly introduced refined oil burning which will eliminate the use of coal altogether! There will be no smoke from factories and nothing to pollute our air. All garbage disposal will be done by chemical, and any trash will be disposed of in the same manner! . . . Yes, 45 years from today, another great worry will be lifted from your life: You will not be worried with headaches, for they will be overcome through a new circulatory treatment!

The Aliyah Group of San Fernando Valley Chapter Hadassah held a luncheon meeting at Bill Storey's Restaurant, 4100 N. Cahuenga Blvd., on September 23rd, with Criswell as a guest speaker.

Halo's mother, Etta Sarah Frances Stonesifer, passed away on October 23,1954, at the age of seventy-five.

October 31, 1954:

What You Will Do in 1999:
It is now November 1, 1999, exactly 45 years from today, and you and your family have just returned from the National Nudist Day Celebration in your local park, where everyone attended nude, in honor of this celebration. There were races, baseball games, a huge picnic, plus a huge community sing. You all had a very good time, and enjoyed the perfect freedom without your clothes. On this day, everyone in this great nation, the United States (which now is composed of Canada, Mexico, Cuba, Alaska and Central America) must go nude or be fined, exactly as they are if they do not vote on Election Day. Men by this time do not vote except on minor problems, for women own and control the nation, lock, stock and barrel! Check up on this prediction!

Coming Hush Hush Events:
One of most famous motion picture stars will return from Denmark an unchanged man, for the operation did not take, and was not successful as in the case of Christine Jorgensen!

Your Headlines of the Future:
Mysterious gas odor penetrates atmosphere of earth from outer space! . . . Science astounded at radio active elements in the Pacific! . . . Japan launches new low priced automobile

to buck European manufacturers! . . . Noted author dies in sleep!

November 7, 1954:

What You Will Do in 1999:
Forty-five years from this very moment, you will be looking out into a clear, happy, understanding world, for every device known to the comfort of the human race will be furnished by your government. You will have free cosmetics, free false teeth, free medical care, free vacations, free schooling, free marriage ceremonies and a free marriage bureau! The only catch is that if you want anything out of the ordinary you will be required to pay for it out of your extra money, which you will be permitted to earn, if you so desire. You will face a brave new world at that time, and life will most certainly be worth living until that time, for so many wonderful things will happen between now and then!

December 12, 1954:

Women Who Will Make the News:
Julie Andrews, the present hit in the Broadway play, "The Boy Friend," a satire on the flaming 20's (sic), will be Hollywood's next greatest star!

Just for You Girls:
1955 will be the year of the return of the Paisley shawl. The famed paisley pattern of your grandmother's day will be high fashion, and the shawl will replace the now popular stole! . . . Your next diet for thinning will consist of raw tomatoes, buttermilk, clear consommé, rare beef, black coffee, plus

eight sticks of celery per day. You will not be hungry or weak, and you will magically thin down!

What You Will Do in 1999:
During the week of mid-December 1999, you will enjoy yourself to the utmost, for during this week, an interplanetary celebration will be held. This space festival will mark the beginning of a new era of peace and prosperity for the entire universe. We will have special telecasts from other planets. This will also mark the unveiling of a machine which will always remain in perpetual motion, alchemy or the making of gold from baser metals, the cheap manufacture of diamonds, and the complete enslavement of the atomic age! This will prove to be the greatest week in the history of the world, for man will have come of age! Please check up on this prediction personally for you will be here to do so!

VERNE LANGDON: Criswell was a novelty in a time, post-war, when people really needed escapism. And things like *Time for Beany* and Korla Pandit and *Criswell Predicts* were really something.

1955 was the apogee of Criswell's career. His *Criswell Predicts* show on KCOP was in full swing and his columns were in newspapers and magazines from coast to coast. He was making numerous personal public appearances billed as a "Famous KCOP Television Personality."

A one-sided 12 inch 78 RPM vinyl record titled *Criswell 1955,* was available from local Philco television dealerships. The recording begins with an announcer stating, "What's in the Future? Criswell Predicts 1955," followed by a plug for Philco, then Criswell gives his predictions for 1955.

When we are forewarned we are forearmed. I predict that 1955, will truly be the pivotal year of the 20th Century. I predict that coming action taken by our government will ensure a peaceful world of the future and although the way ahead may look doubtful at this moment, many surprising incidents will in insure the perpetuation of our way of life. I predict that one catastrophe will follow after another in quick succession and Mother Nature will show man that she is still mistress of the Universe. I predict that 1955 will be the year of woman's supreme independence over men. She will enter and dominate the fields of politics, industry, business, medicine, and invention. I predict that in 1955, it will become apparent that there will be a woman president in 1960. In 1955 woman will control the world's largest corporation. A woman will be the most dynamic business personality of our time. A woman doctor will amaze with her new found control of glandular disturbances and a woman scientist will make the most startling scientific discovery since gunpowder. I predict that a new public health plan will permit every citizen to have the proper medical care free of charge. You will be fingerprinted and your complete identification kept on file in Washington by the end of 1955. Noted pilot in rocket plane goes beyond the moon into limitless space. Law of gravity broken by nuclear device which causes objects to fly off wildly into space. And my final prediction for the year of 1955, is that every man, woman, and child in America will realize for the first time their personal duty to their own happiness, the welfare of others, and our loyalty to our great nation. My friend, there will be violent, turbulent times ahead in the future. Why should we fear the future, when the future is only a continuation of the past and an extension of the present. And so dear friends until January the first, 1956 when the coming days of the future

141

belong to the historical past. This is your friend Criswell who knows we must outlast these things or they will outlast us. It is my earnest desire that good fortune may always be yours.

The five-and-a-half minute recording concludes telling listeners to see and hear *Criswell Predicts* on KCOP-TV Lucky Channel 13 presented by Philco and the authorized Philco dealers where the listener received the recording. In 1958 Philco released the uniquely designed *Predicta* line of televisions promoting them as "The Most Advanced TV of Our Time!" and "TV Today from the World of Tomorrow." The *Predicta* was marketed as "the world's first swivel screen console . . . the most unique ever designed. It provides a fresh look of 'tomorrow' that blends with any decor." The futuristic aesthetic and iconic design was influenced by an interest in space age technology prompted by Russia's Sputnik launch in 1957. It was released as floor-standing pedestal and table-top versions in several console configurations and all the models had the picture tube separate from the cabinet. The *Predicta* proved to be less than reliable with overheating circuit boards and poor picture quality leading to a huge rate of returned sets and warranty service. It was also only available with a black and white picture and color television was then at the leading edge of TV technology. 1960 was the last year the *Predicta* was sold.

There was another "Criswell Day" held on July 3, with jalopy races run in his honor at the Long Beach Memorial Stadium sponsored by Dr. Ross of dog food fame. Dr. Ross dog food, "Get Dr. Ross dog food, it's doggone good!" sponsored a number of early television programs. Criswell was advertised to bring other "personalities" with him "including Paul Marco, who appears with Bela Lugosi in 'Bride of the Atom,' soon to be released." Criswell conducted a special "Criswell Predicts" program from the infield and interviewed fans in the stands. After the races, he gave out trophies to the winning drivers at the Wilton Hotel and appeared in the Sky Room predicting on

"future fashions" during a fashion show presented by the Town Shop.

A photo was run in an issue of *Radio/TV Magazine* showing Criswell signing autographs surrounded by his adoring fans. He was a true celebrity, but not everyone took to Criswell's writing style. "I enjoyed the newspaper section very much until I reached the 'Criswell Predicts' column. It is difficult to ferret out whatever grains of truth this junior Winchell spits forth when the brain is bruised by continuous exclamation points. Did the typesetter misplace the conservative 'period.' Or does the writer sense a desperate need of bombastic punctuation to dress up the stale bits of news and ambiguity in his 'accurate' glimpses of the future?"

February 6, 1955:

What People Will Do:
Due to my TV-radio and motion picture now being made in Hollywood, I will not be able to make a national tour this year, but will hold a convention where you may spend five days with me from June 30 through July 4. For full information you may write Criswell Convention, Hotel Wilton, Long Beach, Calif. Others will come from your area and we will have a wonderful time.

The most expensive piano in the world, all glass, chromium, silver and spun aluminum costing $25,000 will be used by Liberace on his world tour. You will be able to buy a replica for one-tenth the cost by late 1958 . . . Gloria Swanson will appear in a musical version of "Sunset Boulevard" on Broadway with the score by Richard Stapley and Dick Hughes!

What You Will Do In 1999:
I predict that America will not only have a Hall of Fame, but also a Hall of Shame! This Hall of Shame will have the effects of our great criminals, who were statesmen, represented here. All of the men in this Hall of Shame will have committed some grave crime against womanhood, rather than against humanity as a whole! Some of our national heroes who had very violent anti-feminist attitudes towards women's rights, will suddenly find themselves in the same class as the worst despots the world has produced! Yes, my friend, whether you and I like it or not, 1999 will truly be a woman's world!

For People and Places:
Las Vegas: The next motion picture to be produced in your area will concern the building of a huge hotel and the various problems which will arise there! . . . Howard Hughes: Your next aviation project will be based on the rocket principle . . . Eddie Fisher: Your next recorded hit will be "I Wish and Wish".

February 20, 1955:

What You Will Do In 1999:
By trend, precedent, pattern of habit and the unalterable laws of science, I predict that in 1999, you will find that: (1) All disease will have been conquered by the process oxidation,

(2) All climate will have been controlled by radaric principle, (3) All mental problems such as worry, fatigue, distraction and confusion will be eliminated through a brain wave machine which will banish negation of the mind, (4) All traffic on our streets, underground and in the air and in the sea, will be controlled by a rhythmic pulsation which will prohibit any accidents through collision, for each vehicle will carry its own atmospheric protection! Yes, the year 1999 could be very dull and prosaic if we allow it!

February 27, 1955:

What You Will Do in 1999:
In 44 years our world will be one of spun plastic! Yes, clear, bright, new plastic, transparent, bullet proof, shatter proof, and atomically treated for safety! You and I will move in a clean, clear world, where our very air has been washed chemically before we breath it! Our homes, offices, theaters and churches, not overlooking the schools, will have automatically controlled dust and germ collectors which go into action when any foreign substance appears, radarically! Children will be born outside the body in a plastic pouch, and will be carried with safety, and delivered without pain or danger through the severing of the cord! Yes, we will move in a clean, clear, safe world in 1999!

Criswell appeared on the cover of the February 1955, issue of the short-lived science fiction pulp magazine *Spaceway Science Fiction*. Forest J. Ackerman penned a regular movie column for the magazine called "Scientifilm Parade" where he reviewed new science fiction movies and reported on upcoming film projects including some of Ed Wood's. "Bela Lugosi tells me he is interested in the role of a scientist. Lugosi has just finished a scientifilm, *Bride of the Atom.* The cold touch of death with emphasis on the supernatural rather than the scientific will be Bela Lugosi's when he perhaps costars with Vampira in a picture which may be known as either *The Vampire's Touch* or *The Vampire's Tomb.*" Legendary Sci-Fi/Horror artist, special effects, and make-up innovator Paul Blaisdell illustrated the column and designed the cover that shows Criswell staring at a cube shaped space station.

ON OUTER SPACE

Criswell predicts and everybody listens. For many years Criswell has been hailed as the 20th Century Nostradamus and is the first prophet to gain prominence and national recognition since Edward Bellamy and his immortal "Looking Backward".

Criswell has become a household word and is the most quoted personality of our time. You may have read Criswell's syndicated column in over 1,000 newspapers. You may view him on your television set, or hear him on your radio. Criswell holds the record in many theaters and auditoriums throughout the country. We consider SPACEWAY most fortunate in securing Criswell's exclusive predictions on Outer Space.

The Editors

We are all interested in the future, for that is where you and I will spend the rest of our lives.

We must not fear the future, for it is only a continuation of the past. The world of the future will be a place of fantasy, of imagination and bedrock practicability. Man has always been forced to struggle against the elements, but I predict that man will be forced to struggle more than ever before if he wishes to outlast the wraths of cosmic nature—or the wraths of cosmic nature will outlast him.

Outer space can be an inch away from the end of your nose or six trillion miles. I predict that the following will be a short history of man's future—in outer space—and that many of you reading these very words, will live to see the day when many of these things become a reality.

I predict that, within a few short years, man will establish his first successful space-station—and shortly thereafter he will reach the moon. But I also predict that this is as far as his immediate conquest of our solar system will go.

Shortly after man has reached the moon, the all-out war, which everyone has been expecting—yet dreading, will occur . . . and it will leave the earth a radioactive ruin—a place which will become more dangerous to man with each passing year.

I further predict that all the people that have not been destroyed in this 20th Century Armageddon, will unite, and working against time, will construct a huge cube in outer space, which will be ten miles in height, ten miles in width, and ten miles in depth. This gigantic, colossal monstrosity will be held in position by the conflicting laws of gravity between the sun and the planets.

This floating island in space will be inhabited by a selected group of people who will be scientifically, medically, and morally chosen through a mechanical screening device, operated by an electric brain the size of a thimble. I predict that when these people are chosen, they will be propelled into outer space by tiny individual rockets, which will land them unharmed in the more rarefied atmosphere of this new, man-made world.

I predict that this artificial planet will be built from a fund collected as a tithe from every man, woman and child on our

Earth. It will take ten thousand workers ten years to construct this mighty space nation. Materials will be magnetized and shot into outer space, and will be drawn to a huge magnet, which will re-arrange them under an artificial gravity.

I predict that this floating nation in the sky will be governed not by an individual, but by an all knowing, analytical, mechanical brain. The brain will know everything there is to know, except the philosophy and psychology of the female mind . . . and I predict that this will cause its downfall.

Women have always been superior to men, and in this coming age will prove they are even more superior to machinery and the wizardry of so-called scientists.

I predict that tremendous floating world will be evenly divided with masculine and feminine inhabitants. All births will be controlled by artificial insemination, and the bodies of those who have died will be disintegrated. These future scientists, under the guidance of the mechanical brain, will evolve a method of isolating the life-force of all human beings—and this life-force will be kept in storage, so that each entity will have more than one chance at existence.

This cube will be divided into rooms which are all connected by a series of winding hallways, elevators, moving platforms and train service. Everything is on the inside of the cube, for the exterior will be an impregnable fortress to guard against warlike invasions from other jealous worlds, and to protect the inhabitants against the danger of meteors and cosmic rays.

I predict the life of every specimen on this manufactured planet will be as carefully controlled as the atom is today. Every thought, word or action will be policed by this tyrant brain, which will think it is greater than God. Men, women and children will be held in emotional bondage by being permitted to see only selected theatrical programs, attend carefully prepared lectures, read proscribed books, and at any time of the lunar day or night they will have their brain made a receiving station for controlled propaganda.

I predict that it will be a woman who will free all that is left of humanity from bondage under this giant monster brain.

I will now predict the actions of this brave, fearless woman, who will become known as the Joan of Arc of outer space. This amazing product of laboratory breeding will plan with her female counterparts, who are likewise convicts in the most fantastic jail ever conceived by man, a revolt against the tyrannical brain that is their warden.

I predict this is the manner in which this revolution in outer space will take place. These women will construct, in secrecy, two powerful electric generators which, at a prearranged time, will be turned on in unison. The powerful electric impulse will completely destroy the electronic brain by fusing it's relays, shorting out it's circuits and shooting all its tubes, after first overcoming the brain's electronic defenses.

The men will revolt against the change of conditions, but the women will triumph for they will have the power to build a consciousness that cannot be turned by outside interference.

I predict that by this time our present earth will have become a hallow memory in the advanced minds of the people of this floating nation in space. Our world will have vanished as a spark vanishes in a bonfire, and it's charred remains will drift somewhere in the vast regions of time as a cinder floats on the wind, leaving in its stead a gravitational aura which will be an echo of our former power.

I predict that there will be only four things remembered out of the 20th Century—four things they can definitely prove existed. These four things will be a mechanical eggbeater, the music of Liberace, Mae West, and someone by the name of Eisenhower who seemed to accomplish so very much for humanity.

A copy of this Spaceway magazine will be treated with a special preservative in the hopes that this future generation may find these predictions startlingly correct.

For the benefit of those who wish to know more about Criswell, we are reviewing on the following pages his forthcoming picture, CRISWELL PREDICTS TO 1999.

PANIC ON CELLULOID
By CHARLES WIREMAN

The medium of motion pictures has brought us such great revelations as Cinerama, 3-D, Stereophonic sound, Cinemascope, and the magical beauty of brilliant color. We have viewed the classics, comedy, tragedy, musicals, spectacles and science fiction film fare. Through motion pictures, we have had our emotions turned inside out; we have cried, laughed, and clutched at our throats in terror . . . But, there is an even greater thrill in store for us which will create sensations within in us that we never believed possible.

Recently, while at a major sound studio in Hollywood, I noticed a group of important people milling around the doorway of a projection room. There were several notables and celebrities whom I recognized, and, out of curiosity, I mixed with the group and slipped into the theatre when the announcement came that the film was about to start.

There had been some bits of conversation about this being a secret, hush-hush screening, and that there was some doubt about the film being acceptable to the general public, and this aroused even more curiosity and interest.

The room darkened and the title: "Criswell Predicts to 1999" appeared on the screen, in color, accompanied by a rather strange and intriguing musical background. I immediately thought it was simply another futuristic science fiction movie, but soon found that this was DIFFERENT!

The film is narrated throughout with the voice of Criswell, himself, who describes the future of the world and space up until 1999. History had its Nostradamus, who never made a prediction past the year 1999, but Criswell goes into greater detail and brings to the screen, in full fury, the occurrences which he predicts face the 20th Century.

The film deals with a great many strange and horrifying events, almost too numerous to explain fully, but here are some highlights which will cause a many a viewer to shudder.

There is a time approaching when a tremendous stratic explosion will cause the entire world to be without lights for 40 days and 40 nights. All power will be disrupted and crime will take free rein. The earth will be forced to revert to candlelight in order to maintain some semblance of normal existence.

Diseases which science and medicine now are striving to combat will be but a thing of the past, and they will be dwarfed by new and horrible ailments such as blood turning to water, and a wipespread type of leprosy.

The film leaves nothing to the imagination but everything is reveled in full, and the color creates an even more vivid impression. Personally, I found the sequences of an authentic operation quite shocking.

This picture predicts that the hydrogen bomb will soon be nothing but a memory, since it will be rendered useless by a weapon which freezes the atmosphere and all within it. There is, in the future, a terrible human carnage—and the film describes this visibly and without hesitancy . . . no punches are pulled!

Although members of the small audience seem to be edgy and nervous, everyone remained glued to their seats, completely captivated by the scenes taking place before their eyes. Criswell's narration, plus the recurring theme music, will hypnotize anyone!

Some sequences which left me quite stunned and somewhat bewildered including devastating fires, the explosions of dirigibles, nudism, great sea monsters, dying planets, and the sinking of a continent. Words can't completely describe it.

The picture will have an intermission, and I think some people with weak stomachs won't return for the second half, but those that are built more solidly will love it. Frankly, I was glad when the intermission was announced, for it gave me a chance to catch my breath.

When the picture opens for national release, there will be nurses in attendance, for it was felt that some people might possibly require medical attention. This is certainly one film that will never dare be shown on television.

Film was produced by George Richter and Wayne Berk, with a musical score by Scott Seely. Running time is presently 90 minutes. There are some overlong sequences which will evidently be trimmed before the actual release.

Criswell's vast following, through his TV and radio programs and his syndicated column, will prove a ready audience, as will anyone interested in the future.

If you want a glimpse of what is ahead, and if you can take it, go and see "CRISWELL PREDICTS TO 1999."

This description of the alleged film describes and portrays what would become know a few years later as "Mondo films." A sub-genre of exploitation and documentary films produced resembling pseudo-documentaries that depict sensational topics, scenes, or situations. Mondo films began to soar in popularity with the release of *Mondo Cane* (1962). Common traits between the Mondo films of the 1960s, and the 1955, written depiction of the *Criswell Predicts to 1999!* film is the emphasis on taboo subjects such as death and sex, and staged sequences presented as genuine documentary footage. Mondo, Italian for "world," films do include portrayals of foreign cultures that have drawn accusations of ethnocentrism and racism. The last half of the twentieth century saw the popularity of the sub-genre cause it to evolve into its own full-fledged film genre nicknamed "Death film" due to the films' increasing emphasis on graphic footage of the dead and dying, both real and fake. *The Faces of Death Series* (1978–1996), is one of the most well-known, popular, and widely viewed releases of Mondo style film due to the proliferation of video tape technology and increased usage of the VHS tapes and players in the late 1970s and early 1980s.

Scott Seely was a young composer, arranger, and producer working in Hollywood in 1954 when he established his Accent Records label and then met Criswell. During the 1960s he worked with Buddy Merrill who was a featured guitarist on the Lawrence Welk show for over two decades. He also produced the album *Echoes From Nature Boy* by the eccentric Hollywood legend eden ahbez who lived in Griffith Park under the first L of the Hollywood sign and refused to capitalize the first letters of his name. ahbez wrote the song "Nature Boy" about his friend and fellow freegan hippie, Gypsy Boots. The easy-listening tune told a fantasy of "a very strange enchanted boy," "who wandered very far, over land and sea," only to realize that "the greatest thing you'll ever learn is just to love and be loved in return." The song was a number one Billboard Chart hit for Nat King Cole in 1948. Criswell approached Scott to compose some music for him entitled "Criswell Predicts to 1999." Seely had no idea that the music was to be used in a film. He assumed it was for Criswell's television program and produced a demo recording of the composition.

SCOTT SEELY: It's very interesting. It's a simple theme in C Minor with 7 variations. The titles are 1—Ribbon Of Time 2—Theme of The Restless Heart 3—Storehouse Of Memory 4—Hall Of Shame 5—Dance Of Tomorrow's Cadavers (quite far out) 6—Death The Proud Brother 7—The Long Arm Of God. These were Criswell's titles that he gave to me to compose to. I remember Wayne Berk being in my studio in Hollywood. Also remember going over to Criswell's apartment and meeting Mae West there. I don't recall the film.

There are no records of the film *Criswell Predicts to 1999* having been produced much less released. In response to a reader letter in the next issue of the pulp magazine, "Criswell Predicts to 1999' won't be generally released for a couple of months yet. . . ."

In the April 1955, *Spaceway*, Criswell's article entitled "The Dying Planet" details the destruction of a planet named Bellarion after it leaves its normal orbit, sweeps into our solar system and streaks across our heavens.

The following are excerpts:

The pull of gravity during this period will be so diametrically powerful that huge lakes will suddenly empty skyward, rivers will change their courses, and waterfalls will become geysers.

Huge buildings will be loosed from their foundations and will fly off into space.

Houses will fall sideways and crash into hillsides miles distant. No life will be safe and death will strike swiftly and without warning.

The human body itself will become an individual chamber of torture. Human heads will swell to twice their size, due to the blood rushing to the topmost extremities.

Pregnant women will explode.

In cemeteries, the dead will be lifted from their graves through a strange magnetic force which will influence only dead cells. Cadavers will mingle with the living, floating about aimlessly.

The dead bodies of the former inhabitants of Mother Earth will float into limitless space like tiny particles of dust now float in our air.

The skies will rain blood because of the millions of crushed bodies floating in space.

At the end of the rain of blood, Bellarion will come to the end of its course, with a cataclysmic explosion, which will rock the entire solar system. Earth will be showered with cosmic ashes, and great fires will sweep nation after nation, leaving only smoking ruin.

I predict that this will one day happen in what we call the future. Can you prove that it will not? If you have scientific proof to offer, I would be most happy to examine it.

Following the article is a biographical piece named "Jeron King Criswell" by Charles Wireman.

The following are excerpts:

When one thinks of the future, one thinks of Criswell.

This 20th Century Nostradamus has a life that truly belongs to the public, for he has dedicated himself to the problems of mankind and how they can be solved in the future.

Although Criswell knows thousands of people he enjoys nothing better than a friendly chat with someone who comes up and makes themselves known to him.

Criswell's favorite character in history is Napoleon, and his favorite age in history is from 1890 to 1900. His favorite American writer is Edgar Allen Poe.

Criswell has a diet which he claims gives him vitality which is composed of rare meat, buttermilk, peanut butter, raw tomatoes, apples and dark bread. For liquids Criswell drinks hot or cold black coffee and a tart red table wine, sometimes mixed with lemon juice. Criswell only needs five hours sleep a night, can work the clock around without fatigue, has a deep sense of humor, and is much too sympathetic for his own good.

Criswell's next project, besides his coast-to-coast television show, will be when he takes his one-man auditorium show into the Hollywood Bowl on August 18, 1955.

There are no records of Criswell doing a show at the Hollywood Bowl. There also no records of a journalist by the name of Charles F. Wireman. I suspect that Wireman is a non de plume for Criswell due to the nearly exact composition and writing styles of the two articles and Criswell's other writings.

March 20, 1955:

Hollywood: A new trend in audience participation will be introduced by Halo Meadows in her intimate theater in the Hollywood Hotel, which will be novel and exciting.

Tom Hatten: He had a very strange wife named Halo Meadows. An actor friend and I went to a lot of live theatre. Every Friday night in the *Hollywood Citizen-News* there'd be an ad for this Halo Meadows Evening of Drama called *Once Upon an Evangelist* or something like that. We went to this one, one Friday night and it was at the Hollywood Hotel, which of course does not exist anymore, on Hollywood Boulevard. It was a bizarre evening. We were the only two people in the audience. It was in a hotel room actually and the play that she was in with several other people was played in three different hotel rooms in three different cities and of course there was no real need for changing the décor. She was at the door when we came in greeting everybody, my friend and myself. Then she did the show and when we came out she was there at the door to thank us for coming and I can't remember if she said a donation would be appreciated or not. We gave 'em a couple of bucks. It was a strange, strange evening and she sang as I recall, and played the piano abominably.

March 20, 1955:

What People Will Do:
Mae West will pay tribute to this column and the television-radio programs in her newest Decca album "Come Up and See Me Sometime" (No. 87123) when she sings "Criswell Predicts!" I am very grateful to The Sunday Post for helping to make this possible, and to you readers for your interest, and to Mae West, her male chorus, and the Eddie Oliver orchestra. The words and music to 'Criswell Predicts' were written by Mae West, whom we personally wish to thank also!

It was actually the Sy Oliver Orchestra. A minor inaccuracy. Sy Oliver was an arranger, composer, trumpet player, and bandleader who had worked for the Tommy Dorsey band. He is considered to be one of the main contributors to the sound of "swing" in the late 1930s and 1940s. Miss West had handed the lyrics of "Criswell Predicts" to Bob Thompson the arranger, on a napkin detailing her obsession with the Hollywood psychic.

BOB THOMPSON: She was a very complicated personality, to say the least. She believed very much in the spiritual world. There was a columnist named Criswell, and she wrote lyrics to a song called "Criswell Predicts" and I wrote the music!

Dr. Mysterian, a modern-day internet prognosticator, describes the song as, "a hoochie-coochie number filled with salacious horn blasts and drum fills that sound meant for bumping and grinding." The song opens with an ultra-lounge-show style intro quickly followed by Miss West's smoky, husky, contralto voice:

Turned on my television to lucky channel thirteen,
tuned in Mr. Criswell, he sure was on the beam,
with his predictions, with his convictions,
of what the future will be, and it made a lotta sense to me.
Criswell predicts many things in the future,
Criswell predicts what the world's gonna do,
trips to the stars, vacations on Mars, snow in July, the strangest new cars,
and if Criswell predicts it, you can bet it comes true!

Criswell also previewed the song on his television program on March 11. Of course now in the wondrous technological era of the twenty-first century, the song can be found on basically any internet streaming-media service.

Mae became interested in spiritualism and psychic abilities in the early 1940s after a period of deep introspection. She hosted a séance at the celebrity desert resort La Quinta shortly after her fa-

ther's death. She claimed it was conducted by Amelia Earhart and believed that she had made contact with her father using spirit tapping. She continued to host and attended séances and seek counsel from psychics and mediums throughout most of her life. Miss West had a number of psychic friends including Dr. Richard Ireland (University of Life Center), Kenny Kingston (whom she taught to read tea leaves), Sri Deva Ram Sukul (healer and president of the Yoga Institute for America), Reverend Jack Kelly (Universalist minister and her favorite medium from Lily Dale Academy), Reverend Mae M. Taylor (Spiritualist Science Church of Hollywood), and of course Criswell with whom she shared an astrological connection. Her birthday is August 17 and his August 18.

Mae and Cris were longtime friends, and she sold her 1950 Cadillac Fleetwood 75 limousine to Criswell for a dollar as notarized by her attorney. She was getting a new 1951 model. The automobile would later appear in a number of television and film productions including *The Godfather* (1972). Criswell kept the vehicle until his death in 1982 and bequeathed it to his longtime employee, friend, and living companion, Robert George Harrison who sold it in 1991. In 2021, it sold in a Hollywood memorabilia auction for $40,000.

In 1954 Ms. West's chauffeur committed suicide in one of her limos as reported in a newspaper account of the incident. "Authorities yesterday were investigating the apparent suicide of Ray Charles Wallace, 44, personal chauffeur for actress Mae West. His body was found Tuesday in Miss West's Cadillac limousine on a farm near Patoka, Indiana. Miss West, currently appearing at a Chicago night club, could give no reason for Wallace's death. Her manager, Vincent Lopez, said Wallace left Miami on February 7 to drive the car here. Lopez said Wallace called him several times en route to complain of having 'lots of trouble.' Lopez said he notified Indiana State Police to be on the lookout for Wallace. Coroner Robert Kendall termed the death as suicide. He said a hose ran from the exhaust pipe to the car's interior. In the car was a sealed metal box bearing Miss West's name. Miss West, who flew here from Miami, said she didn't know what the box contained." She later recalled that the depressed 44-year-old African-American WWII veteran had threatened to kill himself. He had huddled under a quilt in the backseat of the Cadillac for his final nap.

CLAUDIA POLIFRONIO: He used to give her stock market tips. He told me that he was her press agent for many years. They were very close friends.

He took me to Mae West's home on Rossmore when she was away. He had a key because they were so close. He said, "I want you to see her home." It was like art deco, white, very feminine, white rugs, gold, glitzy, very old Hollywood.

He had a lot of respect for her privacy. He had a way of keeping things in place. But he would talk about her from time to time. Her brother reveled more. Her brother said that Mae West was also a metaphysician and a longevist and a vegetarian, and she doesn't smoke or drink, and she doesn't go out to nightclubs. She was exactly the opposite of the characters she portrayed.

Criswell again appeared on the cover of *Spaceway Science Fiction* for the June 1955, issue. This time he was with his good friend Mae West. They are wearing space suits on the surface of the moon colorfully illustrated by painter and later B-Movie monster maker Paul Blaisdell.

July 4th, 1955, *Reno Evening Gazette,* "A Postcard From Stan Delaplane"

That engaging international gamboleer Mr. Sanford Adler has engaged Miss Mae West to lighten cares of life on the Nevada side of Lake Tahoe. So the other night I hustled over to the Biltmore where what is sin 50 feet away in California ain't no sin at all but a pleasure. I must say that I did not go over to scratch the dice tables. But to see Miss West and her merry muscle men. For I have just read that Miss West will be president of the United States in 1960, and will take a trip to the moon.

When she says, "Come up and see me sometime." You should put on your spacesuit.

Black tie. RSVP.

You are probably not aware of this 1960 forecast printed in Spaceways, a Los Angeles magazine of modest circulation. The prediction was done by one of our foremost predictors, a Mr. Criswell, whose writings in the New York Enquirer are forwarded to me by Mr. Irving Hoffman, Criswell fan and Broadway press agent.

Mr. Criswell forecast for Spaceways as follows:

"You will recall how violent the campaign (of 1960) proved to be! Not only was this campaign unusual but it was waged between an ordinary man candidate and a woman candidate who not only sought to free womankind from the 7000-year old rule of man but also to liberate man from his closed ideas!"

" . . . —women battled against men in the streets and would break up any crowd of men who sought to rally behind the male candidate for president."

"After the battle of ballots. needless to say, Man had underestimated the woman, consequently women won the election by a landslide which placed their candidate, Miss Mae West, in the White House!"

"The first act of President West after inauguration," said Criswell, reaching into the future, "was to immediately start her campaign promises of space travel."

"Many diehards in congress who were swept out of office and replaced by women bemoaned the fact that we had not conquered the common cold as yet. So why should our scientists make the effort to conquer Outer Space." You know what Miss West told them? She had a mighty clever answer. She said the Spaniards delayed Columbus with the same arguments about Spanish fever. And even to this day Spanish fever has not been conquered! That's what she said—or will say when 1960 rolls around.

Mr. Criswell said Miss West will then take off for the moon. She will go to the moon and come back again. Her specially appointed space diplomat with portfolio will be guess who? Criswell. George Liberace, brother of the piano player, will be an aide. Truman will be an air admiral. Mr. Criswell then predicted Miss West's speech on her return.

"Fear has never been the vocabulary of a woman and it was up to a woman to accept the challenge of Space flight! But I was disappointed in Moon!" (There's a woman for you).

She said she was disappointed because it just shows you how half the things you think are true, really aren't. She proclaimed the day as Lunar Day and added: "When my official memoirs are published, I am sure this unforgettable adventure will be recorded for posterity."

It certainly is interesting to be on the inside of such things. And to see Miss West before the election. Walking around just easy and friendly like, feeling the muscles of the muscle men. And halfway to moon if she only knew it.

The August 13 edition of the *LA Times* announced that "Criswell plans a birthday party and invites all to attend at the Hollywood Knickerbocker tomorrow afternoon. . . .

August 14, 1955:

On Jan. 1 of this year, this column predicted that within six months the United States would officially announce plans for a space station . . . We were nationally ridiculed for this reckless prediction and five newspapers dropped the column for this one prediction. Your headlines read "U.S. Space Station to Encircle Earth" on July 29! I further predict that we are much nearer the solution of outer space than you dare think!

In October, with the Carpet Mill company as a sponsor, *Criswell Predicts* was airing two times a week on Thursday and Saturday. The show had a number of sponsors throughout its run including Bill Murphy Buick, Vermont Furniture Company, Brew 102, and Roland Oldsmobile with the tag-lines "TV's most provocative show," "Shocking & Amazing," "What's in YOUR Future," "Happenings Concerning American Security," and "See the 20th Century Nostradamus."

On the evening of November 3 Criswell attended a send-off for the *Carmel Museum Theater*, which was beginning a film revival program of running one silent film and one new talkie each week. Mack Sennent hosted the event which honored Bela Lugosi, along with other stars of yesteryear. Also in attendance were Groucho Marx, Harold Lloyd Jr. and a covey of young starlets that had arrived by motorcade. Bela didn't stay for the entire event.

MAILA NURMI (VAMPIRA): Bela and Criswell were comfortable acquaintances with many mutual friends.

December 4, 1955:

Trends of 1956

I predict that television cameras will record our first penetration of outer space! I predict that a rocket will leave our proving grounds near Las Vegas, Nevada, not later than March 10, 1956, and will record and bring back to 100,000,000 Americans, the first authentic view of the wide-blue-yonder! This will be the most thrilling event of 1956 and will mark a new era in world history in world travel and in world incidents to come!

In the February 1956 edition of "America's Coolest Teenage Magazine" *DIG*, a Criswell Predicts column appeared with the headline "What You Will Do in the Future!" "You will soon live in an all-plastic world! You will live in a plastic house, drive a plastic car, fly a plastic plane, wear a plastic suit, and spend eternity in a plastic casket!" "Atomic tubes the size of a gumdrop will generate enough power to go beyond the moon!"

The article included sections titled "For Boys Only" and "For Girls Only" and predicted future fashion trends.

For Boys Only: I predict that one year from today you will be wearing the new, horizontal cord-weave suits, jackets, slacks, and topcoats!

164

Your shirt will be of the matador style, made of basket-weave linen and other odd materials! It will have a lacy front with a string tie of metallic silver or gold cloth!

Extra-large cufflinks will be the rage, with monstrous coins, old-fashioned buttons, and steel machine parts!

Your hair comb will be very long, and will be curled over your rolled collar! You will comb the temples straight back and hold it in position with a new pomade spray!

For Girls Only: I predict that one year from today you will be wearing new, silky, sheer materials! You will be completely feminine!

You will try to achieve the tall, gaunt look, be pale and interesting, and at all times move with royal grace!

You will use azure green eye shadow, pastel rouge, and pale lipstick. Your eyes will have the dramatic look of injured innocence!

Your hair will be worn quite short, in a Medusa style, with ringlets on your brow giving you that sweet, feminine, helpless look which will stir the romantic heart of any man to protect you!

VERNON KOENIG: My father went to work for Criswell in 1956. He had offices on Sunset Boulevard, which were little more than a turn of the century Victorian house converted into office space (right next door to a miniature golf course). My father had convinced him to get into the food supplement business with a new product called Criswell Family Formula, which was little more than a nickel-size, malt flavored tablet that was loaded with caffeine and a smidgen of vitamins. At that time, the newly formed FDA was hot on the heels of companies producing these types of products

MAILA NURMI (VAMPIRA): His work as an early vitamins manufacturer and salesman (on TV) was pioneering of the first matter. He

Criswell Family Formula, promotional headshot.

was a beguiling salesman, and a rich one I suspect. He was very charismatic and had an odd and delightful ennui.

Classified ads continued to run in local newspapers recruiting people to follow up on "red-hot Criswell Predicts TV leads." The ads offered $50 weekly or $25 daily for part-time work. One classified titled "Criswell Predicts" called for "Food supplement people. Field Counselors needed. Lots of leads" followed by the days, time, and an address. Another proclaimed "CRISWELL PREDICTS An incredible future for you! "CRISWELL'S FAMILY FORMULA needs men & women able to handle salespeople in all areas. We have salespeople waiting for leadership. Also salespeople needed to call on our customers in all areas to repeat our TV sales. THIS is a FIRST-TIME OFFER! A wonderful career awaits those able to see this opportunity! Training, TV support & leads. Send brief resume. Box 135, Hollywood 28, Cal."

VERNON KOENIG: During one TV broadcast something terrible happened. Criswell was sponsoring his own show with his Family Formula. He had invited a very rotund woman to give a live testimonial about how "wonderful" Family Formula was. The studio light on Criswell dims and the live camera is on Bob Shields. He goes into a simple spiel about FF and introduces the obese woman. She tells how great the product is, blah, blah, blah, the lights dim and Criswell returns to his monologue. At the end of the show, the same thing happens, Bob Shields ends the program and gives the last word about FF. The third camera and lights come on for a picture of the FF display . . . AND THERE IS NOTHING THERE. You could have heard a pin drop in that studio. Fifteen people are trying to figure out what happened and what to do next. As it turns out, the woman was a kleptomaniac (a compulsive thief), and she stole all the FF and beautiful alabaster statues before the program ended. That was the first time I ever knew Criswell to be at a loss for words.

Criswell would try most anything to bring attention to his show. A woman had a parakeet she claimed to have trained to say, "Criswell Predicts." Criswell offered her a cash prize if the bird would do as claimed. It did say the phrase in the office before the show but failed when brought on camera. Criswell awarded the woman the cash anyway.

A young and motivated Regis Philbin began his television career at KCOP as a stagehand. He had remarked that it was a colorful place to work, but also grueling due to most of the programming being live, including commercials. Regis and his fellow stagehands would get a kick out of torturing Criswell by holding his cue cards just a little too far away so he would have to strain to see them. It drove him nuts, but they thought it was a scream.

CLAUDIA POLIFRONIO: He was nearsighted, and the teleprompter wouldn't move. He doesn't ad lib very well, so instead of saying something he starts squinting. So that was a little embarrassing.

Verne Langdon also known as Trader Verne, was a man of many talents and passions. He was a musician, producer, composer, writer, legendary horror make-up and mask designer with Don

Post studios, as well as a professional wrestler. A true modern renaissance man. He had befriended many Hollywood legends including Korla Pandit, another pioneer of early television and known as the "Godfather of Exotica." The turban-crowned Korla had a fifteen-minute program on KTLA-TV Los Angeles on-air Monday through Friday, playing romantic compositions and his "music of the exotic East" on a grand piano and the revolutionary new Hammond B-3 organ. Sometimes he would play them simultaneously while gazing alluringly into the camera. He was told by the show's producer Klaus Landsberg not to speak, just gaze into the camera mysteriously. It was said to have been a gaze so sensually mesmerizing that it captivated both women and men alike. As his popularity increased he joined forces with real estate developer Louis D. Snader and began syndicating his show nationwide along with "telescriptions" of popular artists of the day such as Nat King Cole, Peggy Lee, and himself. These could be considered as some of the first music-videos. In 1954 Korla had a disagreement with Snader over his contract and resigned. Snader replaced Korla with a young piano player who had appeared on his own local program on KLAC in 1952. The young man brought his own candelabrum and was the pianist known as Liberace. Korla continued his musical and television career throughout his life. He appeared in Tim Burton's *Ed Wood* playing the composition "Nautch Dance" during the party scene as Ed Wood played by Johnny Depp does a striptease reveling his missing front teeth. Korla went to the Great Beyond on October 2, 1998, at the age of seventy-seven.

VERNE LANGDON: There was no internet in Mae's time or Criswell's time. What you got of them, you got in the newspaper or over local television. That's what Criswell was on. Well, I think he was on New York, and you could get him in California, kind of thing. But that was brand new, and it was in its infancy. So he was one of the pioneers like Spade Cooley and Lawrence Welk and particularly Korla Pandit before Liberace. Korla Pandit was first and opened the door for Liberace when he ixnayed the deal with Snader and left Snader and Snader brought Liberace in and filmed on the same stage that was created for Korla with the billowing curtains and everything, the grand piano, and the only thing they did was add a candelabra and of course Liberace spoke and Korla didn't. But it was Korla Pandit first and then Liberace. Korla was huge on a very small scale. He was huge in L.A. between 1948 and 1953, but if you check your TV history between 1948 and 1953, nothing that much was happening other than it was being developed and Klaus Landsberg was at the center of that development and Korla was a product of Klaus Landsberg basically.

It was during Criswell's tenure at KCOP that he met and became friends with the almost out of the closet, kind of trying to open the door, Liberace. The pair would appear together at charity benefits along with Liberace's mother. Criswell would make numerous predictions on the flamboyant piano player's success and fame.

Cris, Liberace and his Mother.

VERNON KOENIG: At that time, Criswell did not make the bizarre predictions like those in his later years. He accurately predicted a very large earthquake in Peru and it happened about a week later. I once asked him how he "learned" to make his predictions. He told me that he was a student of history and that all history repeats itself. Each and every time I spoke with him, he was kind enough to give me a very intelligent and lucid answer to all of my questions. In actuality, I found him to be quite an intelligent man. He read the St. Louis Dispatch (mailed to him) from cover to cover every day.

February 5, 1956:

What People Will Do:
I predict that President Eisenhower will shock the world with a statement soon to be made to the American public! This statement will explain how Russia has continued to undermine the bulwarks of Democracy throughout the world, while pretending to be friendly to the United Nations! I predict this dramatic speech will go down in history!

Hush-Hush Events:
I predict that Christine Jorgensen will file for divorce in the Paris courts! Her husband will be revealed as belonging to a famous American diplomatic family!

Your Incredible Future:
I predict that our next Outer Space project will be a miniature sun, which will be sent on a mission of its own, to revolve around the moon! I predict this sun will carry an electronic camera device, which will televise the impressions it mirrors! This man-made sun will open up a new vista, and extend our horizons one thousand years, overnight!

Regret Predictions:
I regret to predict that a very well-kept skeleton, in the closet of Hollywood, will walk the streets in broad daylight! I predict this awakened scandal will reveal suicide, rape and murder, and will prove to be one of the most sensational news stories when the History is written, from 1950 to 1960!

Coming Events:
I predict the ghost of Rudolph Valentino will again be seen in his familiar haunts of Hollywood! I predict that this very much alive ghost, will visit many people who will volunteer their stories for newspaper publication!

Criswell appeared for a one-day-only event at the Wilton Hotel in Long Beach on July 9, with Free Admission, Women Only shows at 10a.m. and 2p.m., a Family Party at 8p.m. with Entertainment, Fashions and Door Prizes.

VERNON KOENIG: One thing about Criswell is that he never did a, "I told you so," program. I can't ever recall him rehashing his predictions or taking credit for the ones that did material-ize. At the beginning of each program, he went into his monologue and delivered a new set of predictions. I cannot ever recall him making totally outlandish predictions, such as an inva-sion from Mars.

1956 saw Criswell begin to have his col-umns printed in the tabloids. The first was the *New York Enquirer*, which would later become the world's favorite tabloid, the *National En-*

quirer. The column called "Jeron King Criswell Predicts" was a full page that included "The Answers to Your Problems" and a "Dear Criswell" feature answering reader's letters and the offering of sage advice. The predictions mostly concerned world politics, a few concerning big business, and some showbiz predictions. At one point the *National Enquirer* changed Criswell's column heading to "Thru CRISWELL'S Eyes YOU See the FUTURE." It remained a full page with a close-cropped photo of his piercing eyes and photos of celebrities featured in the predictions with headlines like "News of the Future NOW," "Headlines of Tomorrow," and "Reds Create 3 Headed Human Monstrosities." He continued to answer reader's letters in "Criswell Predicts FOR YOU." Below a photo of his disembodied head, *The Enquirer* asks "Do you have perplexing problems—about love, marriage, finance, job changes or other personal subjects? Let Criswell advise you. Write to: . . . Give name and address. Only initial or code letters you suggest will be used. Letters will be held in the strictest confidence. They will be answered by Criswell in order of receipt, so please be patient in waiting for your reply."

DEAR CRISWELL: This is the end. Life is too unbearable to go on. When I finish writing this letter to you, I'll make plans to kill myself and will wait only for your answer in this paper, before I change my mind. Please save me. Neil R. M.

My dear Neil: You will be the victor in this terrible situation, so bide your time.

This other party will be found guilty, and I know you will have a clear slate, and will be able to resume your old life, free of this blemish that others inflicted on you.

DEAR CRISWELL: Tell me the truth about life. Will it all end sometime? Will 'F' ever be my own? Will I ever forget about "A"? —Moo Moo on the Table.

My dear Moo Moo on the Table: All life is eternal and you are part of that which is also eternal. The true miracle is that you are alive this moment after all that you have gone through. You have outlasted it, rather than letting it outlast you! No one can be owned by another! You have already forgot about "A" and are on to "B" and greener pastures.

CRISWELL'S SPOT PREDICTIONS: Eileen McC: Another job will soon be yours.

Your subscription to the ENQUIRER will start at once . . . Sidney: You have been too good to these children. Demand respect from them and you will have it . . . Jack: Your letter will be forwarded to "18" . . . Grace: This man is a cad, and it is time you found it out. He should be horsewhipped.

In November 1957 the column asked the bold, headline question "Will 1999 Be the End of Everything?"

"The end of the world will come," shouted the German Shepherd, "when the triangle reaches in the sky!" When we examine the starry heavens and note that the three most famous planets will form a perfect triangle in 1999, we cannot help but be impressed!

"The end of the world will come," wrote Nostradamus, "when the only figure in the 20th century adds to 28, and is that last figure of the 20th century!" That is 1999——1 plus 9 plus 9 plus 9 equals 28!

"The end of the world will come," stated Pythagoras, "when three numerals are completion and one is the beginning."

Nine is the numeral of completion—no single number is higher than nine.

One is the numeral of beginning—no number is less than one.

thru CRISWELL'S eyes YOU see the FUTURE

Will 1999 Be the End of Everything?

CRISWELL PREDICTS for Mike Todd: "You will be voted Hollywood's No. 1 citizen for your outstanding motion pictures plus your knack for getting favorable publicity!"

"The end of the world will come," shouted the German Shepherd, "when the triangle reaches in the sky!" When we examine the starry heavens and note that the three most famous planets will form a perfect triangle in 1999, we cannot help but be impressed.

"The end of the world will come," wrote Nostradamus, "when the only figure in the 20th century adds to 28, and is that last figure of the 20th century!" That is 1999 — 1 plus 9 plus 9 plus 9 equals 28!

"The end of the world will come," stated Pythagoras, "when three numerals are completion and one is the beginning."

Nine is the numeral of completion — no single number is higher than nine.

One is the numeral of beginning — no number is less than one.

So "when three numerals are completion and one is the beginning" could make 1999! This 1999 is only 42 years away — so it is in your lifetime and mine.

HEADLINES OF THE FUTURE: Ireland revolts against Crown's taxes . . . Early snows sweep midwest! . . . France in great turmoil! . . . Japan exports new automobile! . . . Freak tidal waves sweep West Coast! . . . Denver plans new water supply! . . . Chicago faces political scandal! . . . Greece suffers new quakes!

CRISWELL PREDICTS for Sen. Margaret Chase Smith: "You will demand full rights for the Negro teachers in the northern school systems!"

Churchill's Farewell On TV

I PREDICT that Sir Winston Churchill will make a final television farewell speech in which he will point out the many errors made by the Allies in World War II and suggest a solution. Those bold statements coming from a famed political tycoon like Churchill will amaze and astound the world!

I PREDICT that T. C. Jones, the mimic, will soon star in a dress in which he will play all 18 roles himself, both the male and female parts! . . . for roominess and for comfort!

'Fair Lady' Role for ← Libby!

Vice President Nixon will preside over a top level diplomatic meet in Paris before 1957 comes history, in which the fate of Gibraltar will be decided! . . . Liberace will be offered the Rex Harrison role in the American company of "My Fair Lady" . . . The best selling item for Christmas will be a glass-enclosed "City of Arts," all alive, and performing every moment for the amusement of we humans!

I PREDICT that Russia will be successful in forcing many nations to accept the barter system of trade. The opening wedge was gained through England's trading with Red China, and now we will all be reduced to the barter system (trading merchandise for merchandise) within a three-year period.

Black Eye For Motels

I PREDICT that motels will prove to be a poor investment next year due to mounting bad publicity and the increasing arrests on narcotics, prostitution and morals charges that are taking place daily in these roadside dens of vice!

The police of many areas have been alerted that the narcotics squads will soon move in! The protection of hotels in towns rather than motels. The motel association must act at once to head off this growing public boycott!

Realty Boom Due

I PREDICT the greatest boom in real estate the world has ever known, for the coming decentralization of cities will create new land values overnight! Remember this prediction!

~~~CRISWELL PREDICTS~~~

FOR YOU

Do you have perplexing problems—about love, marriage, finance, job changes or other personal subjects? Let Criswell advise you. Write to CRISWELL, The ENQUIRER, 1151 Third Ave., New York 21, N. Y. Give name and address. Only replies on code letters only crossed will be used. Letters will be held in the strictest confidence. There will be answered by Criswell in order of receipt, so please be patient in waiting for your reply.

Dear Criswell: I've been taking care of an invalid mother who has controlled my entire life. In fact, my husband left me because he could not stand her. Now he is happily married and I'm still living in a hell. If I leave, she'll say I left her when she was old and sick. I don't want her to feel that way. However, if she doesn't go soon, I'm afraid I'll have a nervous collapse. What do you advise me to do? — RW-77.

My dear RW-77: I cannot say who is the best martyr, you or your mother. The only trouble with a martyr is that they always end up being burned at their own stake. Your mother's power over you is her apparent helplessness. You are both misguided. Get away from her for a month, and it will give you time to think things over. You should both be spanked.

Dear Criswell: Will I ever have any luck if I file for unemployment checks? Also, what does it mean when people say I was lucky to be born in a well? I was born in one. — Mrs. Brooklyn.

My dear Mrs. Brooklyn: When you have money coming for unemployment, you will get it. The old Arab superstition is that when one is born with a veil (or membrane) over the face, you are gifted with a second sight, and you are also a healer. You are quite intuitive, you must admit.

Dear Criswell: Tell me the truth about life. Will it all end sometime? Will 'I' ever be my own? Will I ever forget about 'A'? — Moo Moo on the Table.

My dear Moo Moo on the Table: All life is eternal and you are a part of that which is also eternal. The true miracle is that you are alive this moment after all that you have gone through. You have reincarnated it,

rather than letting it outlast you! No one can be owned by another! You have already forgot about "A" and are on to "B" and greener pastures.

Dear Criswell: I was in love with a man but through a tragic error we both married the wrong persons and both of us have been very unhappy with our lot. Now, I would like to see this man again and I understand he is now leaving for Florida shortly. Do you think we will ever see each other again or whether there is a possibility that we can get together again as we once were? — 1957 WP.

My dear 1957-WP: Let sleeping dogs lie. When you see this man you will find that your past dreams of romance have been shattered. There are other days and other ways.

Dear Criswell: I miss my fat and affectionate ex-wife. When we were married I didn't like her getting so big, and it annoyed me to have her kiss me, and to strangled by her huge arms. But now, at night, I get cold, and have no one to talk to or yell at. Will she beg to come back? — Mark Rt. 3.

My dear Mark Rt. 3: Your wife has no reason to come back to you, after the way she was treated. If you wish a reconciliation, then I advise you to take the first step, and apologize for your abuse and mistreatment, along with a promise that you will be a changed man.

CRISWELL'S SPOT PREDICTIONS: Eileen McC: Another job will soon be yours. Your subscription to The ENQUIRER will start at once . . . **Sidney:** You have been too good to those children. Demand respect from them and you will have it . . . **Jack:** Your letter

will be forwarded to "19" . . . **Tom and J. C.:** The leopard will never change his spots. You will have the last laugh, so make the best of the present situation . . . **C-11:** Your husband needs you more than you need him. The time will come when he will depend on you. You can always name your price.

Elma RD-1: Greeting cards are sold by personal contact. Buy direct, and not from the middleman, for he takes a profit that you cannot afford to lose. We should all have the good health that you have . . . **Jean:** See the August issue of the American Medical Assn. Journal at your public library . . . **A Bothered Bodybuilder:** Why not join the health camps that cater to both men and women? You will find some girl whose ideas coincide exactly with yours . . . **Mrs. Ms:** Let this friendship grow and let it mature. The high rate of divorce among those who married their "first loves" is somewhat alarming in this country, but very low in England . . . **Margie:** You can always have both career and marriage when you balance them properly.

Grace: This man is a cad, and it is time you found it out. He should be horsewhipped . . . IMO: Write to the registrar of voters and the motor vehicle bureau in your state capitol . . . **FM-rt:** His visit can be cut to an overnight one if you so desire . . . **RTJR:** Take a scouting trip to California to determine the employment situation. You will sell the house to a private party when you handle the sale yourself . . . **COD:** Either you must earn more income or spend less. You must find out where you are over-spending, and budget this, making the struggle less and the pleasure more.

NATIONAL ENQUIRER, November 3, 1957

So, "when three numerals are completion and one is the beginning" could make 1999! This 1999 is only 42 years away—so it is in your lifetime and mine.

Another headline claimed a "Fair Lady' Role for Libby" accompanied by a picture of his friend Liberace and the prediction that "Libby" would be offered the Rex Harrison role in the American company production. Sometime in 1958, the column became a half-page and dropped the advice column. The predictions started to be more outrageous, and more celebrity focused with headlines such as, "Scientists Turn 7 Men into Wild Beasts!" "People and Places," "Famed Actress Faces a Mental Hospital," "Leprosy Claims More Victims," "Canada to Become 57th State," "Death Will Knock on 5 Famous Doors," and "Beatniks to Rebel Against All Law." The column ran in the Enquirer until sometime in 1961.

An October 1955, piece headlined "TV Personnel Parade Gives Chest a Boost," tells of the 1955 Community Chest campaign receiving a boost with a parade down Hollywood Boulevard from Vine Street to Highland Avenue. It was staged by television-show figures urging the public to give. It was led by Honorary Mayor of Hollywood, Ben Hunter with Miss Red Feather, and Jolene Brand of Ciro's restaurant. In the parade of celebrities with Criswell were Dick Lane, Rush Adams, Chuck-O the Clown, George Putnam of KTTV, Betty White, as well as "many pretty girls from Hollywood night spots."

A 1956, Los Angeles city directory listed Dr. Jeron King Criswell and Halo Meadows residing at 1559 Cassil Place. This is the location of a fourplex apartment building purchased by Halo, most likely with her father financing the purchase, and where the couple would reside for the next two decades.

VERNE LANGDON: He had that remarkable little piece of property on Selma near McCadden and Crossroads of the World and Sunset Boulevard and a great big Catholic church. As I recall it was just on the other side of Crossroads of the World, maybe down a block. It was between Wilcox and Crossroads of the World and bordered by Selma and Sunset. It was TV buildings one and two, the awnings stated. They were gray buildings, slate gray, with white trim and smart black awnings with white magnificent, printed lettering, Criswell TV Building One and Criswell TV Building Two. They were right next to each other.

CLAUDIA POLIFRONIO: I met him; he was lecturing on health. I was interested in health, vitamins, metaphysics. I looked in the paper and it said "Free Lecture: Criswell" I looked at his picture and thought it was unusual looking. After the lecture, I went up to him and we sort of clicked. He gave me his number. He had just purchased a fourplex on Selma. He had been lecturing and selling vitamins and a chair he called a "Pamper Lounge." He had a sample in his house. A relaxation lounge. He had a vacancy there and he said, "Why don't you move in here?" and so I did with my brother and mother. We had a great liking for each other. Just chemistry or whatever you want to call it. At first he was passing himself of to us as half-Italian.

Storehouse of Memory

Yes, my friend, sooner or later, you and I will join the gallery of ghosts we have known! Short, fat, young and old ghosts will give us the hand of welcome on that gleaming golden shore! These ghosts will be exactly as we remember them! On that golden gleaming shore there will always be the other items or their unreasonable duplicates of secret attics, babbling brooks, sunsets we can't forget or quiet moments of personal tragedy! From the feeling of frustration of failure to the elation of success! Yes, my friend, it is all there and, when you and I join this gallery of living ghosts, we will see it all again!

Criswell

VERNON KOENIG: Criswell seemed to circulate among the fallen angels of Hollywood, such as Mae West, Vampira, Ed Wood. He never seemed to really click with the public. I once took notice at the Brown Derby where Criswell was instantly recognized by the old ladies dining there—and rarely anyone else. He always wore his TV pancake make-up to the after program dinners so that everyone there would know he just arrived from the TV studio.

CLAUDIA POLIFRONIO: He introduced me to Ed Wood, Jack London [the TV producer], Brad Jason, good-looking actor wanting to break into Hollywood, Bill Roberts the brother of Arlene Roberts [actress]. I met George Liberace, Jack West [Mae West's brother]. Mae West would come; she would stay in the car. Because he lived upstairs, she didn't want to climb. She would stay in the car, and I would see him go out to the car and she would give him something, whatever it was. She would call him almost every day.

On August 16, 1956, Bela Lugosi passed away at home at the age of 73. He was laid to rest on August 18 in his full *Dracula* regalia as per his request, at the Holy Cross Cemetery in Culver City, CA. The service was an exotic and publicity-filled event with gypsy violin music, much sobbing and crying, and flash bulbs popping. Prayers were said by a priest from the Blessed Sacrament Church and a fellow Hungarian played a violin dirge. 127 attendees signed the guest book. Paul Marco attended the funeral along with Tor Johnson, who sobbed like a baby and wrote "Lobo" next to his signature in the guest book, as well as Conrad Brooks, George Weiss, Eddie's wife Kathy, and few other Ed Wood regulars. Eddie served as a pallbearer. Criswell's signature is not in the guestbook. He may not have attended due to it being on his birthday and he would usually travel back east to spend time with family around his birthdate.

Ed Wood, Jr., *Hollywood Rat Race*

Bela Lugosi is probably one of the best examples of the character actor who made good his career, as well as making a great deal of money in the process. To the day he died he was always in demand and I know this firsthand. My script, *Final Curtain*, which we were about to film, was found beside his bed when he died. It was opened to page six.

Some accounts have "The Count" sitting in a chair with the script in his hand or lying on his lap, which is not true. Bela's wife at the time, Hope, who discovered his body, said that he was just lying on the bed in his boxer shorts.

On September 2, Criswell was billed as the "popular television star and internationally known columnist" appeared at the Bavaria Hall between 4:30 and 5:00 pm broadcasting "Criswell Predicts Future Events."

Halo appeared on *You Bet Your Life*, the Groucho Marx TV quiz show on December 27, 1956. During the interview portion of the segment Groucho asks Halo why her parents picked such an offbeat name for her. She replies that they didn't pick it. That she had an ordinary name, so she chose it. He also asks her if she had a professional career in mind when she chose her name. She says she was writing, and he asks about her plays. Halo replies, "Well, but not so much. I'm more interested in songs. Writing songs." Groucho inquires what songs and she names "Victorian Waltz" and "I Was Just Around the Corner." Groucho asks her sarcastically if she could sing just around the corner. She replies, "No. But what I'm most interested in is a series that I call a gloom series and a super love. But I'll do one from the gloom." Groucho asks, "Could you sing after you're gone?" Which gets big laughs from the studio audience. During the laughter, Halo says, "Chop My Head Off," the song's title three times then begins "singing" her "song" in choppy and staccato cadence. Groucho stops her after the first line then says, "Oh alright. Sing a little of it. I'd rather you sing around the corner." Halo then begins the song again:

Chop my head off
Kick it around
Hang it up
Lay it down
Look at it dear
Really take a good look
It's me, it's me, it's me
Oh, chop my head off
Make a nice clean chop

179

Chop my head off dear
Chop it off

She finishes to the audience's laughter and Groucho saying in his trademark sarcastic tone, "That's nice. I like it." The audience continues to laugh and begins applauding. Groucho then inquires, "Uh. What kind of music do you use for that? Do you have somebody play on a guillotine?" During the quiz portion of the segment, Halo and her contestant partner answered enough questions correctly and won the one thousand dollar prize. An article in the *Gettysburg Times* reported that the former Littlestown resident was on the show and recited one of her "crazy songs." The article tells of her educational and show business history, and that she lives in Hollywood and married to a "west coast radio commentator" Gerald (sic) Criswell. Her father was part of the TV audience when the show had been filmed several weeks before its airing. A video of the entire hilarious segment is available for viewing online.

December 31, 1956:

Coming Events In Your Future

I predict that automation will help to select you, for any Government job, by cataloging your talents. These monster electric brains will do more to decide the future of the world on a correct basis, eliminating all guessing, where it comes to statistics! . . . I predict that vivisection will be outlawed in many states, due to the strong drive against the needless torture of animals, for so-called medical research! Criswell Answers Your Questions

Q—Love and hate are so close. Sometimes I find my heart filled with love, and in just seconds, hate takes its place. What does this mean? Mrs. Monica 421

A—Perhaps Plutarch has the answer to your question, which is truly a universal one: "Hatred is blind as well as love."

Q—I'm sending you my photo. Am I ugly? People always look at my pictures, and simply say that the photographer has an interesting technique, or the background is very becoming. Forlorn X.

A—Thank you for letting me see your picture, which I am returning to you. You are a very attractive woman, not in an extremely beautiful sense, but not only does your photo show physical charm, but it also portrays a warmth of character, and inner beauty which is far more important.

Criswell participated in the "Parade of Stars" to help benefit the Santa Toy Clinic that collected, repaired, and distributed toys to needy youngsters at Christmas. Criswell would also become a regular at the "Santa Claus Lane Parade" held annually the weekend after Thanksgiving in Hollywood. He would ride in an open convertible waving to the crowds lining Hollywood and Sunset Boulevards.

VERNON KOENIG: I went to a Christmas party at his Hollywood offices. I was twelve-years-old and was wearing a powder blue suit with tie. There were several old ladies there and my mother wanted me to be the perfect little gentleman and ask them to dance to tunes played on an old seventy-eight [rpm] phonograph. I first danced with Mrs. Criswell. As soon as the next song played, I asked another old lady for a dance it was Mae West. She was one of the nicest ladies you could ever meet. When not in character, she was almost unrecognizable. At that party, Criswell announced two things: First, that he had just purchased a "new" apartment building in Hollywood, the Criswell Arms (on La Cienega) and that he would be appearing in a new "scientific" movie that would explain the UFO phenomenon. Little did I realize then, that he was referring to *Plan 9 From Outer Space.*

Plan 9 began shooting under the working title of *Grave Robbers from Outer Space* in late November at Merle Connell's Quality Studios on Santa Monica Boulevard in Hollywood. It was to be Criswell's first movie appearance, Bela's last, and the film that would eventually make Ed Wood a legend. Bela's appearance in the film is from footage that Eddie shot in the spring of 1955.

A SPECIAL NOTE FROM EDWARD D. WOOD, JR. Writer-Producer-Director of *Plan 9 From Outer Space,* (from soundtrack album jacket notes):

When I look back on those hectic early days, I kind of wish that dear old Bela Lugosi could have known that he was making a science-fiction classic in 1956. In point of fact, Bela thought he was shooting a horror film, titled 'Tomb of the Vampire.' But after two days of location work, my good friend dropped dead without a warning and without giving two weeks' notice. Since Bela had the lead role in the film, I couldn't see any way to spread his five minutes of footage through a 90-minute movie, so the entire project was scrapped.

Another friend told me that I was crazy to throw away five minutes of Bela Lugosi footage, and he offered me the chance to shoot an entirely new film around the Lugosi scenes if I could bring it in under $800.00. I told him it would be no problem (don't forget, $800.00 went a long way in those days), and six hours later I handed him the shooting script for 'Plan 9 From Outer Space.' He was delighted and the deal was made.

Eddie's wife Kathy used a chiropractor and hypnotist named Dr. Tom Mason who doubled for Bela in the film by covering his face

Maila Nurmi, Tor Johnson, chiropractor Tom Mason, and Criswell, *Grave Robbers From Outer Space*

with a cape. Dr. Mason was much taller than Bela, but Eddie said his skull structure and ears were similar to Bela's. Also appearing in the film were Tor Johnson, Vampira, Gregory Walcott, Dudley Manlove, Duke Moore, Paul Marco (again as Kelton the Cop), John "Bunny" Breckinridge (introduced to Wood by Marco), Lyle Talbot, Conrad Brooks, and other Ed Wood regulars in the cast and on the crew.

A SPECIAL NOTE FROM EDWARD D. WOOD, JR. Writer-Producer-Director of *Plan 9 From Outer Space*, (from soundtrack album jacket notes):

> Before you could say "Roger Corman," sets were built in my garage, clothes were borrowed from my closet (I personally supplied all the sweaters worn by Mona McKinnon in the film), and stock footage was purchased from Trident Films, Inc. Finally, friends who would work for nothing, and actors who would accept a cut in salary for a good role were hired. By cutting corners and doing 250 camera set-ups a day, we were able to finish the picture on time and under budget. (In

fact, we had enough money left over to take the principal cast members to lunch at the Brown Derby.)

CLAUDIA POLIFRONIO: Right in front of me, Ed Wood took one of those silver pie dishes. Someone asked what are we going to do about the flying saucers and Ed Wood just flipped it like this [frisbee throwing gesture] and it was actually in the movie. A couple of times I think I did go to the set.

The film opens with Criswell in shadowed silhouette sitting at a desk with the title CRISWELL PREDICTS superimposed on the screen. The camera starts a slow zoom-in then stops as lights come on revealing Criswell. In his well measured and cadenced voice he dramatically intones:

> Greetings, my friend. We are all interested in the future, for that is where you and I are going to spend the rest of our lives. And remember my friend, future events such as these will affect you in the future. You are interested in the unknown, the mysterious, the unexplainable. That is why you are here. And now, for the first time, we are bringing to you the full story of what happened on that fateful day. We are giving you all the evidence, based only on the secret testimonies of the miserable souls who survived this terrifying ordeal. The incidents, the places, my friend we cannot keep this a secret any longer. Let us punish the guilty, let us reward the innocent. My friend, can your heart stand the shocking facts about grave robbers from outer space!?

This opening is how Criswell is mainly remembered due to the film's many late night television airings and it's notoriety of being called "the worst film of all time."

It is no *Citizen Kane* (1941), but there are many other films that do not have any of the imagination, independent spirit, or social commentary of the "winner of the Golden Turkey Award." Ed Wood saw it as his *The Day the Earth Stood Still* (1951), and it does have the same message of that science fiction epic. Basically, that we need to take care of the Earth or someone, or something else may take care of it for us. Criswell narrates throughout the film with voiceover that at times segues scenes or fills in missing dialogue and other times is redundant to the on-screen action and dialogue. At the end of the film he appears on-screen again seated behind the desk for a final comment:

My friend, you have seen this incident based on sworn testimony. Can you prove that it didn't happen? Perhaps on your way home, you will pass someone in the dark, and you will never know it, for they will be from outer space. Many scientists believe that another world is watching us this moment. We once laughed at the horseless carriage, the aeroplane, the telephone, the electric light, vitamins, radio, and even television!

And now some of us laugh at outer space. (He rises slowly to standing behind the desk) God help us . . . in the future.

At some point during the filming of *Graverobbers*, legend alleges that Wood directed and produced a recording session

Criswell, *Graverobbers From Outer Space aka Plan 9 From Outer Space.*

of Criswell performing his spoken-word composition "Someone Walked Over My Grave" accompanied by piano possibly played by Halo. The piece was to appear in the film but did not make the cut for some unknown reason. The song was released in 1995 on a seven inch 45 rpm record with Paul Marco as Kelton the Cop on the flipside doing his own song "Home on the Strange." Legend also says that Criswell didn't want the song released until after his death.

"Someone Walked Over My Grave"
by Criswell

Someone walked over my grave disturbing my sleep,
a sleep I thought would last to eternity.
Someone walked over my grave awakening me,
awakening me and bringing me back to reality.
I walk now in a place that is filled with misery,
caused by men in search of their simple destiny.
Friends I've known and family I've loved will have to answer to me,
for they let someone walk over my grave awakening me!

Grave Robbers from Outer Space previewed at the Carlton Theater, Los Angeles on March 15, 1957. Criswell emceed the event and talked about what a great film it was. Just about everyone that was involved with the film got up and said a few words. Dr. Mason thanked "the late, great Bela Lugosi" for giving him his chance to debut in the film. Ed Wood was the last to speak and said, "I'd like to dedicate this film to my great friend Bela Lugosi."

A SPECIAL NOTE FROM EDWARD D. WOOD, JR. Writer-Producer-Director of *Plan 9 From Outer Space*, (from soundtrack jacket notes):

After some minor financial squabbles with the processing lab and several distributor back-outs, we finally premiered "Plan

9 From Outer Space" at the luxurious Brookdale Theater in El Monte. Some of the cast members were there, Tor Johnson and Criswell and Vampira, and we even rented a spotlight. (The damn thing never did work and I refused to pay for it. I also refused to pay for the theater's toilet seat that Tor Johnson broke.) The party after the film was great fun, too. I can still remember the day one of our associate producers came up with the idea of digging up Bela Lugosi's body and propping him up in his coffin in the theater lobby. It would have been a great publicity stunt, but the more I thought about it, the more tasteless the idea became. We ended up putting my plastic octopus from 'Bride of the Monster' in the lobby.

The initial reaction to the film was predictably mixed . . . the fans loved it, and the critics killed it. Some of the reviewers actually made fun of our cheap cardboard sets. I mean, what did they expect for $786.27 . . . the Paramount backlot?

VERNON KOENIG: I think Criswell had ambition. That statement I equate to his friendship with Ed Wood. Despite Criswell's strong persona, I think he could be easily manipulated. Wood was most certainly a manipulator. I also think Criswell believed that making appearances in motion pictures would enhance his career.

Criswell Predicts was cancelled by KCOP-TV in mid-1957.

Wood, Marco, and Criswell continued their collaborative efforts with a script by William Harlow and Kirk Kirkham titled *The Dead Never Die*, based on an original story by Marco and Criswell to be directed by Wood. Like many other Wood & Associates endeavors, this film would never see production

May 14, 1957:

Criswell Predicts About People And Places: Paul Marco: Your portrayal of a ruthless Hollywood producer in 'The Living Dead of Hollywood' will make you a number one character star!"

August 21, *LA Times*:

Hollywood's youngest producer, Paul Marco, accompanied Television Personality Criswell on his lecture tour of Northern California.

Paul would act as Associate Producer as well as reprising his character of Kelton the Cop in Criswell's second appearance in a Wood production which began filming under the working title of *Revenge of the Dead* in late April 1958. Filming was complete by the end of May.

REVENGE OF THE DEAD

Dear Criswell: I know all of the bad luck my husband has been having is merely the revenge of the dead! He treated his own family so mean, and drove his own brother to suicide. They found his body badly beaten with not a clue as to who did it, in front of the place he stole from his sister, who later died in a mental institution. I say, as everyone else says around her, it was simply the revenge of the dead.
        Mrs. VLS, Nashville, Tenn.
        My dear Mrs. VLS: Many unsolved crimes are sometimes blamed upon the revenge of the dead!

PAUL MARCO: Sometimes we would run out of money and have to suspend the picture until Ed could raise more cash. We made *Night*

Criswell with Tor
Johnson as Lobo in
Revenge of the Dead.

of the Ghouls in seven
days and the sched-
ules for the others
would run until the
budget ran out.

Verne Langdon was
friends with Swed-
ish wrestler turned horror movie star Tor Johnson and designed
a mask of the "Swedish Angel" that is one of the most popular Halloween masks of all time.

VERNE LANGDON: Tor Johnson wouldn't shut-up about him. Tor
just thought Ed was the greatest thing in the world because Ed used
Tor in a couple of movies. Tor thought they were good movies and
thought he did well. Tor idolized him. (imitating Tor) "Verne do you
know Eddie Wood?" "No I don't Tor." "You got to meet Eddie. You
would love him. He's a sweetheart." I never did meet Eddie.

Revenge of the Dead also starred Kenne Duncan, Duke Moore,
Valda Hansen, and John Carpenter. The film is paradoxically about
a phony medium named Dr. Acula played by Kenne Duncan who
swindles widows and widowers by conducting séances and allegedly contacting their deceased spouses. The police investigate
the strange happenings at the house by the old cemetery led by
Lt. Bradford played by Duke Moore and assisted by Kelton. Wood
wrote the script as a starring vehicle for Marco as Kelton. *Revenge
of the Dead* is a pseudo-sequel to *Bride of the Monster* and is the

last film in what is now called "The Kelton Trilogy." Criswell opens the film by sitting up in a coffin wearing his sequined lapel tuxedo.

> I am Criswell. For many years I have told the almost unbelievable, related the unreal, and showed it to be more than fact . . . Now I tell you a tale of the threshold people, so astounding that some of you may faint. This is a story of those in the twilight time . . . once human, now monsters . . . in a world between the living and the dead. Monsters to be pitied . . . Monsters to be despised!"

Some of the footage in the film was shot previously for other Wood projects that never saw completion. One scene early in the film is a fight scene between Conrad Brooks and Ed Wood for a movie on juvenile delinquency that was to be titled *Hellborn*. Criswell narrates the scene.

Paul Marco, Valda Hansen, Criswell, and Kenne Duncan *Revenge of the Dead*.

At times it seems juvenile delinquency is a major problem of our law enforcement officers. But, is this the major horror of our time?

Is this violence and terror the small few perpetrate the most horrible, terrifying of all crimes our civil servants must investigate?

The National Safety Council keeps accurate records on highway fatalities. They can even predict how many deaths will come on a drunken holiday weekend.

But what records are kept, what information is there, how many of you know the horror, the terror, I will now reveal to you?

There is also footage from another unfinished Wood television pilot project titled *Final Curtain* shot in 1957, about the star of a vampire stageplay that wanders an empty theater after the last performance of the horror play. Bela Lugosi was to play the lead. This is one of the scripts that were allegedly within The Count's grasp when his wife came home and found him dead. Duke Moore was later given the role. Dudley Manlove narrated the film much in the same way as would Criswell.

Jason Insalaco became interested in the films of Ed Wood after being introduced to them by his great-uncle Paul Marco. Paul mentioned *Final Curtain* to Jason numerous times. After Marco's death in 2006, Jason found a letter on Paul's nightstand detailing Wood's plans for the pilot. It was to be part one of a television series called *Portraits of Terror*. Wood also wrote in the letter that a print of the film had been struck. Owing to the importance of the project to Paul, Jason set out to find the lost print seeing the search as completing "unfinished family business." His five-year search took him to B-movie conventions and film collectors' homes. He eventually received a tip that took him to a collector in the San Fernando Valley. There he found several film cans reeking of vinegar and labeled

"Final Curtain Ed Wood." He purchased the cans for several thousand dollars and began a year long process of having the film restored. The twenty-two minute film saw its first public screening at the Slamdance Film Festival on January 23, 2012. It was well received by the audience that broke into laughter and applause as expected for an Ed Wood film.

Criswell narrates throughout *Revenge of the Dead* much in the same way as *Plan 9* but has a larger role towards the end of the film as the leader of the dead who come to exact revenge on Dr. Acula for his exploitation of them.

> Good evening Dr. Acula. We have been expecting you. You ask who we are, yet it was you who called for our return. Your powers were even stronger than you yourself realized. You have brought us back from the grave. Once every thirteen years when called by a strong medium such as you, we are given a brief twelve hours of freedom from our deep pit of darkness. Those few hours are almost gone. We must return to the grave. You will accompany us there.

The dead surround Dr. Acula causing him to faint, then carry him to the open casket and place him inside. Dr. Tom Mason, Bela's body double, was also an Associate Producer and one of the dead men, which also included Minister David De Merring and Karl Johnson (Tor's son). As Criswell slowly closes the coffin lid, Dr. Acula regains consciousness and screams. Criswell commands, "Take him to the crypt," and the dead carry the coffin out of the room. After the case is wound up by the police, Criswell gives his final words from his coffin then reclines back with his arms folded across his chest. "And now, we return to our graves. The old and the new, and YOU, [pointing at the camera], may join us soon."

Valda Hansen, Kenne Duncan, and Criswell
Revenge of the Dead aka Night of the Ghouls.

The film previewed at the Vista theater as *Revenge of the Dead.* Wood could not afford to pay the lab fees for the film, and it was not released during his or Criswell's lifetime.

CLAUDIA POLIFRONIO: Ed Wood was a very poor person, probably staving, and he would call Criswell constantly, probably wanting his help. So Criswell did that scene with the casket as a way of helping him. And then we all went to the premiere. That movie was so bad. I don't remember where, somewhere in Hollywood. There were a few people there, not anything outstanding.

Criswell came downstairs and said, "Get your white fox fur," which I had, "and dress up, were going to this showing." And everyone thought I was the lead in this picture. They were all coming up to me. That was kind of fun. And I said, "This is terrible." The real

leading lady was standing right over there. I said, "I feel so bad."
Criswell said, "Oh, enjoy it! Fame is very precious."
April 20, 1958:

WHAT PEOPLE WILL DO

I predict that Edward D. Wood, Jr., will start a new trend of 'classic terror' films out of Hollywood utilizing the best combined movie and TV techniques plus a new type of horror makeup. You will be able to buy frightening images of James Moore, Valda Hanson, Paul Marco, Harvey Dunn, Mona McKinnon and Jennie Stevens dressed as they were in the film. This new merchandising method will revolutionize the Hollywood scene overnight.

ANTHONY CARDOZA: I was in a scene with Criswell (*Revenge Of The Dead* aka *Night Of The Ghouls*) in which I was associate producer for Ed Wood. I met him at Wood's parties. All I know is that he was allegedly gay and had a TV show for predicting things to come. Although Ed Wood was a cross dresser, he was not gay as people think he was.

Criswell (they called him Chris) too, was a nice person and he never did come on to me. I respected that. He had a coffin in his Hollywood home (a two family house) and supposedly would sleep in it. Of course I could not prove that. Wood tried to get him to invest in his movies, but he declined. I was one of Ed's biggest investors, that's how I started in the film business. That's all I know about Criswell.

Criswell returned to local Los Angeles television with the *Criswell Predicts* program on KHJ-TV Channel 9 in late 1958, and was on the air until late 1960. The program was at 5:30 for fifteen minutes, Monday through Friday evenings before the local newscast, competing with the other stations children's shows like *Bozo the Clown*, *Popeye*, *Robin Hood*, *Mickey Mouse*, and *Science Fiction Theater*. Sunday evenings saw the "Amazing! Sensational! Criswell Predicts!" running in the 8 to 8:30 p.m. slot with topics like "Your Amazing Future" and "Modern Day Profit!" sponsored by B-Bar-H Ranch, RX 90 Protein, and Wardman Heights. The show was mentioned in the September 29, 1959, issue of *Look* magazine in an article about California's "offbeat" local television.

After the young Claudia Polifronio and her family moved into the Criswell apartments, she became the show's art director.

CLAUDIA POLIFRONIO: And that whole show was mostly my show. Jack London was the producer of that show. The first producer was Jack Capitack. I kind of gave the show some kind of form. Otherwise Criswell would have just. . . . you know live TV, you could do anything. I said, "This prediction is way too out." He would write them up and type them up. Many times I'd change some, give him ideas. His wife was clever. She would give a lot of [garbled].

He'd say, "Ah, they love it!"

Oh, he might say that the Queen of England is going to be decapitated, something like that. Something bizarre. I said, "Really, let's leave this one out." He'd say, "Oh, do whatever you want."

[Q. How did he talk about his predictions? Did he believe them?]

Some of them he believed. In some of course. When you have a show like that all the time . . . I would often say, "Oh you don't want to have the same prediction again this week." He would say, "Oh, just take anything. They'll lap it up." But other times he was serious. He was a great historian. Maybe he majored in history. History was his field. And politics. He was very political. He was a conservative republican. How I fit into that crowd I don't know. But I think it was a destined thing.

Somehow we clicked and he wanted to share the spotlight with me. He kept telling me, "I'm gonna make you a star." But I was very shy. Whenever he would appear in public he would always have me there, but many times I wouldn't go. I was very shy.

Might have been '57 or '58. I was doing art, painting. Yeah, I was getting in galleries. Once I got my paintings in a restaurant. All over the restaurant. He was so excited about that, more than even I was. And she [Halo] was also excited. She said this is fantastic. They were very positive, very interested in me making progress. That part of them was wonderful, because you don't find too many people with that interest. Especially in Hollywood.

Sometimes he would say to me, "Hey, you want to make a prediction?" And he would make predictions about me in his column. "The greatest artist. . . . the young artist is going to be a great artist." He was pushing me, at first he really wanted me to be on his TV show. He'd say, "You're going to stand next to me." I didn't do it. I stayed behind the scenes.

People would tell me, "God, those people like you." They liked John [her brother] too. John did a lot of typing for Criswell for his syndicated column. Criswell was getting tired of the column. He wanted a fast typist.

His wife would tell me very often, "You don't realize that people kill for this kind of fame." So they thought that I was not as enthused as I should have been, in retrospect.

I did this portrait because I thought that he was so handsome. And I like the story of Dorian Gray and being into psychic stuff, it was one of the stories I liked. And then I found out he liked it and Oscar Wilde was his favorite author. He was always quoting him. And I said I'm going to do this portrait, and I asked him for some photos because I knew he wouldn't pose. He was too fidgety. So I asked him for the photos and so I did the portrait in secret. I think I gave it to him for his birthday. We unveiled it and he was shocked.

He went berserk. He said, "Oh my god, this is incredible!" He called Mae West, Liberace, his friends. "Oh, you should see what I have here!" And he was so excited over this portrait. He said, "I'm going to put it on TV! It's going on the show!" But the station didn't want to carry this big thing to the station. So we took a picture of it, you saw it, and used that instead. The head kind of going all around. And then he would come out and kind of stand in the background with kind of a familiar background. It was a very exciting time. For at least three, four years I had a lot of fun with Criswell.

In the beginning it was very exciting. The TV stuff, the Christmas parade, all of that stuff.

At some point, in a fit of rage at him, Halo stabbed the portrait of Criswell as Dorian Gray leaving a gash in the canvas.

Jack Paar started his career as a radio announcer and game show host and has become known as "the original talk show host." His 105-minute nightly talk show called *The Tonight Show*, eventually renamed *The Jack Paar Show* in 1959, was on NBC from 1957 to 1962 and set the par for all late night talk shows that followed. He then left the late night format being replaced shortly thereafter by Johnny Carson. He then hosted a primetime weekly Friday night show called *The Jack Paar Program* until 1965. Criswell made his debut appearance on the Jack Paar show on March 5, 1959. Mr. Paar begins his introduction of Criswell by talking about the unconventional groups and beliefs of southern California.

"California is a wonderful state, southern California is a beautiful part of our country. It is also a lotus land and a strange mecca for weird and eccentric and strange food faddists and religionists and cults and things. One time I was working out there and had a memo blow off my desk of an office building and fell into a park and four hours later a new religion was formed around this." The studio audience laughs. "Criswell is a gentleman who has made a living by making predictions and he has a large following and cult on the west coast. He's syndicated in hundreds of newspapers and people follow his word and listen to him on television. I've always had a lot of fun listening to him. He takes himself very seriously but he's an awfully nice fella. And anyhow. What am I gonna do. He's a hit. Criswell predicts! And let's not start foolin' around here."

Jack and the audience begin applauding as the band launches into Criswell's intro music "Pomp and Circumstance." Criswell walks on stage waving like a dignitary to the audience in his sequined tuxedo and white bow tie. He approaches the dais and shakes hands with Jack and bows and waves to the audience again. As they sit, Jack comments about how Genevieve, a French singer that appeared on the show, thought Criswell's last name was "Predicts." Criswell says that she is a wonderful person. Jack says she thought his name was Mr. Predicts. Criswell pulls a small stack of 3x5 cards from the inside pocket of his jacket that he reads his predictions from throughout the segment. He then immediately launches into his signature line, "You know we are all interested in the future...." The audience chuckles and Jack says, "How 'bout that." They laugh loudly. "You're controversial right off the bat." More laughs. Criswell immediately says, "And my first prediction...." Jack interrupts and says, "You're a tapioca Beatle I think." while he reaches over and grabs Criswell's arm. More laughs. Smiling, Criswell again attempts to launch into his predictions. "Ah, but my first prediction tonight concerns...." Jack again interrupts, "How accurate are you incidentally?" "Eighty-seven percent." Criswell replies matter of factly. Paar asks, "Thirteen percent of the time?" More laughs. Criswell replies, "Thank you." More laughs from the audience.

"I predict beetles in Birmingham." Criswell pauses for the laughs. "Yes, you know there are little red beetles down there now that are just sweeping Birmingham, the entire state of Alabama."

"No kidding."

"And they all get into the woodwork."

"They need to get those police dogs out and go after 'em down there."

"They can even bore through concrete, they are that much, and many buildings have been completely destroyed by these beetles."

"Now what else. That's quite a prediction there."

"I further predict that we will soon have operations in which surgery will adjust your knees to make you either shorter or taller." Pause for laughs. "For under ninety dollars."

"You mean at the knees, they just lower or raise ya?"

"They can either take a piece out or put a piece in."

"For ninety dollars."

"For ninety dollars."

"Ya know we could get Chester on Gunsmoke fixed for about forty dollars." Audience laughs. Jack makes another joke about Chester and then says, "You're hot tonight. You go right ahead." patting Criswell on the back.

"Oh thank you, I predict that Liz and Eddie will find it cheaper to stay married to each other and that Richard Burton already has eyes for another woman."

Jack and the audience sigh an, "Ahhhh..." Jack interjects, "I hate to see a beautiful story like that end that way." Audience laughs. "And may I say something. And why not it's my show." Laughs. Paar tells a joke about Hamlet being played on a leash.

Criswell states, "You know he is very interested in another woman."

"Do you know who?"

"Should I tell you. I thought you knew."

"I don't want any more suits. Do you want to whisper it to me?"

They lean together and Criswell whispers in Jack's ear. Jack leans back up and says, "Gloria Swanson?" Long laugh from the audience as Jack and Criswell nod their heads.

Criswell makes a prediction about a new trend in marriages. How older men will marry older women and that the average person will want complete freedom up until the age of thirty, marrying much later in life. Criswell then predicts about how people will raise fish in their own basement for food. Jack asks sarcastically, "Criswell, what are you on?" getting a huge laugh. Criswell continues with predictions about Castro and the Panama Canal. Jack interjects, "Gloria Swanson?" for a laugh. Criswell then predicts a nationwide price war and how funerals will soon be tax deductible. Jack replies, "Well, ok.—Gloria Swanson?" Criswell continues with his prediction of plastic coins, Senator Margaret Chase Smith being nominated by the republican primary to run for vice-president, and General DeGaulle retiring to the island of Elba. Jack interjects, "with Gloria Swanson?" for another laugh. Criswell gets his biggest laugh about a new perfume for women, "in capsules with millions of tiny pellets that go off all night long." With a smile Jack asks where and Criswell explains that they will be in the hair. He makes a couple more predictions and for his final prediction he says that Jack will return to NBC next season. The audience applauds wildly. Criswell says it will be a new ninety minute special titled "This is the Paar That Was." The audience goes wild again, and Jack says, "Well, we'll cut that out of the tape." Jack reaches over and shakes hands with Criswell and says, "Good to see ya. Good Night." They rise as Criswell says, "Thank you, goodnight and God bless you." He waves to the audience as they applaud, and the band launches back into "Pomp and Circumstance." Criswell walks to the back of the stage and turns around to wave again. Jack waves back then sits down saying, "It's sad, those partings. When he looks back it breaks me up." He pauses for the laugh then asks gleefully, "Isn't he wild?!"

In the Littlestown column of the March 7, 1959 edition of the *Gettysburg Times* ran a piece about Criswell's first national network television appearance on the Jack Paar TV show with his name listed in the article as Jerome Criswell, noting that he was the son-in-law of Dr. Stonesifer and that he was known professionally as Criswell of Hollywood. "Criswell, a newspaper columnist and television personality, writes a daily column and appears daily except Saturday on his own TV program on the west coast. On *The Jack Paar Show*, Criswell entertained by giving a number of his predictions of the future. He was invited for a return engagement next week. Criswell is married to the former Myrtle Louise Stonesifer, whose pen name is Louise Howard."

This is not the first time, nor would it be the last time Criswell's first name was misprinted as Jerome or some other variation on Jeron. Sometimes it was Jared. It would continue to happen throughout his life and even in some of his obituaries.

An April 16 piece in the *Gettysburg Times*, told of Dr. Stonesifer flying to Hollywood "where he will spend several weeks with his son-in-law and daughter, Mr. and Mrs. Jerome (sic) Criswell. Local television viewers know Mr. Criswell from his recent appearance on *The Jack Paar Show*, when he gave his predictions for the future."

On November 30 Jack Paar broadcast his show from Hollywood with Criswell as a guest along with Jerry Lester and Joey Bishop.

Plan 9 From Outer Space (1956) went into general release from D.C.A. (Distributors Corporation of America) in July 1959. Maila Nurmi claimed that Criswell told her the film played in a tiny theater in New York City for a year-and-a-half and made a ton of money. Not for Ed Wood, but for Criswell, who had allegedly invested in it. It has been reported by many people that were involved with the production of the film that no one made any money from it.

Maila Nurmi (Vampira): Criswell, though he denied it because he was a miser who often played poor, did invest in *Plan 9*. He worked two days on it. Not any of the ones I worked.

Dance of Tomorrow's
Cadavers

O my friend, would it have been different had all of the great success-es been miserable failures? What if Alexander the Great had failed to conquer his world of that time, but had lived to be an old, bitter man, dying in poverty? The future is merely a continuation of the past, and success or failure could actually mean very little in the grand sum total of us all!!

Criswell

Criswell returned to the *Jack Paar* show on March 25, 1960, with guests Jerry Lewis, Dody Goodman, Joey Bishop, and Leona Anderson.

The cover of the July 1960 issue of *St. Louis Guide*, "Official Guide ... of the Gourmet-Raconteur Society of St. Louis" featured Criswell's promo photo from *Plan 9*. The text below the photo boldly states "CRISWELL... Whose column 'CRISWELL PREDICTS'—Has rocked America. Mr. Criswell has appeared on Jack Paar's 'Tonight Show' and Art Linkletter's 'People Are Funny' show many times—is presently seen and heard on KHJ-TV at Los Angeles."

Criswell's Mother, Anna B. King passed away on October 10, 1960, at the Duncan Nursery Home in Princeton at the age of eighty. Her obituary stated that she had often supplied news stories to the *Princeton Daily Clarion* and was a correspondent for newspapers in Evansville, Indiana and Louisville, Kentucky. She was a member of the First Methodist Church, WSCS, and the Women's Relief Corp. and was laid to rest alongside her husband at the IOOF cemetery.

In the latter part of 1960, *Criswell Predicts* was no longer airing on KHJ-TV and Criswell was delegated to "Presenting" Milady's Morning Movie weekdays at 10:30 a.m. Some of the movies were *Homestretch* (1947), *Yukon Vengeance* (1954), and *You Can't Escape* (1957). The movies ran up to the noontime newscast. By the end of the year Criswell no longer had a local television program.

Criswell's column appeared in a magazine that catered to the automobile travel service industry called *Exhaust*. These are excerpts from the March 1959 and 1961 issues:

<u>Marching Ahead of Time!</u>

I PREDICT that the inventors will offer four fantastic items for manufacture and distribution next year: (1) A toy wheel that stays afloat like a kite on outer-space principle! (2) Floating homes and apartments that are built on pegs, saving space and conserving light and air! (3) Fast-as-lightning monorail trains and coaches that will zip you there before you know it! (4) Electrically driven autos-small, compact, modern and low priced! . . . I PREDICT that the coming death of an ex-senator will reveal that he has a common-law wife with three children born out of wedlock!

Your Incredible Future:
If animals permitted themselves to be as delicate as humans, they, like the dinosaur, would have died off long ago. I PREDICT that drugs, medicines, chemicals and other remedies will pass from existence before the end of another three centuries. People will learn to cure themselves by permitting their bodies to function as they should. Mother nature can

set up her own resistance in the human body, just as she does in the bodies of animals, if we permit her to do so.

What People Will Do:
I PREDICT that long distance telephone rates on the new dialing system will be reduced in price and a new club plan will be offered industry, to combat the economy wave now growing.

In March of 1961, The Littlestown phone system was converted to dial operation including customer dialing of long distance calls. Dr. Stonesifer, who had managed the Bell Telephone Company exchange in 1908, made the first call with the new service. He talked with his son-in-law and daughter in Hollywood. Dr. Stonesifer was enthusiastic about the success of his across-the-nation-dial-it-yourself phone call and said, "This is sure a change from my days in the telephone business, when it was an event to call Baltimore."

In 1962, the "Criswell Predicts" column began running in a few different pulp tabloid periodicals and adult sleaze and exploitation slicks. Some were respectable such as the *National Star Chronicle*, and some not so respectable that were published and promoted to sell in the "Adult Male" market like the *National Informer*, "Truthful News of All the Facts of Life," and *Rampage*, "Riotous, Reckless." The column would run in these types of magazines until at least 1971.

The cover of the July 1, 1962, issue of the *National Informer* featured a photo of Criswell and Mae

West and stated in the text below it, "Miss West now may read her future in the Great Criswell's columns in The National Informer's Newspapers."

I predict that a new protein powder, mixed with cold or with hot water will give you that extra lift at the end of the day rather than resorting to alcohol! This is one of the new products new to us from the moon flight!

I predict we will all be poor and destitute when we are taxed more to help the poor and destitute! We can place a man on the moon, surely we can place a man in a job and keep him there!

I predict a boom for barber and beauty shops due to the new fashion trend for very, very short hair!

I predict that our Board of Health will demand that all Hippies be stopped and examined for malaria and hepatitis due to the growing epidemic we now face! Decree: in some cities the Hippy will be stopped, taken into custody, given a bath, deloused, given a serum shot, hair clipped and put to work!

I predict an American colony on the moon by 1985!

July 14, 1962: Datelines In The Future
Aug. 18, 1999: Las Vegas, Nev.

Attractions this week along the fabulous strip were Frank Sinatra, Joey Bishop, Sammy Davis, Sammy Kaye, Dewan Martin, Cliff Arquette, Roberta Linn, Freddie Bell and Rudy Vallee and his roaring 20's all star revue with Paul Whiteman, Fifi Dorsey, Helen Kane and Buster Keaton. All acts scored heavily as the new cult of personality seems here to stay! The recent musical revue from the Lunar Palace on the Moon imported by Wilbur Clark will be brought back to earth next season!

Criswell and Marco continued on their quest as filmmakers as evidenced by a contract that Paul had written and was dated October 5, 1962. The contract was with a Michael Linden and stated, "This will confirm our understanding of this date, whereas it was mutually agreed between us that I will provide you with a copy of my story, tentatively titled "Someone Walked Over My Grave" and after reading said story that you will attempt to write the title song entitled "Someone Walked Over My Grave" to be considered by me and my associates for use as the title song in my forthcoming motion picture "Someone Walked Over My Grave."

The contract was signed by Marco and Linden and then by Criswell and Louis R. Spitzler as witnesses. This contract certainly implies that the previously mentioned legend of the "Someone Walked Over My Grave" song being produced and recorded during the filming of *Graverobbers* could be incorrect. The *Someone Walked Over My Grave* film would be another quest that failed to produce results for the pair.

In 1963 Ed Wood started writing for some of the major California adult sleaze and smut publishers just to make ends meet for himself and his wife Kathy. He would write over eighty novels and hundreds of short stories and essays for the next fifteen years under his real name and a large number of pseudonyms and pen names for various publishers including Gallery, Pendulum, Calaga, and Pad.

John Gilmore was an author, actor, screenwriter, and director who's 1997 book *Laid Bare: A Memoir of Wrecked Lives and the Hollywood Death Trip* tells of his time in 1950s and 1960s Hollywood rubbing shoulders with James Dean, Jack Nicholson, Dennis Hopper, Maila Nurmi, and Ed Wood. Gilmore met Eddie through an editor of an adult publisher that he was writing for at the time which led to his meeting Criswell at the Brown Derby coffee shop one morning.

JOHN GILMORE: I found him very clear. That's an odd word, but he seemed clear, his face clear, smooth, his eyes clear and somewhat shining from moment to moment. He seemed very sure of himself and excited by small things; and very observant. I'd gone to Hollywood High School, and he mentioned names of some people he knew, such as an actress named Collen Drake, who had gone to Hollywood High, and the Darrow sisters. I had known Barbara Darrow, dated her a couple times, though she was a little ahead of me. We also brought up actress Sally Kellerman who was trying to get work. Criswell asked if I had ever met Lana Turner and I said no, I hadn't. He looked at Ed, exchanged some look I did not understand. Ed later told me, "You know he knew there would be a murder in her house. He saw it in his mind . . ." I can remember Criswell wore a navy blue blazer and charcoal slacks, which was popular at the time. A very expensive tie, which I complimented him on, and he said it was a gift (from the London Shop on Hollywood Boulevard.) He had some sort of patch on the lapel like a star with an eye in the center of it. Latin words under it.

Gilmore ran into Criswell a number of times in Hollywood and would exchange greetings and small talk.

JOHN GILMORE: I once joined him for coffee at the Plaza coffee shop (across from the Brown Derby, in the Plaza Hotel.) He had some manuscript and was making notes or changes. We talked about Ed, and he said something like, "I feel very badly for him. I wish there was something I could do but he is very determined . . ." Out of the blue, he asked me if I was making any money, and I said well, I was making some, and he said, "But it's never enough, is it?" I know that Ed believed in Criswell, looked up to him in some sense apart from whatever ends of the business both were in. Criswell was the "actor incarnate" according to Ed, and should have played Hamlet. Ed said, "There has never been one so turned (he used word 'tuned') for Hamlet." They made plans together, each, I believe, secretly exploiting the other. I can't recall when it was, but there was a conversation once where Ed was a little tipsy and excitedly talking about a movie idea, during which Criswell (I could tell) thought what Ed was saying was dumb. He kept giving these disdainful looks which Ed was not aware of, so engrossed in the "marvel" of his own ideas.

Gilmore saw Criswell for the last time while spending some quality time with Wood recalling, "Ed was living in a dump on Normandie in Hollywood; desperate, broke, wasted but still scheming ideas for a picture that would 'have them walking on their knees,' as Ed put it."

JOHN GILMORE: I was with Ed Wood on the grass at Santa Monica and Crescent Heights (by the movie theatre that used to be there.) Ed was drinking and Criswell pulled up in a car to tell Ed there was a dead man on the streetcar tracks by Gardner and Sunset, and a dog was pissing on the dead man. Criswell thought it would have been a remarkable sequence in Ed's "next movie"; he urged Ed to get some pictures of the dead man, but Ed had trouble getting up off the grass.

March 1, 1963, Criswell made another appearance on the Jack Paar program and made the prediction that President Kennedy would not run for re-election in 1964, because of something that would happen to him in November 1963. The other guests were guitarist Les Paul and vocalist Mary Ford, humorist-author Alexander King, and comedian Dick Gregory. Criswell's friend and fellow psychic Jeane Dixon had previously predicted in 1952, that the 1960 presidential election would be won by a Democrat who would be assassinated while in office. She even went as far as to try to contact the White House and warn JFK about the danger she saw ahead. On the morning of Friday, November 22, 1963, she allegedly told friends, "This is the day it will happen."

In a March 7, *LA Times* article called 'Bitter End' Is Bitter End as Nutty TV Programs Go by Hal Humphrey. He gives his two-cents on the state of local Los Angeles television.

It is simply this—Los Angeles Television is a nut incubator, and always has been. Everything has been tried on TV here, from bingo to Criswell the fortune-teller. Fortunately for the country at large, none of these weird concoctions has spread beyond the confines of the Los Angeles signal area. The only local talent who managed to blossom onto network distribution is Lawrence Welk, and he is still trying to live it down. The reason for this lack of contagion in TV ideas germinating locally is traceable to Madison Ave., where agency men always have considered the TV audience here as being in the same genre as the Martians. It is one of the rare times Madison Ave. has been right.

It was in Los Angeles that a doll named herself Vampira and played hostess for old horror movies. Another doll baptized herself Voluptua and delivered commercials while lying on a chaise lounge. We also had Renzo Cesana, who posed as "The Continental," a kind of romantic fop who looked into the TV camera and made love to any Los Angeles housewife who had time to look and listen, and apparently there were quite a few.

If these freaks had tried to extend their TV chicanery to any other city in the United States they might have been lynched or at best tarred and feathered. But in the City of Angels, such TV fare is enthusiastically foamed over by a jaded citizenry.

In a future rant, Humphrey would again bemoan the sorry state of television espousing that, "Johnny Carson had Criswell on again recently. Almost any week an assortment of kooks and characters including raw fruit addicts, Nazis, homosexuals, and religious mystics are paraded across our TV screens."

May 20, Johnny Carson's *Tonight* shows' guests were "Robert Taylor, Angie Dickinson, Rose Marie and Criswell, the predictor (remember him?)" said a TV preview listing in the newspaper.

The June 11 edition of *The Daily Independent,* Corona, California, ran an article in the "How the Ball Bounces" feature by staff writer Jo Monich. The article tells of how Jo was in the right place at the right time, for once, at the supermarket, when an announcement over the speakers said the Mr. Criswell of the well-known radio and TV show *Criswell Predicts* was there. Criswell was with Guy Elmore and Marge Grimes and the writer asked to talk to them and was graciously invited over to Mr. and Mrs. Bob Grimes' home that evening for a party they were hosting for Criswell and Elmore. Jo recalled the evening and Criswell's past, recent, and future, as well as facts, fictions, and predictions as told by him.

Criswell has a most interesting family background. One of the Chippendales of the furniture-making Chippendale family came to America when a young man and became a casket maker. He married a girl by the name of Criswell and from this marriage came four generations of Criswell morticians and casket manufacturers.

While this particular Criswell is not active in the business, his family still makes caskets. It was through his association with the funeral director business that Bob and Marge met him.

He told me that he really learned "stage presence" as a boy helping his father and his uncle with funerals. He has never been a mortician himself but two well-known television personalities who have been morticians are Ben Alexander and Art Baker.

Criswell was Mae West's press agent for three years in New York. He started predicting the future of people in show business and before he knew it he was writing a column along this general line.

One of his first stage appearances was in a theater in Long Beach and Liberace was also making one of his first appearances in the theater next door and they have been friends since.

He is married to the former Halo Meadows who is an English recording star.

Oddly enough, she has just finished recording "I Will Be the Only True Mourner at My Funeral."

Mr. and Mrs. Criswells' eight-year-old poodle "Perfect" died last week and like most of us, the loss of a pet is comparable to losing one of the family.

He was telling me the names of some of "Perfect's" canine friends. "Fame" owned by Liberace; "Glitter" owned by one of the Gittlesons, jewelers; "Traviata," Cobina Wright's dog, and Mae West's "Diamond Jim."

Criswell writes all of his own material and commercials. He is also the producer of his new show, "The Unforgettables", which starts next Sunday, June 14, on Channel 13 at 7:30 p.m.

The article then tells of co-guest Guy Elmore being a lyric baritone and that he would be on the new show singing with Vivian Duncan, surviving member of the famous old-time vaudeville team The Duncan Sisters who had appeared on the Liberace TV show in 1956. George Liberace the violinist would also be on the show.

When asked to predict on the town of Corona, Cris predicted, "Corona will grow and grow and grow. The present Sixth Street will become a high rise area. Because of Corona's central location it can't miss. Only a fool will sell Corona short, so don't you be that fool." Jo concluded the article. "In my own mind, it isn't so much WHAT Criswell says, as the WAY he says it. He has a wonderful personality, and is just a real nice guy. Also thanks to two very charming and hospitable people, Bob and Marge Grimes." The article was accompanied by a photo of Criswell, Marge, and Guy.

Criswell and Vivian Duncan appeared together at two social events for the San Fernando Valley Republican Woman's Club and *The Unforgettables* program had a short run on KCOP-TV through July.

October 16, 1963:

I predict that dead bodies entering the United States will be most carefully examined for contraband narcotics! Even the cremated ashes will be sifted to find 'H'! No stone will be left unturned, not even a tombstone, to rid our nation of this growing menace! . . . that 'The 2,000 Year Club' composed of people binding together to live to see the year 2,000 will soon be international . . . that 'Upstage Interlude' the new Hollywood intimate show will pre-record the voices of the cast who pantomime such plays as 'That Morgan Boy' a modern 'Hamlet' by M.L. Stonesifer! This new method will reach wide acclaim!

Criswell made back-to-back Friday night appearances on *Jack Paar* October 18 and 25. His fellow guests on the first appearance were Pearl Bailey, Allen Funt, Joe Louis, and Jackie Vernon. The following week's guests were Alexander King, Helen O'Connell, and Bill Cosby.

October 28, 1963:

Thanksgiving is Allied With "13"

When Nostradamus predicted in 1544 the wonders of the new nation who's holiday would be Thursday (Thanksgiving) and be closely allied with the numeral "13." Over 200 years in the future, we find that there were 13 letters in our moto "Annuit Coeptis" and "E Pluribus Unum" . . . 13 stars in the original flag . . . 13 original colonies . . . 13 rods in our mace . . . 13 letters in "American Eagle" . . . 13 olive branches, 13 arrows in the eagle's talons . . . 13 letters in "Don't Tread On Me" . . . 13 letters in "July the Fourth" and 13 courses in the pyramid which graces our currency! Nostradamus further warns us "That in the last half of the 20th Century, beware of the Red Liberals, for they will try to wreck your world!" Khrushchev claims that "I am first a Red Liberal!"

In the November 26 edition of the *Pasadena Star-News* "Notes From Hollywood" section, Mike Connelly tells of his encounter with Criswell at a seance held at Mae West's Santa Monica beach-house. "Jeron King Criswell (known simply as Criswell to the readers of ESP publications) greeted me at Mae's door. The Savonarola of the '60s steered me through a long, Kafka-like corridor of trellises to an oval drawing room, past paintings and statues, all of Miss West, some dressed, some nude, all sexy, in all of which Mae looks not a day over 30. Okay, 35. You wanna fight? OKAY—40!" He goes on to describe some of the fifty guests, Mae's grand entrance, and her guest of honor, a seer she had met in 1941, called the Amazing Mr. Kelly. After being blindfolded and hitting his head against the wall, the seer "read" questions from the guests in envelopes by tearing, crumpling and caressing each sheet of paper. Many of the questions were the dull, what-will-my-future be?, type with one lady asking if her husband would be true to her while he's on a solo sojourn in South America? Kelly answered, "Yes, he would be, and to stop pestering the poor guy about his fidelity or he'll pop off and leave her."

Jack Kelly was born in Wales and became interested in Spiritualism after returning from World War One and eventually moving to Buffalo, New York which was the Spiritualist hub of America at the time. There he founded The Spiritualist Church of Life, helped the police solve crimes, and worked as a "healer" by using the "laying on of hands" method. He earned enough money from his work as a "healer" that his donations helped build the Healing Temple at Lily Dale, one of the largest Spiritualist communities in the world. He would work blindfolded during seances under the control of spirit guides. Miss West visited Lily Dale frequently and met Mr. Kelly there. He became her favorite medium and she claimed he visited her after his death. "He was the world's greatest psychic and he's come back. I always figured when you're dead, you're dead, but I wanted to know the truth. I had this yogi master travelin' with me for five years, I gave him a hotel suite, a car, everything, but he never convinced me. Then one day a few years ago, I come into this room from my boudoir, and there was Mr. Kelly, sittin' right there where you are, on that couch."

In December 1963 and early January 1964 a variation of the following piece ran in newspapers across the country with the source of the clipping being a different person and source each time:

STRANGE PREDICTION——

Fifteen years ago Mrs. Ira P. Cox of Galax, Va., (Rueben Johnson), clipped a little item by Jeron K. Criswell, (handed us a clipping from a newspaper . . .), from the GRIT; a nationally circulated weekly newspaper, (when President F. D. Roosevelt died, GRIT published . . .), Criswell claimed, "When Congress voted in the 1800's to take land away from the Indians in Kansas, Chief Thunderbird uttered the following incredible prophecy: "Every president elected every 20 years will die in office!" Since that fateful day, Presidents elected in 1840, 1860, 1880, 1900, 1920, 1940—Harrison, Lincoln, Garfield, McKinley, Harding, and Roosevelt—have expired in office. Will this strange prediction by the angry Indian be fulfilled again in 1960? That question, posed some 15 years ago, has now been answered. (The strange prediction by an angry Indian has been fulfilled again.)

The Criswells sent Mae West a handwritten Christmas card that said, "Santa sends Happy 1964. Every year is a better year as we make experience pay off. Criswells"
January 1, 1964:

The Year Of Achievement

My Dear Friend: We are all interested in the future for that is where you and I are going to spend the rest of our lives! And remember, my friend, these future events will affect you! As a tiny pebble is thrown into a quiet pool, the ripples continue forever and diminish but never to nothing! Your voice and your actions in 1964 will be a part of the world from here on out!

Yes, my friend, you are standing on the threshold of 1964, and beside you there is a new born "Baby 1964!" Already the child is old for it's years! "Baby 1964" will be a brat to behold! A very lovable, hateful child! So let us welcome Baby 1964, who took so long to get here! What detained it? What fool detained us? What fool is holding us back? Since the inception of time, you and I have been scheduled to meet Baby 1964, and all of the things, people, places and events he will bring!

We will travel this scheduled journey through 1964, for there will be many others to follow us, for you and I will merely lead a procession of a never ending parade!

I predict that 1964 will be the pivotal year of the 1960's, and when this year of 1964, is over, you and I plus the rest of the world will know we have had it!

Jack Paar had Criswell back again on February 14 with guests Bob Newhart, Marguerite Piazza, the Harmonica Gang, and surfing documentary filmmaker Bruce Brown. This show would be rerun throughout the year when new programming was not available. In April, Criswell spoke for Dr. Harry Douglas Smith at Grauman's Chinese Theatre and his subject was "How to Control Your Future."

On May 1, the *Gettysburg Times* ran an article titled "Halo Meadows In Dramatic Recital." "Three Flames' by M. L. Stonesifer was given, an Upstage Interlude dramatic recital last Friday in the Orient Room of Hollywood Inn, Hollywood, Calif., and stars Halo Meadows and Ed Hickman. The actress writes under her maiden name and plays special arrangements of the classics and sings before the play to balance the mood of the serious drama." "Her plays are being published by French Company of New York City. Last week Miss Meadows introduced 'The Man on the Moon', a copyrighted song by John C. Byers, a childhood friend with whom she played double piano. Mr. Byers conducts an antique shop at his home, 328 E. King St." On August 28, the *Gettysburg Times,* ran a piece titled "Around The Town." "Halo Meadows and Bill DeForest star Fridays in the Orient Room of the Hollywood Inn in Hollywood, Calif., in 'Three Flames,' the life of a successful man and three women who burn like flames in his heart. Halo, under her pen names, M. L. Stonesifer and Louise Howard, dedicates most of her writing to her hometown,

Littlestown, Pa., which is publicized as the greatest little town in the world, being nonpartisan on Mason-Dixon Line."

Frank Edwards is best remembered for his books on various anomalous phenomena, *Stranger Than Science* (1959), *Strange World* (1964), and especially unidentified-flying-objects with the best-selling *Flying Saucers, Serious Business* (1966). He also hosted a popular syndicated radio program, called *Stranger Than Science*. In *Strange World* Edwards relates a short tale called "Fateful Forecast." "In Owensville, Indiana, the citizens were puzzled one winter morning to find a cryptic message painted in huge letters on the sidewalk in front of the public grade school. The message said simply: 'Remember Pearl Harbor!' People commented on the message. But they never knew who put it there—or why. It was really nothing to get excited about at the time it occurred: for the infamous Japanese attack on Pearl Harbor never took place until two years later—to the day." Criswell had told this story to Edwards who printed it without questioning its validity. Owensville is about ten miles from Criswell's hometown of Princeton, and it seems that this story is another one of Criswell's fictions. Charles Coulombe related the story to me saying, "Sadly, Mr. Criswell made that one up."

In 1964, Criswell's column began running in the *Fabulous Las Vegas Magazine,* which was published from 1949 to the mid-1970s, by Jack Cortez and later his wife Etta, who kept it going after his death. Etta had a column on what was going on in Las Vegas and May Mann had one on the Hollywood scene. Criswell was a mainstay of the magazine until its demise. Below are excerpts from the December 1964 issue:

CRISWELL PREDICTS
An Accurate Glimpse of the Future

Can it be another year? What elf has been tearing off pages of our calendar when we are not looking?

Here it is one of the hottest days of the year in Hollywood, and I am rushing you the annual copy for the Christmas issue! Such is Life!

The growth of Las Vegas has been fabulous because of FABULOUS! No matter where I am in the country, people come up to me and make themselves known by telling me that they read the Fabulous Las Vegas magazine every week!

Each time I am in Las Vegas I am amazed at the new hotels, markets, restaurants and shopping centers! And the crowds never decrease, they increase! Surely you have earned the title everyone gives you, Jack, that of "Mr. Las Vegas" . . . and that Etta is the First Lady and Bruce the Crown Prince!

Please tell Governor Grant Sawyer that I am predicting traffic lights all along the "Strip," and to please hurry and make this prediction come to pass!

May all your shattered dreams be mended overnight . . . and may all the riches of the Universe be yours in 1965! Always in your future, gratefully,

Criswell

Criswell with his "startling predictions for 1965" joined his old buddy Regis Philbin on his short lived network late-night talkshow, *That Regis Philbin Show,* for his New Year's celebration with Zsa Zsa Gabor, Mort Sahl, Ken Murray, The Standells, Lance LeGault, and Susan Barrett.

Criswell at unknown gathering. Courtesy of Jason Insalaco.

In 1965, Criswell began making appearances on Johnny Carson's *Tonight Show*. Sadly, most of the tapes of *The Tonight Show* up until 1969 were inadvertently taped over and erased by an NBC employee. Following standard procedure at the time, they decided to use the videotapes for other purposes. The following is from a rare audio recording excerpt:

CARSON: Wanna bring a friend that we always have when we come to California because, uh, no trip would be complete. Uh, Criswell as most of you know out here in California, and uh, he writes, he has a syndicated, uh, column I guess in quite a few papers around the country.

(audience applauds and "Pomp and Circumstance" plays as Criswell walks to and sits at the dais next to Carson)

CRISWELL: We are all interested in the future for that is where you and I are going to spend the rest of our lives, whether we want to or not!

CARSON: Well, there are not many people who can argue with that. (audience laughs) Do you have some exciting predictions for us tonight?

CRISWELL: Yes, here are some predictions, advance predictions which will appear in the syndicated column. Such papers as the *Fabulous Las Vegas* and *St. Louis Guide*, the *Anderson South Carolina Daily Mail*.

CARSON: Ah.

CRISWELL: And my first prediction is. . . .

CARSON: Okay.

CRISWELL: I predict that food will be raised on your wall. (audience chuckles) All you have to do is pick it and eat it. (audience laughs)

CARSON: See now, people laugh at these predictions. (audience laughs) How will you do that?

CRISWELL: It's simply this. It will be mixed in a little bucket of glue. And you take the glue and you simply spread it on the wall and the seeds will sprout through the air. And it's very, very simple because they fertilize themselves and right from the wall your food will grow. (audience laughs)

CARSON: Good. (audience laughs)

CRISWELL: I predict that President Johnson will be placed on Mount Rushmore. (audience and Carson laugh)

CARSON: Well I know some people that would like to put him under it. (audience laughs and applauds) (audio cuts out and back in)

Carson attempts to name the presidents on Mt. Rushmore.

CRISWELL: I predict that your own funeral service will be pre-taped for your own criticism. (audience laughs)

CARSON: Now that's not bad, that's not bad. That would be interesting. In other words, you pre-tape it. . . . (audio cuts out and back in)

CRISWELL: I predict that Jello will come out with a new flavor called Nothing. (audience laughs) (audio cuts out and back in)

CARSON: It's there sitting in the glass. Okay.

CRISWELL: I predict knit suits for men along with high boots of gold, silver, and copper.

CARSON: Knit boots for men?

CRISWELL: Yes

CARSON: Alright.

[recording ends]

THE AMAZING KRESKIN: He was on Carson for a while fairly regularly and of course he wore the black tuxedo with a glistening black jacket that had iridescent lapels on it. It looked like an outer space tuxedo. When he walked on they usually played "Pomp and Circumstance" and he sat down next to Carson. He started with "We are all interested in the future. . . ." which is a very, very old phrase. I don't know how many decades even before him I remember reading it. But he of course dramatized it most effectively. Then he went on with his predictions. My favorite was when he said there would be an outpouring of bedbugs in Boston. And Carson played it exactly what he wanted it for, as a mock, ludicrous, ridiculous set of predictions. He spoke in a very kind of pompous way, which is the role he was playing on the show. I had no idea except seeing him in the movies, how he behaved in front of audiences in other situations, but on the Carson show it was done with a great pomposity, which made it all the funnier. And of course nobody took him even remotely seriously. It was interesting, because Carson never pursued anything about his personality or his interests or his background or anything else. He just had him come on, sit down, and make these quote, asinine, close quote, predictions and then he finished. I think most people that's the only place they knew him or heard of him from these appearances. I don't believe Carson would have had him on had he taken himself seriously. Everybody the next day would remember of the predictions he read, the most ludicrous things that he said.

VERNON KOENIG: One of the things that kind of upset me was the way he was treated on the Johnny Carson show. Criswell basically told me that his predictions were made as a result of history repeating itself. Over the 60 years of my life, I've found him to be correct in that assumption. Carson seemed to taunt him during the programs, and I think it frustrated him to the point where he came off to the audience as some kind of buffoon—which he was not. You could hold a straightforward conversation with him and come away with the realization that you were speaking to a very intelligent man.

In March, Criswell attended the funeral service for silent-era actress and dancer Mae Murray. It was held at his future haunt, Valhalla Memorial Park in North Hollywood. Murray was known as "The Girl with the Bee-Stung Lips" and "spent her way through a $3 million fortune she made in the movies." She was seventy-five at the time of her passing at the Motion Picture Country House and Hospital in Woodland Hills. Other mourners included Vivian Duncan, Ramon Navarro, Fay Holden, Claire Windsor, Isabel Jewell, and Wild Bill Tucker.

Criswell's third and final appearance in a full-length film began shooting in early 1965. It was based on Ed Wood's eighteen-page script called *Nudie Ghoulies*. It was composed of ten topless dances intermingled with a story of a horror writer and his fiancé being held captive in a graveyard where the dances occur after their car crashes while searching for the ancient cemetery. It was directed and produced by A.C. Stephen aka Stephen Apostolof. Wood worked as assistant director, production manager, and helped with casting. For a time it was known as *Ghouls and Dolls*. Criswell suggested *Orgy of the Damned,* but Apostolof changed it to *Orgy of the Dead* (1965). The film stars Fawn Silver, William Bates, Pat Barringer, Bunny Glaser, Texas Starr, and a "bevy of beautiful girls." Criswell would have more on-screen time than the two previous films playing the lead role of the Emperor of the Dead and of course narrating the film. Rising from a coffin, Criswell opens the film and begins speaking almost exactly the same lines as the opening of *Revenge of the Dead*:

> I am Criswell! For years I have told the almost unbelievable, related the unreal, and shown it to be more . . . than a fact. Now I tell a tale of the threshold people, so astounding that some of you may faint. This is a story of those in the twilight time . . . once human, now monsters, in a void between the living and the dead.
>
> Monsters to be pitied, monsters to be despised . . . a night with the ghouls . . . the ghouls reborn, from the innermost depths . . . of the world.

After the opening credits roll, the writer and his fiancé are driving to the graveyard, "Ah, the curiosity of youth. On the road to ruin! May ever be so adventurous!" and have the automobile accident. Criswell then begins a voiceover while the cemetery is revealed. "It is said on clear nights, beneath the cold light of the moon, howl the dog and the wolf, and creeping things crawl out of the slime. It is then the ghouls feast in all their radiance." Criswell then walks out of a mausoleum and across the graveyard with a cape held over his face Dracula style. The cape was Bela Lugosi's in *Abbott and Costello Meet Frankenstein* (1948). He continues his speech. "It is on nights like this most people prefer to steer clear of, uh, burial grounds. It is on nights like this, that the creatures are said to appear, and to walk!" He then walks up the steps of an alter and sits on a stone seat and begins speaking as the Emperor. "The day is gone, the night is upon us, and the moon, which controls all of the underworld, once again shines . . . in radiant contentment . . . (pause, eyes searching the cue cards) Come forth, come forth, O Princess of Darkness." The Princess of Darkness, played by Dawn Silver aka Ghoulita, walks to the Emperor's throne and bows to him. He nods as she places her hand on his. The Criswell voiceover continues. "Time seems to stand still. Not so the ghouls, when a night of pleasure is at hand!" He then speaks as the Emperor again. "If I am not pleased by tonight's entertainment, I shall banish their souls to everlasting damnation! (pause) And who is to be first?" The Princess of Darkness claps twice to summon the first dancer, an "Indian" girl wearing a headband and Native-American style dress that she quickly removes. The Princess explains the girl's demise. "One who loved flames. Her lovers were killed by flames. She died in flames." As each dancer appears, the Princess introduces them telling of their downfalls. Criswell comments on each one as they dance; the Gold Girl: "Throw gold at her. More gold. More gold! More gold!! For all eternity, she shall have gold!"; the Cat Girl: "A pussycat is born to be whipped." And the Slave Girl: "Torture! Torture!! It pleasures me!" The dances continue throughout the film with the writer and his fiancé forced to watch the "dancing" while bound and held in the foggy graveyard. In the end they escape as Criswell's voiceover explains. "As it is with all the Night People (The Emperor of the Dead and the Princess of Darkness) they are destroyed by the first rays of the sun. But upon the first appearance of the deep shadows of the night, and when the moon is full, they will return, to rejoice, in their evil lust, and take back with them any mortal who might happen along." Then back in his coffin he concludes the film. "Yes, they were lucky, those two young people . . . May you be so lucky . . . But do not trust to luck, at the full of the moon, when the night is dark . . . Make a wide path around the unholy grounds . . . of the Night People. Who can say that we do not exist . . . Can you? But now, we return to our graves, and you [pointing at the camera] may join us soon!"

Stephen Apostolof commented in later years that Criswell was a problem on set. He couldn't remember his lines and you can see in the film that he is looking down below the camera at cue cards that Eddie was holding for him. After lunch breaks Criswell couldn't be found and would be sleeping peacefully in his coffin. The greatest satisfaction Apostolof received was at a screening of the film when Criswell started crying and exclaimed, "You made me look so regal!"

TED V. MIKELS: I do remember Criswell sleeping in a coffin. The set was fantastic, and it excited me to light it so it would be best to see, with the proper atmosphere. I especially loved backlighting fog, etc.

Orgy of the Dead was released in June 1965 by Astra Productions and promoted as "Filmed in Gorgeous and Shocking ASTRAVISION-SEXICOLOR." It played in Los Angeles area adult theaters and is tame by today's standards and silly by the standards of the 1960s. *Torrid Film Reviews,* a Yucca street skin mag of the mid-1960s, called it, "a refreshingly different motion picture with a wild new premise and a cast of 12 beautiful girls caught in the void between the living and the dead, all doomed for their moral looseness." It was also shown under the title *Orgy of the Vampires* even though there were no vampires in it. A Wolfman and a Mummy do make an appearance. Criswell's involvement and the "name" strippers began to generate a small following for the film in adult movie houses and drive-in theaters. This prompted Wood to use the title for the

Dawn Silver as the Princess of Darkness, Criswell as the Emperor of the Dead with the Wolfman and Mummy. *Orgy of the Dead* Lobby Card.

name of a short story collection. Forrest Ackerman related that Eddie would call him while Eddie was inebriated at all hours, and so to end the intrusions, Ackerman agreed to negotiate a deal with the adult publisher Greenleaf Classics for publication of *Orgy of the Dead* in 1966. Ackerman wrote the introduction to the book which included the stories; "The Night the Banshee Cried," "Final Curtain," "The Day the Mummies Danced," along with a number of stills from the film. The book is about seventy-five percent photographs and twenty-five percent text. The outstanding Robert Bonfils who had produced countless adult covers, created the lurid cover painting. Allegedly, Wood had previously produced a recording of Tor Johnson reading "The Day the Mummies Danced" and Criswell reading "Final Curtain" in 1963, but that has not been found or released.

Earl Kemp was the editorial director for William Hamling's adult publishers that included Greenleaf Classics and a few other imprints. Shortly after the deal was negotiated, Eddie called Earl and said he would be in San Diego and wanted to get together. Earl was amused at the prospect and invited him for lunch. Wood said there would be two of them. At the scheduled time Eddie showed up with Cris.

EARL KEMP: They erupted into the office reception area in a flutter of flapping wings and flying, billowing, twirling capesmanship that was enough to rival an entire ballet troupe. There were also giggles and twittering . . . and they didn't come from the office staff that had become an unknowing audience to the spectacle of their "beingness."

Criswell was ablaze in heavy layers of theatrical makeup that made him look like a run-away circus clown. His clothes were extremely shabby and almost threadbare.

They had clearly seen much better days . . . and they were meticulously maintained as if they were actually the last real remnants of a once-great wardrobe.

Criswell had a remarkable voice; it was almost mesmerizing in its intensity. He could use it with real force and easily project it across an entire restaurant, causing every head to turn and . . . admire . . . the professional at work. Then, just as quickly, he would lapse into almost childish glee, once he knew he had them in his hands.

Once they were in the office, Earl realized he couldn't take the outrageous pair to anywhere he routinely frequented with other visiting dignitaries of Bill Hamling for fear that he might be recognized. Earl was reserved and easily embarrassed at the time, but looking back he wishes he had treated them more like true visiting dignitaries. He had to go all the way across San Diego to an area he never visited to find a restaurant where he felt he could be seen with them as they took center stage in one of their blatant attention gathering routines.

EARL KEMP: They were fantastic together, moving like a well-oiled machine, empathetically communicating with each other, each finishing the other's sentences, etc. . . . I didn't know if I should be scared or amused most of the time. Fortunately, amused won out, and rightly so. Had I not really accepted them, I would have missed out on one of life's really rare moments . . . sharing in fleeting touches of greatness.

Eddie and Cris visited Earl a number of times at his office in San Diego. Earl got to know the pair better than he really needed to or cared to. Every time they visited Eddie would tell Earl what kind of female undergarments he was wearing and offer to show them, especially panties, even though Earl showed no interest. He somehow avoided the exhibition. He never saw Eddie without Cris and believes they made a special trip to pick up the $500 check that was payment for the text portion of the book.

EARL KEMP: When I handed him that check, time froze. He looked at it in disbelief, then lit up like a Christmas tree, broke into a big grin, and did an involuntary quick two-step dance in excitement, all in double-time. I guessed that $500 check represented the largest amount of money Ed Wood had seen all at once in a long time. 1966 dollars went a very long way.

Wood had two other books published by Kemp that year, *Parisian Passions* and *Side Show Siren*. Kemp can't remember why the first book was credited to J.X. Williams, the house pseudonym, especially since Eddie was so insistent about using his real name which does appear on the latter book.

Criswell appeared on Johnny Carson's *Tonight Show* October 2, 1965, and plugged his latest movie, *Orgy of the Dead*. The other guests on the program were Roy Rogers and Dale Evans, Mamie Van Doren, Melinda Marx, David Allen, and Ray Hastings.

THE AMAZING KRESKIN: Interestingly, Criswell came on and sat on the dais right next to Carson on his left. Sat right next to him. This was very, very unusual. I don't remember anybody else doing that. Even Ed McMahon sat to Johnny Carson's right. Every person on all the talk shows sit not on the dais but on another chair, on the series of chairs to the right of the host, camera left. But Criswell came on and sat camera right to the left of Johnny Carson. Right next to him. It was very interesting. It made it stand out as a kind of intriguing set and of course he was so pompous with this lemon meringue hairdo.

VERNE LANGDON: I remember Criswell wearing the sequined tuxes on all of his shows or most of them, he certainly did as a guest on *The Tonight Show*. He got more and more flamboyant and heavier as the career wore on.

THE AMAZING KRESKIN: He seemed like a great, specialized comedic character even though I think, I'm sure, he would have liked to be taken seriously. His character was so well honed that it was a narrow position in the business. It would have been difficult for him to expand on it and do other things in television.

Criswell was again on the *Tonight* Show on December 31, 1965. His fellow guests were Woody Allen, William Walker, Gila Golan, and the Muppets. He predicted that Ronald Reagan would be the next Governor of California with the audience responding with huge laughs. In 1966 Reagan did win the election by defeating incumbent governor Edmund G. Brown. It would become one of

Criswell's most famous and quoted prognostications. A rare video that survived of this appearance is available on YouTube.

On January 5, 1966, the *Gettysburg Times* ran a piece entitled, "Rotary Hears Predictions by Criswell" reporting on Criswell addressing the Littlestown Rotary Club. He recalled his last visit to the community and his participation in the town's bicentennial parade. He told the Rotarians that one of the important rules of self-improvement was to "pamper yourself just a little bit more and have positive outlook; do not crowd your future with a lot of things that will never happen." He announced that he would be co-host on the Mike Douglas Show in about a month, and and that he would appear on the Johnny Carson Show on New Year's Eve. He entertained the group for about a half hour with his predictions and then answered questions. His "I Predict" items were: universal fingerprinting for every person in the country, moving into the world of the vending machine when even false teeth can be purchased for a few dollars, opening Medicare to everyone, refusal of 10,000 doctors to practice under the Medicare program, a price war on frozen foods, a round trip ticket from New York to Paris for $50, the present as the twilight zone for the unions, development of new civic and nationalistic pride, fixation of legal fees in 1966, a lot of tragedy in conjunction with the Olympics in Mexico, a nation of people to emerge from underground, the reaching of the highest point of prosperity in the nation on March 27 of that year, and then a slight recession for a year and a half, the replacing of all coins by currency, and a double wedding in the White House. He told the audience that he based his predictions, which are his own opinions, on research and trends. One Rotarian claimed that Criswell had predicted the date for the ending of World War II. He then told the attendees to circle the date of August 18, 1999, on their calendars when it would "rain comets." He also said that small towns are the backbone of America. A photo of Dr. Stonesifer and his son-in-law accompanied the article.

Born in New York City in 1959, Charles A. Coulombe moved with his parents to Hollywood at age six. He has been called "the youngest member of the Ed Wood set" due to his living under the Criswell roof and his recollections of that time. Roy, his nickname of his youth, grew up in Hollywood with his brother Andre and a group of close friends that still get together on occasion. I attended one of these get-togethers and was regaled with and amazed by the stories they related about the wild and bizarre adventures of growing up in Hollywood during the mid-to-late 1960s. Charles is now a prolific author and lecturer and has written a number of books and articles on a wide variety of religious, political, historical, and literary topics including, monarchism, drinking and the influence of alcohol on literature, haunted houses, the supernatural, the Catholic Church, the Popes, and the supernatural in the Catholic Church. He made a pact with his brother that he would include a Criswell quote in all of his books. In his 2004, book, *Rum; The Epic Story of the Drink That Conquered the World*, he quotes a bartender at Boardner's, the closest bar within stumbling distance of the Criswell residence. "I walked Criswell home a few times—even when he couldn't walk!" In his 2003, history of the Papacy; *Vicars of Christ.* "The famed 1950s-60s television psychic Criswell, as un-papal a man as one is ever likely to meet, said, 'We are all lighted candles in a darkened room, weary travelers on the road of life.' It is the contention of the Catholic Church that she and her popes continue the work of Christ, that she is the Mystical Body of Christ; through this body alone, she maintains, can such travelers find the way to salvation."

CHARLES COULOMBE: Criswell was, when my family and I first moved here to Los Angeles, our landlord (1966-69). A mere child then, I remember Mr. Criswell, his wife, and their friends horrifyingly well. My father nearly did a movie with him. I still have the script somewhere. It was a Bigfoot movie and featured himself making a typical intro and sign-off. [The script was titled *Garga* written by Charles' father, Guy Joseph Conrad Coulombe, who was an actor and patron of the arts.] With Criswell came into our lives a parade of intriguing folk; apart from various bygone third-tier film people, there were such luminaries as Maria Graciette (dubbed "the psychic who helps you" by one supermarket tabloid) and Madame Juno, the "Psychic to the Stars." Hot and cold running predictions were the order of the day at Criswell House, and the prophecies of Nostradamus and Edgar Cayce were constantly discussed and speculated over. At the master's renowned Sunday Brunches, various experts took up such important questions as UFOs and Bigfoot, reincarnation and hauntings of all kinds.

JOHN DOUCETTE: A childhood friend from school, Blessed Sacrament, which was right next door to where Criswell and Andy (Andre) Coulombe, Charles' brother, lived with Criswell. I got a kick out of him because the first sight of him, (he was an imposing man, at least 6' 3", and when you're a kid he's bigger than life), [was] when I went to visit Andy. Criswell was coming out of his bungalow in a purple sequined tuxedo jacket and the whole package, ruffled shirt, cummerbund and patent leather shoes and a big smile, he looked like he was going to a premiere and the only thing missing was the paparazzi.

ROBERT HANKS: Mr. Criswell was a colorful, entertaining, and extremely bright individual with a wonderful flair for entertaining and holding the attention of anyone that he came in contact with. My grandmother, Nancy Lowery (mother of actor Robert Lowery, my father) knew him for many years—he later became her landlord when she took a flat in a fourplex that Mr. Criswell owned at 1542 Cassil Place, in the heart of Hollywood. This house was a faux Mediterranean/various combination of styles.

CHARLES COULOMBE: His wife was quite mad. Mrs. Criswell had a huge standard poodle (named "Buttercup") which she was convinced was the reincarnation of her cousin Thomas. She spent a great deal of time sunbathing—, which given her size, was not too pleasing a sight. She had a bellybutton as big as a silver dollar. She had been a former speak-easy dancer, under the name of Halo Meadows. All of this is by way of prequel. You will have heard, no doubt, of Mr. Criswell's famous Brown Derby lunches. Well, none of us ever attended those, but, like the other tenants, we were expected at the Sunday afternoon brunches. These were potluck affairs, held (to my then incredible embarrassment) in the front yard on long folding tables. The guests were an amazing assortment, including both mega-stars like Tor Johnson and Ed Wood, and others, like Jean Harlow's Understudy, and Madame Juno, psychic to the stars. But the highlight would come after the food was cleared away, and Mrs. Criswell would dance on the table, in her bikini, accompanying herself by singing songs of her own composition. (Incidentally, a friend of mine who had long doubted this story, ran into Vampira at a Comic Book Convention, and she confirmed the details!) At Criswell House, truth was stranger than fiction.

CLAUDIA POLIFRONIO: Ed Wood would come (to the potlucks) and he would sit in the corner and not talk to anyone. He was not an animated man. I didn't know his wife. I didn't even know he was married. He was always dressed as a man. Criswell shielded me from many things.

Ed Wood was a nobody. Very good looking, no personality. Very shy. I was shy but he was shyer than me. They sent him downstairs to look at my paintings and he didn't say anything, just sitting there.

JOHN DOUCETTE: I grew up in Hollywood and I always loved meeting new people and celebrities. My Mother was a homemaker, I was born in 1954, and my father [John Arthur Doucette] was a character actor, so meeting Criswell felt like he was a friend right away, he always said hi and smiled, his wife was also very nice to us, she even made us chocolate-chip cookies as we sat on the front porch one summer afternoon.

ROBERT HANKS: Criswell was married to Halo Meadows, who was a well-known eccentric and new age type long before it was fashionable. She was delusional and could often be seen hanging out one of the many windows of the house. She had an interest in writing both poetry and short stories, as well as essays that frankly were difficult to understand—and some compared to the ravings of a lunatic. Halo was all over the place, and would often drop in at neighbor's home unannounced. She also liked to plan and hold parties, which, sadly few would attend.

Love
By
M. L. Stonesifer
Love is a word meaning absorption,
And that is a big word.
Does anyone want love?
Does anyone want oblivion?
Maybe some think oblivion could be nice,
But not oblivion in another.
Self oblivion is still self choice,
And who doesn't want to keep self choice,
Even self choice for oblivion.
So love is really a lost word,
Just hanging on by a thread that it offers more self.

CLAUDIA POLIFRONIO: Halo, oh my goodness. If I told you about her you wouldn't believe it. That's the problem. She was brilliant, very educated, played the piano, was a metaphysician, a longevist, influenced me a lot. Gave me a lot of advice about life and people. A woman of wisdom. I think she had a nightclub career singing. She didn't have a good voice but a gimmicky type thing.

I thought she was an attractive woman. She had a certain charm. At the time I met her she had mental problems; she had been ill. But I saw pictures of her, in Claudette Colbert bangs, one of the silent screen types. But her personality, I've never met anyone like her. She was eccentric. Maybe now she wouldn't be considered eccentric, but the things she talked about, that you can live forever. She was a storyteller. Both of them were story tellers. You could sit and listen to them for hours. And she knew everything, she could dramatize every situation, act it out. She'd tell me personal things, this I can't tell you, her life with Criswell.

It's a sad story. I mean, it was funny at the time. I could see that she had a mental condition. And he actually could have done more with his career than he really did.

CHARLES COULOMBE: Well, way back in 1966, after we first moved in, but before I began school, Mother and I were hungry. She asked Mr. Criswell if he knew of a reasonable place for lunch. He replied, in stentorian, he had no other tones: "Certainly! The Gold Cup, up on Las Palmas and Hollywood!" This was a place he frequently went to in search of young lads—. This we did not know then. Ensconced at a table, I noticed that the clientele were staring at us. I asked my mother why this was. She looked about rather stiffly and answered, "they are celibates, and rarely see mothers and children."

[On Criswell's suspected homosexuality] . . . he did lock his bedroom door at night, for fear she [Halo] would stab him while he slept; I suppose that on some level she was not pleased.

Charles also relayed that during the family's weekend strolls around the neighborhood they would run across Criswell at the local newsstand reading and purchasing "bodybuilding" and "weight-lifting" magazines.

CLAUDIA POLIFRONIO: He might have been bisexual, I think. At that time I didn't understand these things. But he had a lot of men around him. But he had women, too. He had me and Mae West.

[Did he have romantic relationships with women?]

I don't know. I didn't really delve into that. But because of his looks and Hollywood, I could see why. He was an attractive man.

[Did he have any romantic interest in you?]

Oh. . . . the same way he has for Mae West. He appreciated certain types of women, but I can't say that it was romantic. There were many times I thought he was fatherly. But he appreciated who I was, he thought I was very attractive. He was looking at it artistically.

He would want me with him all the time. So he would like women. He was not apathetic toward women. He liked them in friendship. You could tell he appreciated the female. That's why he was married, even though it was supposed to be an arrangement.

JOHN DOUCETTE: Criswell you will always remain in my heart, as a young boy, you let my friend Andy (your next door neighbor on the corner on Selma Avenue & Cassil Place) and myself go into your air raid bunker, we also opened your garage once and a huge coffin was staring at us! It scared us, but we still loved you.

CHARLES COULOMBE: You must understand that I started school at Blessed Sacrament, a Catholic school on the same block. Criswell's back yard was directly under the convent windows;

there was an empty lot (now part of the church/school parking lot), which had been a house, two doors down from the Criswell House. One day (when I was in second grade, so 1967/68) some of my friends called me over to the fence separating the school-yard from the lot. There, in the middle of the field, was Mrs. Criswell, in her bikini, on all fours eating grass (she was much into health foods).

"Isn't that your landlady?" asked my friends.

Mortified, I nevertheless, even then, sensed that the slightest hint of embarrassment on my part would set me up for endless ridicule.

"Yes" I replied, "that's Mrs. Criswell."

"Well, what's she doing?"

Looking matter-of-factly at her, I said. "She's grazing."

"Why?"

"It's lunch-time. I expect she's hungry. Is that all?"

It appeared to be, and so we went away. But when I got home you can imagine my shrieking at my folks. (on Mrs. Criswell's house-keeping) She also did not clean their apartment, saying that "dust must form its own patterns."

CLAUDIA POLIFRONIO: You see, she was way out. I didn't want to see that. Well, she was a sick woman. But when she would come back from the hospital she was very lucid. You could see it. She was loving. That would last for a few months, six months maybe. And those were the times. . . . she had a strong need to be in the limelight and being married to someone that showy. See Criswell is the type that no matter how fabulous you are, his presence takes the whole room. His voice and yet he was not a competitive person. No ego.

Because you know how it is with long marriages. There was a competition between the two of them. Because here you have a woman who is a longevist, an immortalist, who believed that you don't have to die at all, married to a man who is an undertaker with caskets in the house. Look at that scenario!

So she was, I would call it, an extreme eccentric, Schizophrenia, you know. She spent some time in and out of institutions.

STACYA SILVERMAN: My mother was an artist and no great house-keeper herself, but she would not allow me to eat at those famous brunches, saying the tines of Halo's forks were crusty with old food, the designs in her china caked with gray grease. Her house was full of dust and grime, she never cleaned. She told my mother she didn't believe in cleaning.

CHARLES COULOMBE: He had the unfortunate habit of wearing boxer shorts (and nothing else), and coming out on the front porch to confront whatever events displeased him.

My activities often provoked his porch outbursts; but then again, he would wax melancholic, and contrast my upbringing with his.

ROBERT HANKS: As a child attending Selma Avenue Elementary in Hollywood, both Criswell and his wife were prominent in our neighborhood. He often could be seen in his yard, barely clothed in a robe and house slippers, tending his garden, or entering his bomb shelter in the front yard (Criswell believed in being well prepared). Mr. Criswell's was the first I had ever seen that had a bomb shelter. The kids from Selma Elementary School across the street were invited over to tour it, which we did. It was spooky down there. One of the high points (or low points) was watching Mr. Criswell water his yard in his house robe without any under-garments. Looked like a large cow udder down there. Quite spectacular.

The Criswells' bomb shelter was reported in a UPI Hollywood story saying that the eighteen-foot by eight-foot shelter was underneath the front lawn and had sleeping accommodations for six people. When asked who his guests might be, Criswell asked airily, "Are there four other people worth saving in Hollywood?" Asked about the chances of a nuclear bombing he replied, "Within a year, there will be need of fallout shelters." suggesting that the need would arise not from a war but fallout from nuclear testing. He added, "I hope I'm wrong on the prediction that there will be use for the shelter" but that, "forward looking people are building them. If someone had described TV sets 50 years ago we would have locked him up and should have." Construction wasn't without incident as a hapless bulldozer driver drove into the hole leaving a tangled pile of dozer and operator. A passerby asked if Criswell had foreseen the accident, which left the operator unharmed, he replied knowingly, "I told the driver that if he didn't get away from the edge of the hole he'd fall in." He claimed the driver was an unemployed actor who kept looking over his shoulder hoping to be discovered by a movie producer.

VERNE LANGDON: I remember when my wife Dawn and I first came to Hollywood before I met up with Mae again. We took great delight in driving around the block with the top down on our convertible and as we passed the buildings, Criswell TV building number one and Criswell TV building number two, I would holler at the top of my lungs, "Criswell predicts!" And it was great fun. I don't know why. It was just something we enjoyed doing. Give you a rough idea of our frame of mind.

Somebody told me, that was really close to him or he discussed it with Mae and I and it's always stayed with me, that he slept in a coffin. And it was his own personal coffin, and he came from an undertaking family. His father was apparently an undertaker and there were people in the family besides the father that were undertakers. So he grew up playing in the mortuary. Which I suppose has an interesting effect on you.

MAILA NURMI (VAMPIRA): His family owned many funeral parlors in San Francisco, and he loved them all and wished to be an officiator at any and all funeral parlors. So he spent a great deal of time at Utter-McKinley on the corner of Argyle and Hollywood Blvd.

I used to work there as a professional mourner. It was right in my neighborhood. The elderly folks said, "If you need money, you can stop in at Utter-McKinley when you are passing." And just stop in and see if there is a funeral going. If there is, you can get three dollars if you stay a few hours and be a mourner grieving for the dearly departed. But if you cry, you get five dollars. I have loose tear ducts.

When Maila's mother passed away, she didn't know how to conduct the business of arranging a funeral. Criswell came to her aid saying, "I come from an undertaking family."

MAILA NURMI (VAMPIRA): But when my mother died, my mother didn't have any friends, because she was a good woman, right? ... My mother was a chambermaid, and a sweet human being, didn't have anyone to carry her coffin. Criswell loved to officiate at that sort of thing. He took full charge. Well, he came, and he acted like the "hand-shakeur" [posh French accent]. He wore a dark blue suit and a little white silk handkerchief, a white carnation. And he greeted everyone, he was very comforting, very gentlemanly. And he got all the pall bearers. Paul Marco was one. Ed Wood was not. He may have been, but I don't know. I was too busy mourning.

CLAUDIA POLIFRONIO: He was in the funeral business, related to Utter-McKinley funeral directors. A couple of times he took me to the funeral parlor and that gave me the creeps. And he would still do some undertaking. He had a couple of caskets in the house. They used one in the Ed Wood movie where he comes out of the casket. So his family were undertakers.

Paul Marco attended a gathering of morticians with Criswell where one man related taking particular notice of the beauty of a deceased young woman that was brought to him. Upon examining her, he noticed the edge of an object sticking out of her private area. When fully removed with one of his instruments, it turned out to be a twenty-dollar bill. Apparently she was the proverbial "$20 whore." The mortician had one of his workers wash it off and go out to buy some liquor. Paul said that Cris laughed first and loudest at the bizarre absurdity of the whole situation.

On January 1, 1967, Criswell made a prediction in his column that would become one of his most famous and quoted on his future book covers. "I predict a blonde sex symbol will suffer a Dixie death." On June 29, 1967, Blonde Bombshell actress and pin-up model Jayne Mansfield was killed in a car crash on her way to New Orleans after a performance in Biloxi. A blonde bouffant wig that she was wearing had flown off in the accident. The wig was photographed, and a reporter stated that it was her head. The story of her decapitation then spread through the press as fact. The *New York Times* contacted her undertaker who confirmed that her body was intact, including her head, but the myth of her decapitation still continues to this day.

March 7, Criswell was back on Carson's *Tonight Show* with fellow guests Bob Stevens and MacDonald Carey. April 13, "television and radio star Jeron K. Criswell" appeared as a guest speaker at a luncheon in honor of Annual Secretaries Week.

Seven Seventy Publishers of Southern California began publishing adults only, pulp girlie magazines in the early 1960s as Seven

Seventy One Publications. Exploitative titles included; *Banned, Shocker, Shocking World, Girls A Go-Go, Sassy, Torchy, Lusty, Way Out,* and *Today's Breed.* During the Summer of Love of 1967 they released a special issue exploiting the free love, nudity, and openness of the hippy generation. It was appropriately titled *Hippies.* The cover has a full color photo of Criswell next to a nude woman with the text "CRISWELL PREDICTS: BOTTOMLESS" strategically placed covering the woman's breasts. Criswell is featured in an eighteen-page spread that includes a number of photos of himself alone and with the nude model. Of course there are a great number of photos of women baring their behinds. After an Editor's note with a short bio on Criswell, the column begins with; Criswell Predicts: For Men Only.

I predict that 1967, will be the year of the federal ruling on alimony payments . . . for two years only . . . but child support will be required as usual! Divorce laws and marriage laws will be federalized, that is, the same in each state! Community property rulings will exist in many other states, but it will be up to the woman to prove her aid in the acquiring of said property, which can be made difficult! . . . I predict that in some states common law marriage will be recognized both on the part of the man and the woman! Many injustices will be evened up and it will take two to make a bargain! I predict that Wife-Swapping Clubs will lower the bar to any one who will bring a woman, whether it is his wife or not to swap! The Clubs feel that this will bring new and exciting members, who must of course, sign a 'non-blackmail' pledge and also post a $10,000 bond for secrecy! I predict a boom in the wife swapping clubs in 1967! . . . I predict that Nudist Camps will increase in 1967, under new licenses of 'Health Camps' which will outlaw all immoral acts on the premises! However, there will be an off-limits area, which you may wander at your own risk! Membership fees will be low and attendance high! I predict that there will be stern laws against 'blackmail baby bandits' who are children, trained by their parents to accuse and to frame you of 'child molestation' and to demand that you pay off quickly to avoid the scandal! . . . I predict that in 1967, it will be you, the man, who will take the birth control pills and not the woman! . . . I predict that a new vitamin-mineral for men only will restore flagging powers and you will again feel tip-top no matter what age or what condition! You will welcome the year 1967!

He then daringly predicts, "Daring Fashions for Women"

I predict that 1967, will be the year of daring fashions for women! You will remember 1967, as the year of the new see thru cloth, which leaves nothing to the imagination! It is thin, light weight and clings to the body in a most enticing way! . . . Skirts will be split to the thighs, showing ample legs and sides of the stomach! The hair will be worn piled high to give the wearer a taller appearance, and also a thinner one! . . . Backless and frontless gowns for evening wear will be the rage, with the hips as the focal point of styling! . . . Women's briefs and panties will have enticing invitations written on them and this will be the new fashion for the jet set! These transparent garments will be the ideal birthday or holiday gift in 1967! . . . Hats will be large and elegant with tule floating from each side, crossing just over the almost visible breasts! Yes, 1967, will be a daring year for the girls and the girl watchers!" Then: Shocking Predictions "I predict that a well-known airline will secretly offer an 'all stag flight' from New York to California with very willing and experienced party girls as hostesses. On the screen you will see the latest of the smut films and nudity will abound! I predict that LSD will be the enemy of the Teen-Age set in 1967! Many of these youthful narcotics takers will turn themselves into a vegetable with brain damage, and will spend the rest of their lives in institutions and jail! Many of these takers will be moved to violence, and as many as 1,000 a month will die directly from the results of LSD itself! . . . I predict that you must be aware of the angry girl who can infect you with syphilis with the mere jab of a needle when you are not aware! The contraband from China has the hypodermic hollow needle filled with active syphilis germs, and one jab can do it! . . . I predict that 1967, will be a very good year for the single man and the single girl as a great restlessness is creeping over the land and people are seeking new mates and new friends! Yes, I predict that wherever you are, you will definitely make out and score out in 1967! And finally: "Criswell Predicts Our Top-Less, Bottom-Less World"

I predict that 1967, will be the year of the top-less, bottom-less world of entertainment! . . . I predict that the topless craze will hit the nation, followed by the bottom-less! I predict that luncheon places will boom for the tired businessman where his appetite will be sharpened by unclad waitresses, jouncing cocktail girls and uppity hostesses, all included in the menu price! I predict that there will be topless lady barbers who will cut your hair to your liking! I predict that you will be able to play a friendly game of pool with a topless partner! I predict that your program at a wrestling match or boxing match will be sold to you by either a topless or bottomless usher! I predict that you will be able to get a shoeshine by an energetic topless shoe shine girl for one dollar per show! I predict that hockey games will be enlivened by topless players, and then an all-girl nude football game (of the touch variety) will play to a full stadium! I predict that you will drive into an enclosed gasoline station and be served by a topless gasoline jockey! I predict that men's stores will use topless saleswomen to gain more business! I predict that after you see a baseball game with a topless team versus a bottomless team, baseball will become then, a new American top fad! I predict that topless players will give polo a new life, not to mention how much more zip will be added to nude swimming contests and sporting events!" A caption to a photo of Criswell in the coffin from *Revenge of the Dead* says, "Criswell says this coffin could be used sooner than the hippie clan think —each reefer is another nail in the coffin!

A two-page spread culled from this magazine was featured in a 1968 issue of *Shocker*, but changed the year of the predictions from 1967 to 1969.

Criswell's birthday was honored at a luncheon party held in the Garden Room of the Hollywood Roosevelt hotel. His cousin, Mrs. Hopkins Bellah hosted the event which was attended by Halo, Miss Ayllene Gibbons, and Bill Gass. A September 1 newspaper mention of the event listed the honoree as J.T. Criswell.

August 6, 1967, *Bridgeport Sunday Post*:

I predict that June Wilkinson, the Hollywood personality, will create a new image as an actress, which will be copied for years, as she will set an endless trend you girls will unconsciously imitate.

June 6, 1968:

I predict that June Wilkinson as the sophisticated hippie in the new TV series will be the most impersonated actress in all television next year.

June Wilkinson was born in Eastbourne, England and began her showbiz career on the stage at the age of twelve as a trained dancer and by the age of fifteen was performing topless. In 1957 she joined the legendary Windmill Theatre in London as a fan dancer and was soon discovered by Hugh Hefner who brought her to the United States in 1958 for her first appearance in *Playboy* magazine in September of that year. Hefner appropriately dubbed her "the Bosom" on account of her incredibly endowed and voluptuous 43-22-37 contoured figure. She became one of the most popular and most frequently photographed cheesecake pin-up models of the 1950s and 1960s with subsequent appearances in *Playboy* and appearing on the cover and inside scores of girlie magazines, newspapers, tabloids, calendars, posters, and record album covers. Like her fellow "bombshell" personalities, Jane Mansfield and Mamie Van Doren, June sought stardom in the movies. She was under-billed in a handful of B-grade films from 1959 to 1961 garnering her little attention as an actress. Thought the 1960s and 1970s she kept her name alive returning to nightclubs and the live stage. She performed as a sexy foil to the legendary comedic bandleader Spike Jones and his Musical Depreciation Revue. She started acting in live stage productions of sex comedy teasers such as her most successful vehicle, *Pajama Tops* (1964), which amplified her still-gorgeous figure as well as her comedy timing. She portrayed the glamorous villainess Evilina on the *Batman* television series in 1968 and also made appearances on the *Doris Day Show*. Being a savvy and health-conscious businesswoman, her later projects included running a successful string of fitness centers in Canada; hosting the Encore cable show *The Directors*, in which she interviews filmmakers; and a historical fashion television show called *Glamour's First 5000 Years*. In 1997 at the age of fifty-seven, June returned to *Playboy* with a nude-shoot featured in *The Best of Glamour Girls: Then and Now vol. 2* (Winter 1997) and in 1999 was ranked as number thirty on *Playboy's* list

"100 Sexiest Stars of the Century." June is a compassionate proponent, advocate, and supporter of the humane treatment of all living creatures. She became acquainted with Criswell after being introduced by her friend Christine Jorgensen.

JUNE WILKINSON: Yes, Christine Jorgensen did introduce us. I think it was in the early sixties. I had met Christine in Seattle during the Seattle World's Fair. I was doing *Pajama Tops* at the Moore theatre and she was doing a nightclub act. We became friendly (she was always interested in my clothes) and later in L.A. we met, and she introduced me to Mr. Criswell, whom I did not know as an actor but as a foreteller of your future in the newspaper. He then would call me and would use me in his column. I never went to his house, but I met his wife several times at various openings and at several parties. It was not until much later that I found out he was an Ed Wood favorite. I did meet Mae West, but she was not very friendly to me and did not want any photos taken with me and I never met Ed Wood, but I would have loved to.

December 27, 1967, *The Daily News*:

> I predict that rock and roll will come to an end with recordings selling for 10 cents just to get rid of them! . . . I predict Salvador Dali will cast aside his present art form and become famous for his religious paintings!

In 1967, Stacya (Shepard) Silverman and her family moved into the Criswell apartments. She was only two-years-old at the time, but later in life her parents related to her many stories and recollections of their time living in the eccentric, unique, and at times volatile world of the Criswells. Her father told her that the first time they met Criswell, he had taken her up with him and Mae West was

247

there. Miss West threw her fur coat on the floor of the apartment so that the infant Stacya could crawl around on it. At that time her father was trying to revive his career as a folk and country music singer, songwriter, and recording artist. The elusive and fascinating country singer Richard Riley Shepard was born in Wilmington, North Carolina, on October 21, 1918, and taught himself to play guitar by the age of twelve. At that same age, he broke the glass storefront window of his Grandmother's grocery store to hand out food to the poor families in the town. He was sent to a psychiatrist who suggested he be sent to the Eastern Carolina Industrial School for Boys in Rocky Mount, North Carolina. It was basically a prison and labor camp for children, except they also took young men as old as nineteen off of chain gangs to give them a second chance. The older "boys" were mixed in with boys as young as eight with no real supervision. Some of the boys were there for stealing, like Riley, others for simply skipping school, but some for rape and assault. Riley was raped there, and he ran away three times and each time he was caught. The older boys were sent to chase after him, but sometimes he was out for a long while and the sheriff would come after him. After being returned to the "school," they'd shave his head and put him in "The Jug" which was solitary confinement where he would only be feed crackers and water. During one of his escapes at the age of thirteen, he began his quest for stardom performing professionally on the vaudeville circuit as a black-face minstrel-show inspired character named Lanky Bill. Fully aware that black-face promoted terrible stereotypes, he later remarked, "I performed with other kids, most were black teenagers. We simply didn't know any better back then, and we were lucky to have work. Times were tough. It was the Depression." The black face was a good disguise, but he was eventually caught and returned to the "school" where he remained until he was fifteen-years-old. He then began playing and singing with a number of bands in the Raleigh, North Carolina area and toured as an actor during the latter half of the 1930s with the famed Bert Bertram Players. During the uncertain war torn years of the early 1940s he landed in Chicago and began a series of lectures that reflected that ambiguous, fearful time in the world. He promoted himself as an Author, Historian, World Traveler, and Philosopher, while using Doctor or Reverend preceding his name on flyers advertising free weekly lectures presented by The Cosmopolitan Church. The "educational lectures," held in the Aviation Room on the third floor of the Hamilton Hotel on Dearborn Street, mirrored the uncertainty in the world at that time because of the raging world war and not knowing what type of government rule was on the horizon. The topics were "God, Man and Science," "Marriage, Sex and Morality," "Jesus, and the Rise of Christianity," "Democracy and Capitalism," "Origin and Growth of Fascism," and "War, Revolution and the New World." In 1943 another series of Saturday night lectures presented by The Better Humanity League were promoted on a flyer with the bold headline: "Forward to a Brave New World!" The polemic topics included "The Necessity for Radicals," "The Tyranny of Marxism," "The Menace of Science," "Enemies of the People," and "Slavery Vs. Freedom." Riley then began promoting himself as Dick Scott the "Cowboy Philosopher" and "the worst act in show business." In 1945 he went East and dropped the pseudonym reverting to his real name and began appearing with Shorty Long's Sante Fe Rangers on WFIL radio in Philadelphia. He signed a recording contract in the Fall of 1945 in New York City while also employed by a music publishing company. The postwar era was his most prolific and the height of his popularity. He recorded and performed with a number of bands while using different names, signing a copious amount of recording and publishing contracts that were often legally in conflict with previous contracts and agreements. During this time he also worked in booking and management and was a driving force behind the Federation of American Folk Artists (FAFA), an early organization that strove to bring greater prestige, pay, and respect to professional country musicians. For a few months in 1947, he was based in Oklahoma City with his friends The Thomas Family Trio and hosted the weekly CBS broadcast of The Oklahoma Roundup. He finished the 1940s back East signing with and recording for a number of record labels often breaking or not fulfilling the contracts. By the mid-1950s his career was in decline, and he was mostly forgotten largely due to his scams, shifty dealings, and wearing out his welcome in the recording industry. Disc-Jockeys were asking *Billboard* magazine what happened to him, and the magazine called him "the one-armed paperhanger of folk music." For the remainder of the decade and into the 1960s he occasionally worked under pseudonyms such as Dixon Hall while performing on western and historical recordings and as a disc-jockey under the name Riley Cooper. He struggled financially to make ends meet.

When Stacya was born in 1965 her father had used at least eighteen different pen names including the previous mentioned nom de plumes as well as Richard James, Ben Thomas, Johnny Rebel, Hickey Free, Dick Gleason, Klym Hawley, Rex Cross, Milton Cross, Zachary Quill, Logan Stanwyck, Jan Yakish, Paul Lester, Richard Alexander, Albert Reilly, Richard James, Floyd Riley Shepard, Melody Barr, Jean Gilmore, Henry Paul, Riley Kirk, Annasuss Coleridge, and Rebman Shaftesbury. These shifting aliases were used for songwriting, ASCAP royalties, radio shows, avoiding detection of infidelity with several girlfriends while married, eluding the victims of his previous schemes and scams, and penning pornography. In the late 1960s, he authored a considerable amount of pulp-paperback pornography, sometimes under his actual name of Riley Shepard. Some of the books read like "history of sex" textbooks, with titles like "The Sexual Instinct," "Erotica Around the World (Marvels of Human Sexuality)," "Sex Potential Through Astrology," and "Satyricon of Petronius Arbiter, Translated and Adapted by Riley Shepard. Erotic Realism Press, 1969." As Zachary Quill; "Whoring Through the Ages, A History of Harlotry, Illustrated," "Lesbianism Through the Ages," "Heterosexual:ity," and "Sex and Sexcraft (Animal and Human)." Using a mix of the mentioned names, he wrote provocatively titled paperback pulp novels such as "Pick a Country Piece," "The Sex Fighter," The Homosexual Motif," "The Sex Screamer," The Starlet and the Satyr," "The Proud Prostitute," "The Dirty Producer," and "The Pussy Hunt."

Riley would search used books stores for novels published before 1909, to avoid copyright entanglements and would modernize the story by changing things like, horse and carriage to car, changing names and locations, and then adding the sex scenes. He rented an office on Hollywood Boulevard near the Hollywood Theatre and hired a typing pool of women to add his porn scenes in specified spots of the stories. When he ran out of money to pay the typists or the rent, he would go home and make huge trays of his special recipe cheesecake and sell it to Musso & Frank's Grill. He would get about thirty dollars a tray and with that money would finish the books and have them sent off to the printer. He was eventually locked out of the office by the landlord for back rent and lost his typewriters, unfinished manuscripts, and even some paintings done by his wife and mother of Stacya.

On moving into the Criswell apartments, Riley set up a "wacky" barter to help Halo with her songwriting skills in exchange for rent.

STACYA SILVERMAN: My father was supposedly helping Criswell and Halo with their show business aspirations in exchange for rent. We moved into the apartment right under their place. Criswell was already publishing books and doing well as a celebrity psychic, while Halo struggled to write songs and plays without success, so Dad was coaching her. She told him that SHE was really the psychic one and came up with many of Criswell's predictions. She insisted that ghostly fingers directed her piano playing, and that's how she wrote her songs. She adored my father, hated me most of the time, and my mother couldn't stand her. When I was three, she told my mother that I wasn't really a baby, that in fact, I was an old lady, reborn. "Children are born to suck the life out of adults. They are the reason we wither and die. If no more babies were born, we could live forever," she said. She used to wander over to my school yard at Selma Street School and hover over our sandbox, saying crazy things. Back then, random people could just wander over to the school yard. Strange.

She sunbathed obsessively, lost and gained weight on yo-yo diets, all the while drinking gin all day, it was hard on her body.

My mother told me that Criswell had her institutionalized once or twice. One time after she took out a bunch of cash and handed it out to random people on Hollywood Boulevard. She found out Criswell was telling everyone that his wife was dead and she was so angry that she withdrew a few thousand dollars from the bank and was handing out $100 bills to people. Criswell had her committed and had her family restrict her allowance to five dollar-a-week spending money. By the time I was five years old, Criswell and my father were having small disagreements. My parents told me he was a bigot, and that he'd chased my black friends off the property, and once he chased off Maria Graciette's kid, because he saw a brown kid and forgot the child was Maria's. One day, they had a shouting match that seemed to shake the walls. I remember the day well. After that, we moved quickly. I never found out what the actual disagreement was, my parents said it was a political argument that spiraled out of control, but I wonder if it was about money.

In 1968, Droke House Publishers, Inc., Anderson, South Carolina published Criswell's first book of predictions, *Criswell Predicts*

From Now to the Year 2000! Wilton E. Hall Jr., who also owned the *Anderson Daily Mail,* which had been publishing Criswell's column for over ten years also owned Droke House which would publish all three of his books of predictions. Hall also owned the *Anderson Independent* newspaper, two radio stations, founded a television station, published the magazine called *Quote,* and was appointed to the United States Senate as a Democrat on November 22, 1944, to fill the vacancy caused by the death of Ellison D. Smith. He served until January 3, 1945, and did not run for re-election resuming his newspaper publishing business.

Lewis N. Schilling, Jr. designed *CPY2K* and its eye-popping op-art cover featuring Criswell's disembodied head, along with illustrating some of the predictions vividly with surrealistic, graphic, black and white line drawings. The page opposite the copyright page has a picture of Criswell's disembodied head staring intently. The next page has a photo of Baby Criswell opposite the first page of the Preface which begins "I wasn't always Criswell Predicts: Once I was Baby Criswell!" He then continues to recount his past as previously quoted, closing the Preface with:

> When Droke House Publishers approached me to do this book, I merely released to them "Journal of the Future:"—my private collection of what will happen between now and the end of our civilization—1999!
>
> My predictions are not written to win literary attention. I am not sure what they all mean. Some are frighteningly explicit. Others are somewhat vague. All are based on conscious study and sub-conscious "realizations."
>
> I pass them along to you as I have recorded them.
>
> Over the next thirty years, you may keep your own "score" as to their accuracy.
>
> After that, it will not matter.

The first prediction after the preface is titled:

HOMOSEXUAL CITIES

I predict that perversion will flood the land beginning in 1970. I predict a series of homosexual cities, small, compact, carefully planned areas, will soon be blatantly advertised and exist coast to coast. These compact communities will be complete with streets, churches, bars and restaurants which will put the olden Greeks or Romans to shame with their organized orgies. You will be able to find them near Boston, Des Moines, Columbus, Philadelphia, Washington D.C., San Francisco, St. Louis, New Orleans, Dallas and Miami."

He then foresees that birth control chemicals will be placed in the water system of every major city in the country and that "the electricity that comes into each home will have certain ionic particles that cause contraception." He goes on to say that birth control will be a function of the Federal government. In another prognostication he says that by 1982, a full medical education will only require six months of study. Criswell had attended pre-med school in his college days but dropped out.

He then turns his sights on outer space:

SPACE STATIONS

The U.S. and Russia will, separately and jointly, during the 1970s, begin to set up space stations. Progress will be slow until the late 1970s, when discovery of anti-magnetism forces will free man from the laws of gravity and make space travel without rocket propulsion possible.

I predict that man's exploration of space and the building of space stations will be the salvation of the human race.

By 1999, there will be more than 200 of these space stations in existence. They will house entire colonies—men, women and children.

When the earth is destroyed on August 18, 1999, these space colonists will be the only Earth-humans left in the Universe. But they will not be able to return to Earth for many years because this planet will not support human life for more than 400 years after the holocaust of 1999.

He then predicts a Hollywood suicide, television education, and an "Aphrodesian Era" caused by "a spray that is almost odorless but when breathed stimulates the most basic sexual erotic areas." This would lead to mass nudity and sex acts performed openly on the streets. An antidote would be found, and the entire nation would be dusted by airplanes, effectively stopping the shameless activities.

Edgar Cayce has been called "the greatest prophet of the twentieth century" and been compared to Nostradamus. He would put himself into a self-induced sleep state or trance that enabled him to place his mind in contact with all time and space. Questions would be put to him, and he would respond with what he called "readings." Cayce came to the public's attention when it was told he was a "healer" and gave "health readings" in which a patient would be diagnosed and a cure prescribed. His business card described him as a "psychic diagnostician." He gave 25,000 to 30,000 "readings" over a forty-three year period of his life. A stenographer took notes during some of the sessions which produced over 14,000 transcripts. Cayce channeled information on many esoteric subjects, now called "New Age," including reincarnation, astrology, meditation, ESP, the secrets of Atlantis, and the "Cayce Diet." He also prophesied on religious prophecy telling of the unknown life of Jesus and how he was a soul like us who reincarnated through several lifetimes, making many mistakes, finally achieving "Christhood" to which we also should aspire. Some of his "readings" allude to pole shifts of the Earth, which would bring about the rising of Atlantis, the sinking of California, or another coming of Christ. This was to have occurred in 1998. Criswell of course aligns himself with Cayce.

It was Edgar Cayce, known as the, 'Sleeping Prophet,' who beheld visions of our future which have come to pass. And it is in interpreting his visions, that I have found visions of my own regarding the incredible future.

Elsewhere in this book I have written of the shifting coastlines of our Eastern seaboard and the disappearance of such cities as New York and San Francisco. Edgar Cayce and I share this vision.

We share, too, the vision of the lost continent which shall arise from the depths of the ocean in the mid 1980's. It will comprise a virtual bridge between western Africa and eastern South America. And upon it we will find the ruins of a lost civilization which has come down to us through the annals of time as the continent of Atlantis. When this body of land rises from the depths of the ocean, where it has lain hidden thousands of centuries, the ruins man explores upon it will answer many mysteries about the history of our world. Particularly we will know the secret of the Mayans and Incas. It will, in many ways not yet clear, convey to man how this earth shall end in 1999.

Other predictions in the book include the destruction of Denver, the assassination of Fidel Castro, floods, droughts, earthquakes, London destroyed by a meteor, widespread cannibalism, predictions for each of the fifty states, and many more too numerous, far out, and outrageous to reprint here.

He takes the reader on a trip to future and what a day in their life will be like on:

June 1, 1995

Let us venture, you and I, to the year 1995. Dismiss the present moment filled with personal worry and grief. Shake off the shackles of man-measured time and man-made distance, and let us, in the twinkling of an eye transplant our personalities to June 1st, 1995—a mere few years ahead. You doubtless have anticipated a visit to a place that you've never been to, in fact you have projected yourself so thoroughly that when you actually were there you were slightly disappointed! You lived for the moment in reverse. Let us do the same thing now! . . . What is a mere few years to the millions of years already past? Even five minutes from now is the future—so why fear it? Come with me to this day in 1995!

You awaken in the bright sunshine of your room. As you lie in your boxed bed and look up to see a glass ceiling of stainless gervo, so transparent that it is hardly visible to the naked eye!

He goes on to guide the reader through a day filled with nudism and easy leisure. The only division between the peoples of the future seems to be based on choices in diet, with the "Pill Takers" and the "Bulk Takers" as rivals in "public debate and riotous demonstrations . . . You will no longer class yourself as a 'Republican' or 'Democrat' but as a 'Pill Taker' or a 'Bulk Taker'—and these are true fighting words in 1995!" After you enjoy your breakfast reconstituted from concentrates, you notice "a voice that seems to float on air—soothing, clear and in measured sentences, giving you the news of the day: 'And here is the news of the day—and today is a very routine day—The scheduled flight to Mars, Venus and Neptune by a group of holiday seekers was suddenly called off today because of the full eclipse of the sun. The authorities feel that they do not wish to be responsible for a similar accident as happened last year when the moon eclipse was visible and caused a shift in gravity, which ripped the ship apart in midair. The Government will no longer be responsible for the health and welfare of individuals who rebel against the new edict of the eight hours of sleep requirements, careful watch on the calorie totals consumed and flagrant violation of not using the outdoor swimming pools three times a week. All law breakers will be segregated until their habits are corrected. In your homes tonight you will enjoy one of the treats of 1995—it is the famous film, all talking, color and music—of a novel called 'Gone With the Wind' circa 1939—and although the film is only 60 years old, it clearly shows the misdirected thinking of that period. You will laugh all the way through it at the quaint language, customs and philosophy. Other items will be an antiquated Mickey Mouse Cartoon, a travelogue showing our National Capitol before it was moved to Wichita, and a style show of 1962. The style show is excruciatingly funny—This all-request period of revivals of 1940 to 1965, is of extreme interest to everyone as it clearly shows how the misdirected energy of that period brought ruin. And now if you will stand by, your complete daily paper will be delivered to you." The visitor to the future tears a long roll of paper from a slit in the wall and reads from the clear and bold type "Children's classes in Occultism, Astrology, Spiritualism and Hypnotism will start as planned in the City Park, with a special course in Numerology added for the semester." After reading the paper, "You decide to go out into the street and find it a thriving place" with small buildings and shops neatly spaced with vegetable gardens because "There are no real shopping malls, no actual cities, as population has been scattered and decentralized after the disasters of the 70's and 80's." All the products in the shops are generic with no variety, trademarks, or brand names and this "mono-market" extends to automobiles, autogyros, tires, etc.... "The civilization of 1995 is absolutely through with the frills and the fancies that once kept man and woman constant economic bondage. The change has been gradual but severe. No garment has a tight bodice or an uncomfortable stiff collar, and they continually stay in style. The most popular cloth is of balloon weight, semi-transparent, an equal conductor of heat or cold, made from 'gervo." The time traveler then takes a ride on an atomic driven bus that noiselessly runs "on a column of air above the surface of the highly polished street." Fellow passengers are all taller than average, thin, and have all their hair and good teeth because "The full socialization of medicine has forced each and every individual to have perfect health! Scientifically developed health is the order of the day and the law of the times. Everyone seems in a very pleasant frame of mind. There are no personal worries and no one is in a great hurry, as everything is running on schedule." He goes to describe a new way of life in a world populated by equally and uniformly educated offspring of artificial insemination and that there are no deformities, slums, poverty or hunger and "The question of love is purely put on a scientific basis without emotion and tenderness. There are a few that are romantically conceived, but they are of inferior stock." "Basketball, football, soccer, tennis, boxing and racing are extinct. People find looking on any sports events as very dull, and only enjoy sport if they are active participants." "Religion has ceased to be cultish, but there is an overall concept that everyone agrees to. The leaders of religion are women because men have

259

misused this great truth and caused wars, privation and want! But all of man and woman's efforts to perfect this imperfect world will have been in vain, for this day, June 1, 1995, is a scant four years, two months and seventeen days before the end of this civilization we call Earth." The section called "Beginning of the End" starts to wrap up the book proclaiming "Yes, the fate of the world is in your hands. But our greed, plus the genius of science will destroy. The final war, the most terrible war, is at the very end of the Ribbon of Time." The next piece is his "Vision of the End" followed lastly by:

THE END

The world as we know it will cease to exist, as I have previously stated in this volume, on August 18, 1999.

A study of all the prophets—Nostradamus, St. Odile, Mother Shipton, the Bible—indicates that we will cease to exist before the year 2000! And if you and I meet each other on the street that fateful day, August 18, 1999, and we chat about what we will do on the morrow, we will open our mouths to speak and no words will come out, for we have no future . . . you and I will suddenly run out of time!

A trade paperback version of *CPY2K* was published without illustrations in 1969, by Grosset & Dunlap.

February 24, 1968, *The Daily Mail,* "THEY Likely Are Watching Us"

I predict that when you step outside tonight you will feel a touch of insecurity, and you will know that they are watching from another world! In the past 30 days we have had repeated reports of strange radio coded messages . . . of moving lights in the milky way . . . of strange vibratory actions which hamper TV reception and stop delicate mechanism of our watches, clocks and automation machinery! Could they be on the lookout for a safe place to land? Could they be planning an invasion foretold by H.G. Wells, Jules Verne or by Lewis Carroll? Perhaps they could be upon us before we knew it! How will it happen? This is what you will read on your front page: "THEY ARE HERE!" will be the headline and the story will follow: Dateline Bridgeport Conn. Jan. 30, 1978. Yes, contact today was made with the invading army from the other side of the moon! The invading armada landed from the air in the Long Island straits opposite Bridgeport tonight. "They are awaiting dawn for action!" exclaimed the mayor of Bridgeport as he exchanged greetings by instant thought wave mechanics. "They are using solar rays for power and can only operate full strength when in the sunlight," he thoughtfully added. "This could be no worse than the great freeze of last year when even the air turned to solid ice and we had to resort to our powerful personal oxygen making machines to survive. The moon general was evidently a woman as she became very intimate in her conversation with me!" In the meantime, Bridgeport, Conn., stands by!

May 1, Criswell was back on *The Tonight Show* with Joan Rivers, Jon Lindbergh, Paul Newman, and Harry Belafonte. In a promotional mailer/pamphlet for his book, Criswell claimed that the predictions in the pamphlet were recorded and sealed along with the video tape of the entire program to be opened and shown on the future *Tonight Show* on December 31, 1985.

He made the cover of the May 10 *Princeton Daily Clarion* with a story titled "Criswell Predicts on Walnut Street" by Frank Roberson. The article tells of the writer's visit and informal interview with Criswell at his aunt Ruth Mullhall's home in Princeton. He was in town for the funeral services of his second cousin, Helen

Hopkins Bellah who had passed away the day after Thanksgiving at her home in Santa Monica. The writer said of Criswell, "Without the make up and sequin suits we are used to seeing him wear, his manner changes and off stage, although he's a performer and you wouldn't mistake him for the man next door, he seems like a warm sympathetic man with a great personal charm. In spite of four decades spent away from southern Indiana, the Hooiser in Criswell is identifiable, and he seems more than a little proud of it." "Something about the man, perhaps his speech, or maybe his poise, creates a quiet sensation of success. It's a bit disconcerting to discover that he's not what you expected and, once you've met him, you're never quite sure what you did expect." During the interview Criswell spoke of his memories of Princeton, its people, his family and friends. He talked quite a bit about the creative side of writing and his predictions. He said most of his predictions result from analyzing the financial pages. He claimed that if you interpret the information in an average newspaper, you can predict many things at least six months in advance. When asked about the hard time he and Johnny Carson sometimes seemed to give each other on *The Tonight Show*, he laughed and said it seemed unrehearsed, but was done off of cue cards. He called Carson a quiet, nice guy type of performer and gentleman. Criswell gave the writer a copy of his *CPY2K* book from which the writer quotes several of the "best" predictions. A photo accompanying the article showed Criswell reading from the book to his aunt. The article told of his plans to return to Halo and their Hollywood home over the weekend and how the couple were both animal lovers and would spend much time with their two dogs, a Kerry blue terrier named Buttercup and a Spaniel named Mr. Chips. He also stated that he was the national president of the St. Francis Animal Welfare Society and an honorary officer in the Mercy Crusade. The article related Criswell's plans of going on tour to promote the new book and the making of two films over the summer. One called *Capitol Dome* and the other entitled *Somebody Walked Over My Grave*. The article concluded. "As an opportunity to look for a moment behind the scenes with a celebrity in the quiet confines of a Princeton living room with a real personality instead of an image, the hour with Criswell was well spent." Criswell also visited Littlestown and again addressed the Rotary Club as reported in the local newspaper. A photo accompanied the article showing him explaining his published book to his father-in-law and the president of the club.

After Bobby Kennedy was assassinated, an article appeared in the *Sheboygan Press*, June 5, 1968, with a man-in-the-street reaction: Everett Larson of Hinsdale, Ill., a publisher's representative for Grosset & Dunlap, opened a brochure he was carrying and pointed to the name of a book, "Criswell Predicts to the Year 2000." "Criswell in this book predicted another tragedy in the Kennedy family." said Larson.

June 26 the "psychic The Amazing Criswell," appeared on the *Mike Douglas Show* with co-host Joey Heatherton. Other guests were folk singer Trini Lopez, comedian Joey Villa, and Flamenco dancers Julio Piedra and Company.

On July 7 the headline, "The Amazing Predictions of Criswell" appeared on the cover of the tabloid *Candid Press*. Inside the sensationalist magazine is not one of his columns, but a single page book review "exclusively for Candid Press" by Jeff Lee. The article is accompanied by the promo photo from *Revenge of the Dead* of Criswell rising from the coffin. The review begins with the more racy, prurient predictions from the book then tells of his appearances on the Carson and Paar shows and the laughter he received for his outrageous prediction about Ronald Reagan becoming Governor of California. It points out his other correct, but vague predictions concerning JFK, MLK, Nick Adams, and Jayne Mansfield, as well as "America's top folk-rock singer will commit suicide during Easter

Weekend 1969. This could refer to Bob Dylan—and it could also refer to one of a dozen other folk-rockers—all of whom are noted for fits of blue depression which could lead to suicide." "Criswell's book itself is not a gem of literary merit. Since this is a book review, we are forced to admit that Criswell the writer leaves a great deal to desire, but then, as Criswell himself admits, 'My predictions are not written to win literary attention.' Like many people who predict the future, Criswell masks his predictions in vagueness and the reader must then decide what he is saying. This is part of the fun of reading Criswell's book." The review goes on to say, "Criswell predicted that nudity and sex will infiltrate Broadway—and 'Hair,' the newest folk-rock play on Broadway does just that." This is followed by a list of more specific predictions from the book. The last section of the review is titled "Sex Transplants."

Some of Criswell's predictions are funny such as 'clamp on bikinis for men,' sex organ transplants in 1971 and John Kennedy Jr. becoming U.S. Senator (but not president). Some are interesting such as proof that there is life on other planets and the emergence of a Negro named Sanders in 1972 who will lead all Black men to Mississippi. Criswell's book must be read with many grains of salt as well as with a sense of humor, because until we know if Criswell is actually putting us all on or not, his book "Criswell Predicts" can either be one of the funniest books ever written—or one that is cause for monumental alarm throughout the world.

The lower portion of the article has "CRISWELL'S DEATH PARADE!" in large bold print with photos of Martin Luther King, Nick Adams, the planet Earth, Bob Dylan, and Jayne Mansfield.

July 8, Criswell was back with his predictions on the *Merv Griffin Show* with comics Soupy Sales and Nipsey Russell, singers Bobby

Goldsboro, Monti Rock III, and Gloria Loring. Then August 13, back on *The Tonight Show* with Don Adams, Don Rickles, Sonny and Cher, and Sherry Jackson.

Criswell began making public appearances at department stores and bookstores promoting, selling, and autographing his new book advertised as the "amazingly accurate historical and political foreseer . . . now author." On September 13, he started a string of appearances at Bullock's department store through November in honor of the store's tenth anniversary called "Ten to Remember." An advertisement for the gala event stated:

Visit with Criswell Predicts in Person. This September's Friday the Thirteenth, Criswell will visit our Book Gallery, Second Floor, to autograph his book, Criswell Predicts . . . the significance of the date had prompted him to predict once again . . . this time. . . BULLOCK'S 1978!

I predict that I will again visit BULLOCK'S on September 13, 1978 . . . but at that time you will see Bullock's as a towering merchandise mart . . . ten floors with automatic moving sidewalks . . . where you may choose your purchases in an unhurried manner . . . a beauty salon where you may have your face instantly lifted and your hips reduced by ten pounds in ten seconds . . . a huge dress emporium where a dress can be instantly designed, fitted to your figure within ten minutes . . . the choice will be made by automation and if it does not do the best for you, it is rejected by the machine . . . your husband will have his figure trimmed in a high school fashion . . . a new head of hair transplanted by radar . . . and a brain transplant if he has the time! Santa Ana will be a thriving city of high rise own-your-own apartments, sport and park pavilions . . . you will live on Bullock's vitamin and youth pills . . . and under the sky dome roof you will find everything that you need from cradle to coffin . . . in fact you could enter Bullock's at birth (or even be born there) and never leave, for everything is a Bullock's service! Yes, in 1978 Bullock's will be a city within a city yet your every personal need will be met personally!

We have a date on September 13, 1978, just ten years from now, so meet us again at the new Bullock's! Always in your future, Criswell.

On September 13, Bullock's hosted their "Ten to Remember" ten-year anniversary event in the gardens surrounding the Bullock's Fashion Square in downtown Santa Ana. Proceeds from the event would benefit seven Orange County charities. The event included a buffet supper, open bars, parking for 3,000 cars, dance music by the Lynn Willis Orchestra with a repertoire of 1958 tunes, "of course, included will be the sounds of today. . . ", a fashion show, art galleries, the "Up With People" young people's singing group, and of course the well promoted chance to "Meet Mr. Criswell . . . let him predict your future." On October 18, he performed two shows in their tenth floor auditorium with "his astounding predictions from now to the year 2000!" He appeared that evening at the Studio City Theatre with Judy Canova and Tor Johnson along with the costars of the movie *Shalako* (1968), Stephen Boyd, Woody Strode, Chief Elmer Smith, and Rodd Redwing. Sean Connery and Brigitte Bardot were the stars of the film but didn't appear. November 22, Criswell held two book signings at Bullock's Pasadena in the Toys and Books section on the upper level.

September 18, Criswell spoke at the first annual "Past Boss of the Year Night" hosted by the Santa Monica Chapter of the National Secretaries Association held at the Surf Rider Inn in Santa Monica and made a personal appearance on December 3 at the Ventura Club, For Single Adults over 25 . . . Meeting Place for Dance Lovers, in Sherman Oaks.

The last year of the turbulent, change-filled 1960s, proved to be a chaotic and eventful time for the United States, the World, and Criswell as well. His record album of predictions was released, his second book of predictions was published, Halo moved from Hollywood, and he was arrested.

January 1, 1969, *The Daily Mail*:

Russia To Pose International Shock
I predict that many readers of this column will be amazed to find how far ahead this series of predictions and forecasts are compared to the newsletters of the commercial world! Time after time this column has scored weeks before in an exclusive prediction and here is another for you to ponder! I predict that Russia will invade the Middle East before the snow, so be prepared for an international shock!

The Soviet Union would not invade Afghanistan until Christmas 1979. This prediction was only about a decade off the mark.

January 22 he was back on the *Mike Douglas Show* co-hosted by Ethel Merman with guests Tony Lynch, Buddy Rich, and Sandler & Young.

Criswell's vinyl record album of predictions was released on Horoscope Records and called *The Legendary Criswell Predicts! Your Incredible Future.* The 12-inch LP is forty-two minutes in length and chocked full of some of his most outrageous and best remembered predictions. A number of them are from *CPY2K* book. He opens the album with his signature line followed by this bold and somewhat accurate political prognostication.

I predict that politics will make stranger bedfellows than ever before. I fearlessly predict that the once politically in-active South will rise again in no uncertain terms! I predict that every vote South of the Mason-Dixon line could easily be conservative! I predict there will be two political parties in America, one will be the Conservative party and the other will be the Liberal party. There will be a clean cut division which no one could consciously cross over. This startling trend will become most apparent before the next election and you will join heartedly in this stand whether you want to or not. Now don't say you won't, because I predict you will!

He then goes on to predict a new "unisex" trend in fashion followed by a prediction on one of his favorite topics.

I was not allowed to say on television, radio or have it appear in my column, as the advertisers would clomp down on me, and clomp very heavily. I further predict the new age of nudity for the human body will be glorified. Body designs, self-painted, will take up most of your spare time. Women will decorate their breasts with startling colors, while men will decorate their genitals!

He boldly predicts womankind's domination over men and the world saying, "So what are we poor men to do? Personally, I welcome it, because we men have made such a mess of things that you women must naturally come to our rescue and do better!" He then follows that with this prediction that shows that all is not lost for the male race.

I predict that you will not be able to turn this record off as they turned me off on the Johnny Carson program with my following prediction. I predict every able-bodied man in America will be asked to contribute to a sperm bank! This will later be used in artificial insemination if and when a holocaust should occur. This sperm bank will be open twenty-four hours a day and a night depository would be accepted. This for the eventuality that the male of the species might become extinct!

He goes on to forecast medical attention by vending machines, embalming by radar which turns the body into indestructible stone, a sacred cremation where your ashes are placed in a warhead missile and fired into outer space, a push-button world, celebrity scandals, years of "riot, rape, and revelry," when "some gutters will flow with blood as rain after a spring shower!" He then looks at the problem of overpopulation with this insightful remark, "I predict there will always be more people, but there will never be more land." He continues with prediction after prediction including; the death penalty for freeloaders, a new world government, flying saucers landing on the lawn of the Whitehouse on May 6, 1991, nudist funeral processions, nude bathing on all public beaches and pools within ten years, a one shot serum that will cure every disease, public executions on TV sponsored by the local gas company, floating cities suspended by anti-gravity, and education pills. Criswell then warns that squeamish listeners and children should leave the room as he reveals the scourge of our time. "I predict that there is one enemy we have not conquered and in our lifetime we never will conquer . . . and that is leprosy! Leprosy, yes, leprosy! The curse of the ancients, the blemish of the present and the scar on the festering face of the future!" He gives graphic descriptions of the dread disease and questions why the "modern men of medicine" have not yet eradicated it. He rants on the subject for over four minutes. He then predicts a "twilight of terror" when the Panama Canal is closed due to international scandal concerning its use.

Being one of his favorite ancient prognosticators, he quotes Nostradamus extensively saying, "Remember the words of Nostradamus for he has yet to be proven wrong!" After more quotes from Nostradamus, Criswell makes this bold statement "Oh my friend, coming events have already cast their shadows and whether you believe it or not, this is all to be a part of your INCREDIBLE future! Mother Nature destroys as Mother Nature creates, for this is the law of life. Time is endless and the future is only a continuation of the past!" He then goes on a five-minute rant about medicine and doctors reporting that "In the past, medicine was far from enough, at this very moment it is only adequate, but in your incredible future, medicine will conquer that which plagues us today and even the common cold and the simple headache will become a thing of the past, excepting of course . . . leprosy!" He predicts organ transplants and the extensive use of hypnosis in medicine from birth to death. He next predicts a golden age when women will dominate the world, controlling everything from finance to politics.

Men will take a backseat and lose their influence in your very, very incredible future. Remember, it was also a woman back in 1448, Mother Shipton by name who foretold, "The day of shame will come to pass, no clothes will wear the lad or lass. Who doff the shawl, and trousers too, and romp amid the morning dew." Yes, Mother Shipton was quite right. Never in the history of our world, have we dressed so briefly on the beach, in the garden or on the streets. I predict that it will only be a matter of time, when you will join a nudist camp or health farm and enjoy the complete freedom of nudity. The human body is nothing to be ashamed of, for we were all born in the likeness of God. And remember it will be in your lifetime, when you will walk down the street, you will shop and you will attend the theater in the nude. And perhaps in this very same city.

He continues with more predictions from Mother Shipton followed by a Black Friday started by a madman dictator that prints every currency of the world then releases it into the markets, causing anarchy and a wave of suicides. He reiterates his prediction of the world coming to an end on August 18, 1999, with a four-minute spiel on its destruction and aftermath. "The fortunate few who survive must find new worlds. Perhaps the Moon, Venus, or Mars. Or perhaps a far-off undiscovered universe beyond the sun." He follows these apocalyptic revelations with some innocuous and obscure Hollywood predictions but with the same force and conviction as his visions of Armageddon. He then goes on a patriotic rant.

Oh my friend, I only hope you realize at this prediction what we face in the future. The days will grow long, the nights will grow shorter, and I predict that truly nothing will change. Because the precepts of America, of God, of home, mother, and honor will stay. And we will always know within our hearts, no matter what the atheistic cry from the hilltops may be, that prayer changes things. And you and I in the still hours of the very short nights will come to this realization, for nothing can defeat the human heart of the American. No matter where we go, we are the indestructible, the incorruptible, and the unconquered.

Criswell then makes a forecast about unprecedented weather and natural disaster over the following three years and begins closing the album.

And in closing, I would like to say, oh my friend, when all else is lost, remember the wonderful future still remains. Now when you see me on the street, come up and speak to me, for that is the only way that you and I can ever win our war against our loneliness. I'll be lonely without you. And may all your shattered dreams be mended by morning and may success overtake you overnight. Goodnight my dearest friend and God bless you."

You can hear the exclamation marks as Criswell reads his prognostications in his stentorian, Toastmasters trademarked voice. The sound of rustling papers is heard at times, and he stumbles on certain words and phrases but recovers quickly like any good public speaker would. Apparently the budget of the recording session didn't allow for any retakes of the mistakes and stumbles. A number of predictions are verbatim from the *CPY2K* book.

Your Next Ten Years—Criswell Predicts was published in 1969, by Droke House and distributed by Grosset & Dunlap. Like *CPY2K*, it was designed and illustrated by Lewis N. Schilling, Jr. with an op-art cover and more bizarre illustrations. A trade paperback version of *YN10YCP* without illustrations was published in 1971.

The page before the Preface is inscribed "Dedicated To My Wife Halo Meadows." The Preface gives more insight into his past and has been previously quoted. After the preface he introduces the book.

LET THE RECORD SHOW...

My predictions come true at an amazing rate. In my first book, *Criswell Predicts to the Year 2000!*, I predicted "the assassination of the nation's top Civil Rights leader" who, of course, was Dr. Martin Luther King. And many other of my predictions in that book have come true or are coming true. Many of the predictions in this book will refer to my more expansive commentary on the subject in my earlier book

Then, as now, I invite the reader to "keep record" of my predictions and see for himself whether these things come to pass.

Cruswell

The next page is the FOREWORD:

O my Friend...
    Let us pause for a moment!
    For after us the deluge!
    Our glittering world will soon be a smoldering cinder of a world!
    The sins we do one by one are paid for two by two!
    And in the next ten years, the story will be told!
    Do not ask for whom the bells toll for it might be for you! Scientists tell us that we are a world of duplicates, triplicates, and trillionates...for this world and every item in it is duplicated a trillion times over in the vast universe of nearby space! Why should you feel lonely when you have a trillion counterparts? Do the other trillion feel as lonely as you? Are you fair to them?
    The coming ten years may frighten you, but remember, of all the times to be alive, this is the time!
    On this purgatory planet, I predict we will survive. But, while we live...the deluge!

Cruswell

On the first page of predictions:

CURTAIN GOING UP

Yes, my friend, the curtain is going up on the most exciting ten years of the 20th century! You have a front row seat... reserved just for you!

Of all the time to be alive, the time is now!

The orchestra is in an overture!

The actors, you and I, are moving into our stage positions!

The lights brighten . . . the music swells . . . and the curtain rises!

You and I among every man, woman and child on earth are in the cast . . . all controlled by the Supreme Puppet Master Himself . . . and motivated by orders from above!

We are both the cast and the audience and the world is the theater!

We laugh at our mistakes and make our own jokes!

We are at the core of every crisis, every event and any joy!

We keep our eye on the program, and can hiss the villain and applaud the hero!

For that very villain and that hero is a part of you and me!

The marvels of the next ten years will seem like miracles to us now, but in 1980 we

will take them all for granted!

On with the show!

In this volume Criswell predicts the events that will befall America and the world during the decade of the 1970s, like a new science called "Femology" (the rebuilding of women), electricity without wires, the first divorce in the White House, a new black America, a mind machine, a cannibal cookbook, and:

THE CONTENTED DISCONTENTS

I predict a new breed of civilians in the next ten years! The Contented Discontents!

These will be the disgruntled citizenry who are and will be content with merely complaining! They will gripe, gripe, gripe from morning until night, and yet will not do one thing themselves about it! They will gripe on the way of government, taxes, crime, sex, death costs, insurance, landlords, weather, transportation, traffic, bi-sexuality, homosexuality, heterosexuality and no sexuality at all. You will find this breed of the discontented very happy just criticizing!

Criswell then answers the 101 questions most-often asked him:

Q: Have you chosen your epitaph and where will you be entombed?

A: I will be entombed in my hometown where I was born . . . Princeton, Indiana, where the White, Patoka and Ohio Rivers converge. It will be either in the Archer Cemetery or the Odd Fellows. I am yet to decide as I have a space in both. I had chosen my epitaph "All we golden boys and girls must, as chimney sweeps, return to dust!" but now I have changed it to "World weary Criswell Predicts, Back home again in Indiana!" However I do not plan to make use of this tomb for some time, as my plans at the present time are endless!

Q: What do you predict new in music?

A: I predict a new sound—a new beat! This will take the place of Rock/Roll as this sound is dead and the market glutted with the corpses of many well-meaning artists and song writers! I predict that the new beat will be known as "One

World Jazz" and will inherit the musical earth! The Dixie Land Beat will live again in a more glamorous way!

Q: Can you predict where the Homosexual, the Bisexual and the Heterosexual Capitols will be located?

A: I predict that the Homosexual capitol will be Des Moines, Iowa, the Bisexual capitol will be Pasadena, California and the Heterosexual capitol will be Erie, Pennsylvania.

Q: What will be the next trend in radio and TV, business wise?

A: I predict that TV and Radio Sponsors will give definite orders to their advertising agencies NOT to buy commercial spots on any TV or radio program which campaigns for the "legalization of marijuana," is "pro-hippy and praises the student demonstrations and racial protests and shows a disrespect for the flag, for religion and for the government! This tends to create a "subconscious boycott" of the sponsor's products as no one will buy a recommended product by a radio-TV personality supporting the new left!

He ends the book and wraps up the decade of the seventies with:

THE NIGHT IS DARK

It is December 31, 1979, the night is dark and we are far from home!

We are leaving the sensational seventies and into the eventual eighties!

The prologue has become our epilogue, and Time has become a huge pot of seething lava!

Already the clouds of more wars, more deaths, and ultimate destruction are on the horizon!

America will be invaded from within, but the mighty fortress will stand!

We will emerge in 1980 without a friendly nation in the world! We will recall the words of Benjamin Franklin who told us we could not buy loyalty, respect or friendship! We will also bitterly reflect on the warning of George Washington against foreign entanglements! But it will be too late, much too late!

Let us not cry out to the Heavens, but seek the peace within, our only saving grace.

For we have but *twenty more years* of this world as we know it!

TWENTY YEARS from 1979—in the year of 1999—all will cease.

And we will cease with it!

Criswell

1969

Writer Ken Hollings gave his impressions from a reading of the book.

Your Next Ten Years reads like the *Prophecies* of Michel de Nostredame rewritten by the staff of the Saturday Evening Post. For a work supposedly produced during the full flood of the Aquarian Age, it is strangely redolent of 1950s suburbia and its attendant preoccupations: a combination of fashion tips, financial forecasts, amazing labour-saving devices, spicy gossip and gloomy tales of impending social collapse.

And why not? During the fifties Criswell had made an entire career out of offering his audience a chance to peek inside the peepshow of the future. With the strident tones of a sideshow barker, he called the people away from their modern homes with their gleaming kitchens of chrome and formica, enticing them into his tent to watch the space-age burlesque that was in store for them. Nearly all of his predictions in *Your Next Ten Years* can be read as a nostalgic extension of that decade. It was, after all, a period that Criswell understood completely, and he shared its concerns. He also spoke its language, making its vaulting confidence and breathless sense of destiny his own. It is a rhetoric conspicuously absent today, where the future seems to be over before it even reaches us.

Myrtle's father, Howard, passed away on February 26, 1969, at the age of eighty-nine. His obituary outlined his life of community service and noted his $150,000 grant to the community of Littlestown, which made possible the construction of the town's swimming pool. Myrtle returned to Littlestown to live as she had threatened many times before. "Don't come back." her father had told her before in that Sunday sidewalk tone of his. "All you want to do is play music and raise dogs. You'll never be able to take it if you come back here." She returned to Littlestown to live in the family's pre-Civil War home with a black cockapoodle named Champ, and took daily four-mile walks.

Posted by Comely Mike on a blog site called "Unremitting Failure:" "Myrtle Louise Stonesifer was the town character when I was growing up. Every day, weather permitting, this old eccentric sat on the front stoop of her house on South Queen Street in some outrageous new getup, strumming a ukulele. When the town pool opened (built with money from her father's grant to the town), Myrtle had to be restrained from swimming topless. In other words, she was a total boho, living out her final days in our crappy one-traffic-light town. We called her Myrtle the Girdle. It was only later that we found out she was the ex-wife of the Amazing Criswell."

In a March 2, newspaper article Criswell claimed "Nixon in '72 will be a shoo-in" and then went on to predict that the big fad in 1969 would be transparent clothing, resembling shower curtains, for both men and women, Shirley Temple Black would be the first lady Governor of California, Tony Curtis would win the Oscar for *The Boston Strangler* (1968), but Barbara Streisand wouldn't win for *Funny Girl* (1968), Grace Kelly would get a divorce and marry into a big Chicago family and return to movie stardom, pregnant women would be the first astronauts to land on the moon, and a young Arkansas man would ask to be legally wed to his pet cat. When asked if it was true he once predicted that Mae West would become president he said. "No, that was misunderstood. I predicted that the first lady president would be someone *like* Mae West—with a magnetism for people, and who could be easily imitated." Nixon did win the 1972 election by a landslide, but Tony Curtis wasn't even nominated for an Oscar that year, Barbara Streisand did win one for Best Actress in a Leading Role for her portrayal of Fanny Brice in *Funny Girl*.

In April, Criswell was a celebrity auctioneer on the local Los Angeles Public Broadcasting Station KCET for their fundraiser called "Of Moonshots, Monkeys, and Minks!" Up for bid were reservations to the moon, a trip to Cape Kennedy to see the Apollo Ten Moonshot, a monkey with an organ grinder, a mink coat, a year's supply of bananas, Art objects, original Disney artwork, luxurious trips, a bucket of La Brea tar, and celebrity items like a Peggy Lee painting, Marlo Thomas' sun glasses, Fess Parker's original Daniel Boone buckskin jacket, and the highest bid would take Barbara Streisand's bikini (size 10). Other celebrity auctioneers included were Steve Allen, Joey Bishop, Buddy Ebsen, Henry Fonda, Henry Gibson, Michael Jackson, Sheriff Peter Pitchess, Chief Tom Reddin, Jack Warden, and Mayor Sam Yorty.

Judith Scobee was seventeen when she visited Criswell at his home in the month of May 1969. Someone at a poster shop on Hollywood Boulevard told her where he lived. She went by and looked, then later went back with two friends and a camera. They knocked on the door and the legendary Criswell came down to greet them in a robe. Judy asked if it would be alright to do a magazine article. He of course said yes and told them to wait a moment while he got dressed. He came out into the yard dressed in his business suit and gave Judy and her friends autographed copies of his *CPY2K* book along with some promo photos for the article. He also posed with his guests for a series of Polaroid photos. Judy said he was gracious to answer all her questions for her article, which is published here for the first time.

CRISWELL; Newsreporter of the Future

Right now you are all probably wondering what in heaven's name is a Criswell? Well, I'll tell you—he is the person who wrote the book called *Criswell Predicts—From Now to the Year 2000!* He also wrote *Your Next Ten Years* and now he has a record album called *Criswell Predicts.* In all of these he tells of things to come; some of which have all-ready come to past, afterwards.

He has predicted many things, for example, in 1965, (on the Tonight Show), he predicted that the next governor of California would be Ronald Reagan. At the time, people laughed and thought he was some kind of a nut. But, like many of his predictions which are laughed at, it came true! Another prediction, that came true with astounding accuracy, was when he was on the Jack Paar show when predicted that something would happen to President Kennedy in November of 1963 that would cause him not to run for re-election in 1964!

Criswell, as he is just called, has been prognosticating for about thirty or more years concerning not only America but the World, as well. The scorekeepers have noted that his predictions are about 86% correct!

When I got to meet him, in Hollywood, California, I asked him how he goes about predicting these events. He told me very simply that he predicts through "trend, precedent, pattern-of-habit, human behavior and the unalterable law of cycles." He told me too, that he doesn't do any "wishful thinking, for when you think wishfully, you're not predicting." He always remains impersonal.

At present, he writes a syndicated column, which is published in 600 newspapers and is translated into seven languages. It also is the number one column in Japan! In his Criswell Predicts, column (which is weekly and consists of about 1,000 words) he tells what is to come.

He predicts that after we land on the moon, we will find a remnant of lost civilizations! He also, says that the world will end on August 18, 1999 (His birthday, coincidentally)!! When I asked him about this he said that "Nostradamus predicted that it would end on that day."

Now living in Hollywood, California, he appears a lot on local TV programs and occasionally on nationally known shows such as The Tonight Show, Merv Griffin, Dick Cavett, and a few others.

He likes to be known as "the news reporter of the future" and indeed he is!! He is now predicting—Queen Elizabeth II will confront the world with a very shocking personal problem —Mrs. Martin Luther King will be hailed as the "Joan of Arc of the 20th century," and will take complete charge of the civil rights movement— One of our major TV and radio commentators will undergo a sex change and his attorneys will advise him that his contract will still hold with the network— the self-called "Queen of the Hippies" is really a man, who heads an all-girl revue, which will soon tour Europe! This will become known when his passport is made public!—A recent royal marriage will end in disaster, with the bride cutting her wrists in suicide when she finds out about the past of the groom—a famed woman doctor of London will be executed for performing abortions as the Crown rules that "abortion is murder" . . . These are but only a few of the many things he predicts will come true.

Like any other author of books, he plans to write more books; *What Time is the Funeral?*, *What the Great Prophets Predict*, and others.

God in heaven only knows what CRISWELL will predict in the coming years!!

Criswell was arrested at his home on May 21 on charges of receiving stolen property during an investigation that started with the arrest of an Alhambra carpet salesman on suspicion of burglary. Police said they recovered a number of alleged stolen office machines including four electric typewriters, two power saws, and a wood cutting router from Criswell's apartment. He was booked and released on $1875 bond. A newspaper article reporting on the arrest titled, "Unforeseen 'Guests' Pay Criswell a Visit" said, "Seer Criswell could be reached neither for comment, nor for prediction on the outcome of his case." Criswell was ordered on September 18 by Municipal Judge Vincent N. Erickson to appear in Superior Court September 29, for arraignment on the five counts of receiving stolen property. A co-defendant, Earl J. Costello, a sixty-two-year-old mortician, who lived at 1230 N. Berendo Street was arraigned with Criswell. Criswell pleaded no contest to one of the counts on November 18, and was sentenced on December 12, with the four other counts dismissed. As reported by the Associated Press, the "Self-Styled Seer" was fined $500 and placed on probation for two years. "Dr. King" told the court he was selling the items for a friend, and he had no idea they had been stolen.

On July 20, 1969, the Apollo 11 lunar module Eagle, landed the first humans on the moon. Criswell's previous predictions for the moon landing were not accurate as the astronauts were not pregnant females nor were they Mae West, George Liberace, and himself. Also, just for the record, contrary to the beliefs of modern-day conspiracy theorists, twelve humans have visited the moon during six missions to the Earth's closet celestial body and the moon landings were NOT an elaborate hoax perpetrated by NASA with the help of legendary film director Stanley Kubrick.

November 16, "Mr. Criswell of Criswell Predicts!" appeared at the Church of Religious Science in Glendale.

The November 1969 issue of *Saga: The Magazine for Men*, included a six-page article entitled "Criswell Predicts Your Next Ten Years." The article is comprised of excerpts from the book of the same title "covering everything from assassinations to zoology—and including such subjects as communism, crime, campus, Congress, marriage, medicine, space science, sex, sin and scandal." The article is accompanied by illustrations by Jerry Contrerras of a presidential suicide, flag burnings, and rioting.

February 18, 1970, saw Criswell back on *The Tonight Show* with Don Rickles, George Hamilton, Hugh Hefner, Karen Jensen and Carol Wayne. March 21, he was with *Philbin's People* with guests, Don Adams, Ernest Borgnine, and Robert Hoffman. On April 4 and 5, Criswell appeared at ARI Trailer Sales with free orchids for the ladies, coffee & donuts, and music. July 5, he was on the *Virginia Graham* local TV variety show with Kaye Ballard and Robert Ettinger. Then *Life with Linkletter* on July 12; "Scheduled: Criswell Predicts fashions for the next decade; Hannah School prepares a recipe; Mason Wong talks of San Francisco's Chinatown youth."

June 16, 1970:

I predict that great inroads will be made to return the nation to prohibition with the target year of 1980 in mind! Mark this on your calendar of the future! . . . I predict that you will no longer see any 'Flower Children' of any of the 'Psycho-dellics' around, for by this time their minds will have become so deranged from marijuana and narcotics, they will be vegetables or better off dead! . . . I predict that a 'safe' sex change operation will be performed in many hospitals for both men and women! . . . I predict an American colony on the moon by 1995!

July 21 saw Criswell on the local Los Angeles program *The Real Tom Kennedy Show* with Jack Albertson, Maureen Arthur, and David Brenner. August 14, he was back on the *Merv Griffin Show* featuring Arthur Treacher with guests Ethel Merman, Abbe Lane, Mort Lindsey Orchestra, and Jackie Vernon. On one of Criswell's appearances on Merv's show, comedian Slappy White predicted, "Criswell, you will go home broke tonight." Slappy had relived him of his wallet, which he returned after enjoying Criswell's reaction and the roar of laughter from the audience.

Criswell visited Halo in Littlestown as often as he could, usually around her birthday or his, and would make personal appearances during the trips.

On his birthday in 1970, the *Gettysburg Times* reported on Criswell predicting in Littlestown. He conducted a radio show from the town by phone. The half-hour program was on station KDKA in Pittsburg and broadcast from 12:30 a.m. to 1:00 a.m. on Tuesday mornings. The program also appeared from 1:00 to 3:00 in the morning on the Miami, Florida station WOID. Telephone callers would ask him questions that he would answer with predictions of future events or his view on current events if asked. The article states that the program normally originated from Hollywood and that after he concluded his broadcast early that morning that he would be back there next Monday. He had been in Littlestown for the past several days with his wife, the former Myrtle Louise Stonesifer, daughter of the late Dr. Howard S. Stonesifer, at the former Stonesifer home. The article concludes with plugs for his two books of predictions and stating that he was scheduled to attend the Littlestown Rotary Club meeting at James Anthony's Fishing Lake that night and was scheduled to fly back to Hollywood on Wednesday. Three days later a follow-up article told of his visit to the Rotary Club and that he presented a recording of "Criswell Predicts" to the club and that $17 was collected for fishing fees and given to the local Boy Scouts.

After leaving Hollywood, Halo began corresponding through the mail with Paul Marco up until her death. She would write to Paul about her ideas and plans for having her plays produced as films, having her poetry published in the local paper, and other schemes for prolonging her relative fame and continue to stretch her creative wings.

Letter dated October 15, 1970

Dear Paul,

Ann Noble wrote that she is starring in sex movies and one was in Film Festival and she wants to premiere one here as I have cousin owner-manager of movie house and he is interested and if he does he knows other managers. Also my play "Live Again" in which Sharon Tate made her first Hollywood appearance may be movie independent for the dough that husband has publicity on front page of N.Y. Enquirer and he may direct it.

Cris said you go to doctors—don't be guinea pig for them.

Best, Halo

Actress and writer Ann Noble and her husband Lester Philcox moved into the Criswell apartments after Maria Graciette and family moved out. Ann's real name was Irene Philcox and was from Portsmouth, United Kingdom, and also used the name Vicki Mills in one film. Her husband used the name Stephen Lester for his film roles and appeared with Ann in the few films she appeared. They worked together on Ted V. Mikel's true-grindhouse movie about cat food made from dead humans which leads to the cats developing a taste for human flesh called *The Corpse Grinders* (1971). Ann then wrote and starred in the *Sins of Rachel* (1972), a grindhouse exploitation movie about a murdered over-the-hill lounge singer and her sexually confused son. The low-budget feature was filmed in a process called "Texturetone" and produced and directed by mid-century homoerotic beefcake, stag short-film maker Richard (Dick) Fontaine. It has been described as "with threadbare production values and [the] grungy vibe of a seventies porn film, *Sins of Rachel* is sometimes misrepresented as a gruesome horror movie (it *could* be loosely categorized as 'hagsploitation' and there is one gory Herschell Gordon Lewis-style close-up of the murder victim's blood-drenched face, but the special effects ain't exactly convincing). *Sins* is truthfully more of an ultra-lurid, heavy-breathing soap opera crossed with a crime who-done-it, all overlaid with a frankly queer sensibility and an ineffable veneer of sleaze." Ann (and Lester) had also been in Dick's *Threads of Man* (1971). Her (and Lester's) last two roles were in the triple-x gay porn flicks, *Hollywood Cowboy* (1972), as "Barfly," and *The Light from the Second Story Window* (1973) with Ann billed as Vicki Mills.

October 18 and 23, Criswell appeared on a "Special" that was a projected weekly local television series variety show on channel 9 hosted by Wally George and his wife Linda Lowell. The other guests were Mayor Sam Yorty, Joann Castle, Henry Gibson, Father Hogart, and Suzy Brent.

Ralph Story was born in 1920 as Ralph Snyder and began his near half-century career in broadcasting after returning from serving in WWII as a fighter pilot in 1948. Hosting and directing a morning show on KNX radio Los Angeles, his casual style and witty observations about life in Los Angeles made him a popular host and garnered him national recognition and a spot hosting the network television gameshow *The $64,000 Challenge* in 1956. The show was canceled in 1958 after allegations of network scandals and that popular contestants on that type of gameshow were supplied with answers in advance. Story wasn't implicated in the scandal but returned to local Los Angeles broadcasting in 1960 on KNX radio then KNXT-TV with a news program segment that developed into a local news magazine program about the people and places of Los Angeles called *Ralph Story's Los Angeles,* airing from 1964 to 1970. In 1971, Story went to KABC-TV co-hosting a morning show that eventually became the network-produced *Good Morning America.* When the show moved to New York City, Story stayed in Los Angeles where he continued working as a writer, producer, and reporter for several TV stations.

The Weird World of Weird (1970), presented by Metromedia, is a forty-seven minute made-for-TV special hosted by Story in which he explores ESP, Witchcraft, Astrology, "various psychic fads," and "all those mysterious secrets hidden in the mythical world of the occult." It features a visit to a psychic "balloon reader," a seance to contact Houdini at the exclusive and private Magic Castle in Hollywood, Lotte Van Strohl who exorcised ghosts from Elke Sommer's home, footage of Anton Levay from *Satanis: The Devil's Mass* (1970), Astrologer Carroll Righter, actors such as Terry Moore, Anne Francis, Tige Andrews, some witches, some hippies, some gypsies, snake charming go-go dancers, and other followers of the occult in the dawning Age of Aquarius. It has a groovy, trippy-hippy late 1960s psychedelic and humorous up-beat vibe with cool, pop TV show style music by the Body and Soul Orchestra. Throughout the program, there are person-in-the-street clips with one filmed outside of Criswell's apartment building in which a woman spells out the word W-I-T-C-H, then proclaims "Women's International Terrorist Conspiracy from Hell!" Criswell makes ten appearances espousing his predictions in different locations like the Magic Castle, from a car, on the back of a concrete lion, and rising from a coffin. His first prediction is certainly one of his most accurate. "I predict that I will predict and predict. Remember that prediction!" Other prognostications were "I predict you girls have taken such an interest in politics, that within ten years, we will not have nine old men on the Supreme Court, but nine old women." and "I predict men and women will use the same washroom within three years." More of his forecasts of the future included, a new star in the sky lousing up astrologers, the White House would prove to be haunted, the return of national prohibition by 1982, a political career for Christine Jorgensen, and katydids in Kansas. For his last prediction he rises from a coffin surrounded by mourners including Paul Marco and pointing at the camera proclaims that the end of the world would occur on August 18, 1999. "You be there! Remember this prediction." The program aired a few times on Southern California local television and is included on the Something Weird Video twentieth anniversary special edition DVD-R, *The Weird World of Weird* (2009).

November 26, 1970:

Q: What predictions does Criswell have up his sleeve for the New Year? And what did he do for a living before he became a clairvoyant? P. Campo, Las Vegas.

A: "I worked in a Los Angeles funeral parlor for 20 years," says the seer. "But I prefer my present calling. As my prediction for '71, I'll go off on a double limb: I predict there will be a divorce British royal family. And that Prince Charles will mount throne within 18 months."

On January 17, 1971, "America's Foremost Prophet," was back on the *Mike Douglas Show* with co-host Robert Morse and guests E.J. Peaker, Skitch Henderson, Izumi, and June Gittelson.

I Predict by Criswell was published in January 1971 by Peacock Press, Chicago, Illinois, and distributed by Aladdin Distributing, Franklin Park, Illinois, who were also the owners and publishers of the *National Informer* tabloid which had been running Criswell's column for some years. The publication is comic book size but with a slightly better quality slick paper than your average pulp comic book and is twenty-two pages in length. W. Phillips illustrates some of the predictions with provocative line drawings, while others are accompanied by stock clip-art images. It cost fifty-cents and was comprised of predictions mainly from the tabloid columns and the *YN10YCP* book, including the cannibal cookbook, the hornet terror, the automatic atomic plague, forced marriage, sex changes and transplants, and an insane President which is illustrated with a drawing of President Nixon with long hair and Elvis sideburns. The prediction differs slightly from the one previously published in *YN10YCP*. The original lines that were omitted or changed are in parentheses.

I predict that a coming American tragedy will shock the world! (in about 20 years!) (I predict that) The President who will hold office at that time will become incurably insane because of a brain tumor! This raving man will be restrained and the White House will become a private mental institution! The Vice President will quietly assume all duties and the (business of)

Federal government will continue as before, (When historians write of this event, they will marvel at the courage shown by the American citizens!) except that golf will be banned in Washington, D.C.!

POPE ASSASSINATED!

I predict that an assassination attempt, possibly successful, will be made upon the Pope. I see the papal throne empty—and smeared with blood!

THE DEATH OF OUR PLANET

I predict that we have reached the point of no return in our plunder of our planet! We have drained the oil from the underskin of the earth, dug the metals out which gave the earth consistence, hacked and mutilated the natural areas, tampered with the climate by irrigation, false rivers, lakes and canals. I predict that this will take a heavy toll on existing protective forces. The insect world, the animal world, the fish of the sea and the plant life will prove to be no friend of ours in the final showdown, when the world will return to a former unspoiled, unoccupied state—a point of no return!

One section taken from the *YN10YCP* book is titled "Maria Graciette," the name of Criswell's friend, fellow prognosticator, and tenant at his apartments. The section states that she is the Chairman of the Board of Directors for the International ESP in Hollywood and features her predictions for the period of 1971 to 1980, and that the predictions have been verified by the membership and accepted in their annual meetings. One of Maria's somewhat accurate predictions was that tobacco and cigarette companies wouldn't be permitted to advertise on the radio, TV, newspapers, magazines, or outdoors and a fine of a million dollars would be levied against all lawbreakers. In 1970, Congress passed the Public Health Smoking Act banning the advertising of cigarettes on radio and television starting on January 2, 1971. After that most cigarette advertising took place in magazines, newspapers, and billboards until 1999.

Maria billed herself as a countess, a former Miss Portugal, UFO Contactee, and was known as "the psychic that helps you" in supermarket tabloids such as the *National Enquirer* as late as 1994. Graciette was a guest speaker at the 1966 Giant Rock Interplanetary Spacecraft Convention and a number of other 1960s saucer happenings like Daniel Fry's Understanding Conventions at the "Understandorama" in Harmony Grove, California. In November 1964, Maria hosted a forum called "My experiences aboard a spaceship." Little in the way of specifics regarding Graciette's purported UFO contactee experiences have been found. She authored *Astrology and Your Sex Life* (1965), and recorded a vinyl LP album called *Astrology, Know the Language of the Stars*. Maria conveyed to *The San Bernardino County Sun* newspaper the story of her ability to read auras and her mystery box. "Since I was a little girl, I've been able to see auras around people. When I was very young, my teacher gave me a mysterious box and told me never to lose it. I've had the box for a long, long time! I had always used it in my studio to store things. It was by accident that I discovered the mysterious power of the box. I had thrown some pictures in the box and when I took them out I could see auras around the figures in the image. I have always been able to see auras in photographs, but now it seems to me that it is much easier to read the auras in an image when it has been placed in the box . . . I do not know what it is, I cannot explain it but when I write a statement on a sheet of paper and put it in the box, the statement is always true." Graciette reportedly foresaw the Manson murders and predicted that Tom Cruise would become bald due to a stress related illness. Some of her other prophecies that appeared in the *Enquirer* were "A UFO base, thousands of years old, will be found deep in the Mexican desert." "Vice President Quayle, attending a World Series game, will impulsively interfere with a play." "A meteorite will crash into the White House Rose Garden, placing President and Mrs. Bush at risk from radiation." A Mexican UFO website called *Marcianitos Verdes* could find no evidence to back up Miss Graciette's claims of being a countess or Miss Portugal and suspect that she constructed those claims. Maria and Criswell would be both given awards for their 1971 best sellers in the non-fiction field for *Your Next Ten Years* and *Astrology and Your Sex Life.* A photo from a newspaper story shows the pair together with their books and awards and claims the awards were presented on national television from New York City.

I Predict is one of the rarer Criswell publications due to it becoming a part of copyright infringement lawsuits filed by himself and his publisher against Aladdin Distributing Corp. et al. The suits were filed in U. S. District Court for the Central District of California (Criswell later dismissed that case) and Atlanta, Georgia District Court. Criswell was not awarded any damages in the latter case, but Aladdin was ordered to cease publishing and selling the publication.

Predictably, the *National Informer* quit running Criswell's column and replaced it with "I Predict" by Mark Travis with this announcement.

We knew it would happen someday. Every star must eventually burn out. So many readers have complained about Criswell's column not being what it used to be that we decided to release him from his weekly obligation to us. It is our judgement that Criswell has run his course and has burned out, just as the stars in the sky will someday burn out. In his place, however, a bright new star, full of vitality and a talent to foresee that which Criswell never passed has arrived on the scene. Mark Travis. Remember his name. It will be a household word soon.

Travis predicted with each prognostication starting with "I predict . . . that bull fighting will soon be legalized in the United States and will soon eclipse baseball in popularity . . . a successful reverse sex-change operation soon. A woman will successfully be changed into a man, capable of performing as one in every way . . . the first birth of a baby to a man! . . . video tape ca-

"I PREDICT"
By MARK TRAVIS

I predict that every city will have, by 1986, a TV station owned and operated by the federal government. This will be used not for news or for "public service" programs, but for increasingly spectacular and expensive dramas and entertainment features. The reason for this will be that the government will be trying any measure to take the population's mind off such hardships as the energy crisis, and fascinating TV shows will be a good way of doing this.

+ + +

I predict the discovery of active volcanoes under Greenland's rugged mountains about the middle of the 21st century will lead to that huge island's becoming the next popular frontier. The heat from underground will be harnessed for energy, hot water, and even to alter the arctic climate, eventually making the southern half of the island into a tropic paradise. By the beginning of the 22nd century, the same techniques will be used to

start making Antartica habitable.

+ + +

I predict the next major advances in medical science will be in preventative medicine — most especially, the nutritional needs of the human body. It will be discovered that those who now say the body needs massive amounts of many vitamins are largely correct, and the new knowledge of the nutrition, coupled with other medical techniques, will extend average human life to nearly a century and a half.

+ + +

I predict that Brazil will be one of the top half-dozen world powers by the year 2075. With the opening up of the vast land area and natural resources of the Amazon valley, and the combining of modern technology with vast amounts of inexpensive labor, Brazil will come to rank right after the U. S., the U.S.S.R. and mainland China in the list of rich and influential nations.

settes (sic), played on your television set, will replace movies and books. People will collect libraries of video tapes . . . the birth of a baby in the White House in 1978." The Mark Travis column ran until the mid-1970s, eventually dropping the Mark Travis byline and just being titled "I Predict."

Another competitor to Criswell in the field of foretelling the future in the tabloids was the exotic, alluring-eyed Celestia. The *National Spotlite* was another "For Adults Only" weekly sleaze tabloid that featured absurd, sensationalized, eye-grabbing headlines and stories like "Satan Rules Our Bodies: Sexual Witch Cults, U.S.A." "Top Fashion Models Reveal Why They Dig Lesbian Love" "America Needs

293

Nudism to End Crime" and "Lesbian Rock Band Holds Orgies On-stage." Celestia had a full page spread headlined "Sex and the Stars" in a whimsical, new-age font. Bordering the page on the sides were graphics of the twelve signs of the Zodiac. Text above a centerpiece photo of the smoky-eyed, hypnotically and magnetically attractive astrologer asks, "Have any questions about your stars and your sex life? Celestia will answer them all. Besides being a beautiful chick, she's our staff astrologist and fully qualified to tell you just where your sex life's at, according to the stars." This is followed by an address for the reader to send their questions. Surrounding the photo is a typical astrological forecast based on and for each of the signs of the Zodiac written in a cheeky manner with vague, half-veiled sexual references. The bottom third of the page is titled "Celestia Answers" where she replies to readers' typical marriage, romantic and sexual relationship questions based on the sender's birthdate and astrological sign. As the sexual revolution of the 1960s continued on into the 1970s, people were looking for answers and direction in the new uncharted seas of sexually liberated love and astrology was a popular place to look.

In 1971, Ed Wood began working on his second X-rated movie, *Necromania: A Tale of Weird Love!* (1971). His first was *Take It Out in Trade* (1970). *Necromania* came about because Pendulum books wanted a feature film. Ed jumped at the opportunity to make another film. He wrote the twenty-page script that was about a haunted hotel where couples and lovers went to cure their sexual problems. Maila Nurmi (Vampira) was asked to play the role of the ghoul in residence but refused saying that it would be professional suicide. Cris loaned his coffins to the production, and one was used for some of the hardcore sex scenes. He and Buddy Hyde spent a hot afternoon at the shoot at Eddie's request. The film took a weekend and $7,000 to shoot and would be the last full-length film that Eddie would direct. For many years only a soft-core version of the film was available until Ed Wood biographer Rudolph Grey discovered the hardcore version in 2001 at a Los Angeles warehouse after a seventeen-year quest for the film. Fleshbot films released a DVD that includes both versions of the film in 2004.

Criswell addressed the members of the Friday Morning Club on March 5, 1971, in the clubhouse auditorium located at 940 S. Figueroa. St., Los Angeles. His topic was "Your Next 10 Years." Following a luncheon he gave predictions on questions asked by the audience.

Halo sent a copy of her plays to Paul Marco along with her ideas for how she thought the film versions should be produced and also gave advice as to how they should be promoted.

Letter dated May 4, 1971

Dear Paul,

On back page of "Live Again" is "That Old Gang" and this could be filmed so cheap with women's lib group and you could guest on TV as producer and with one of their groups or go alone and show the film as that is popular now.

"Live Again" could be special exploitation as Sharon Tate made her debut in Hollywood "Live Again." That would sell it and you can have showings at town and area and good review and photos as our local weekly is across street from movie house.

Our movie house has stage and lights and only shows movies on weekends so a school-theater can tie in with off-Broadway and operate for summer or six-week courses during year. There is coffee shop next door. House is modern and seats 550 and has great marquee. If age barrier limits you our town is great place. Colleges are everywhere and good restaurants.

I bicycle and houses are warm in winter so going out is for refreshment. Anyway, here is another way of life so hang on.

Best ever, Halo

Thanks for birthday card-every year-better and better. To Nicky from Buttercup and Mr. Chips.

In a letter dated June 6, 1971, she seems somewhat bitter about where life has taken her and where she has been.

Dear Paul,

Call your script "Everyone Wants to Walk Over My Grave," and then you will have a true love story.

I'll continue promoting my plays and then my relatives, the legal enemies, cannot say I'm too feeble, as around here everyone with money is ushered into rest homes to be finished by nurses and doctors. They are sitting like death row so named crazy, murderer, or assassin all end in same boat.

We're all puppets of the Power Line that can wipe us out in a second, but I still prefer dogs to humans. The Great Scheme, or Schemer doesn't care who hinders or helps, it's just keep going and Life Plan is served. You and Cris should go far, or must you find a better sucker than I. I feel in Futility of Effort Cris won grand prize and I the booby for being prize sucker. All a man has to do is find a striver and pretend he will help her and then call her crazy for wanting to continue and society goes with him, and if she stands up she is crazy and if she gives in and she is sick and doctors reap either way.

After this point the letter becomes unreadable and indecipherable.

Halo sent Paul her xeroxed booklet of poems simply titled *Poems*. On the front cover she lists her names: M. L. Stonesifer King, Louise Howard, and Halo Meadows, then "Wife and Associate Editor of Criswell Predicts Syndicated Column" with her address below.

Dog
Warm body,
Cold nose,
Soft touch,
You want
to repay,
You want
to play.
You need
the who-man
Who knows
Who you are
for him.

On the back of the booklet was a clipping as published in the *Adams County Illustrated Press,* November 12, 1970:

To the Editor:
As wife and editor of Criswell Predicts syndicated column, I give my predictions far beyond 2000 as he sees end.
(1) Outer Space crust break will cut down population.
(2) New concept of birth-death cycle and those just going on.
(3) Animals will be a luxury and not eaten.
(4) Mermaids and winged humans and people with features more resembling animals and birds may popu-

late this earth in the 21st Century, with more diverse variations in the 22nd Century.

(5) Nature or man can't stop man; we just go in return cycle or super variation cycle.

Most truly,

Mrs. Criswell

On May 20, 1971, the Pantages Theatre in Hollywood hosted a "Colossal Old Fashioned World Premiere to Honor Mr. Vincent Price for His 100th Motion Picture." The movie was *The Abominable Dr. Phibes* (1971). The event was nationally televised by Steve Allen and featured "Antique Cars and Stars of the Past and Present." Criswell was among the huge list of the "great and near great of Hollywood" including Vincent Price, John Astin, Ruth Buzzi, Judy Canova, Sebastian Cabot, Bob Crane, Hans Conreid, Sammy Davis, Jr., Vivian Duncan, Sam Elliot, Jamal "Buckwheat" Frazier, Christine Jorgensen, Agnes Moorehead, Forrest Tucker, Doodles Weaver, Betty White, Johnathan Winters, Joanne Worley . . . and many more. In July and August, Criswell appeared on the syndicated *Virginia Graham Show,* a daytime variety and talkshow program with fellow guests, Kaye Ballard, Robert Ettinger, the Ellie Frankel Sextet, Joanie Sommers, Rubin Carson, and Pattie Deutsch.

Harold Greenland was a businessman who operated on the fringes of the entertainment world. Mr. G. had adult movie theaters, burlesque houses, and cocktail bars in cities across the U.S. including Seattle, Buffalo, Los Angeles, and San Francisco. He was fortunate when he booked *Deep Throat* (1972), at his Garden Art Theater where it played for years. Somehow, Mr. G acquired ownership of *The Citizen-News,* a respectable daily newspaper that was a reasonable alternative to the *LA Times.* Starting in September 1971, *The Citizen-News* began running a weekly column of Criswell's predictions. The first installment was run on the front page, above

Front left: Titus Moody, unknown, Paul Marco, Criswell, unknown, and Hale Smith. Technical conference for *The Last of the American Hoboes.* Courtesy of Jason Insalaco.

the masthead, which includes the line "It Tells the Truth" under the paper's title. One of the predictions includes the mention of a man named Titus Moody. "I predict that Hale Smith, the Hollywood Hobo, will zoom to the top of the heap with his forthcoming film to be premiered in September, 'Last of the American Hobos.' This remarkable production by Titus Moody will win many of the coming awards for its freshness and new approach! . . . I predict a grassroot boom for 'Ralph Nader for President' will be most evident in the coming months. Ralph Nader is most popular from Wall Street to the Bible Belt, Dixie and Non-Dixie! . . . I predict that rampant crime on the streets of New York will discourage tourist trade this Summer, but that will clear up by October under stern police measures."

Titus Moody, born Titus Moede in 1938, was an actor, photographer, editor, cinematographer, producer, and director that worked on the peripheries of the exploitation and underground alternative cinema and the adult magazine trade for over thirty years. He acted in and was associated with some of what are called, "the worst films of all time," such as *Rat Pfink a Boo Boo* (1966), with the sidekick role of Boo Boo, and *The Incredibly Strange Creatures Who Stopped Living and Became Mixed-Up Zombies* (1964), in which he plays a hobo. Both of these films were directed by Ray Dennis Steckler, another cult movie director cut from the same cloth as Ed Wood. Titus began his career in the industry in 1958, with small bit parts in teenage-themed movies which lead to a few parts on television shows such as *The Twilight Zone, Have Gun Will Travel, Wyatt Earp,* and *Combat.* He directed and filmed his free-form, mondo-style documentary *Outlaw Motorcycles* (1965), before the Roger Corman and A.I.P. "bikesploitation" flicks like *The Wild Angels* (1966), and *Hell's Angels on Wheels* (1967), and well before the film that is now known as the quintessential biker movie, *Easy Rider* (1969). *The Last of the American Hoboes* (1967), released in 1970, is a do-it-yourself, cinema verité, pseudo-documentary starring Coleman Francis, director of *The Beast of Yucca Flats* (1961), as a hobo riding the rails and celebrating the vagrant lifestyle. Moody had also previously starred in Francis' *The Skydivers* (1963), along with Kevin Casey and Tony Cardoza. Titus co-stars in *Hoboes* as a hobo cross-country traveling with Coleman to the annual Hobo Festival in Britt, Iowa. The nearly impossible to find film has been called, "a sprawling mess of half realized ideas made with a lot of heart." Photos show Criswell and Titus together along with Paul Marco and Hale Smith apparently filming a scene for *Hoboes* in a train car with a President Lincoln replica casket that was owned by Criswell. He doesn't appear in the released film. Beginning in the 1970s, Titus mostly worked in the sexploitation and hard X-rated film industry and the adult magazine trade with countless photos he shot, scene shots from his own films, and photos of himself "in action." He is in a number of photos in the previously mentioned *Hippies* adult magazine. For many years Titus had the constant companionship and love of his chihuahua named Chi Chi. The dog lived to be twenty-eight-years-old, but after Chi Chi passed, Titus couldn't let go and kept the dog's frozen body in his freezer for about two years. Titus died of cancer and was cremated in 2001. A memorial service was held for Moody in the parking lot

of the Mondo Video store on Melrose Avenue in Los Angeles and a portion of his ashes were put into a goblet and drank. The remainder of his ashes are reportedly on display at Mondo Video.

October 2, 1971:

Total Women's Lib Coming?

I predict that we men must soon face a new world of women! The Women's Liberation League will sweep every man before it, and soon! I predict that the right to vote will soon be taken from all men as they will be proven 'inferior and second class citizens' in every state of the union! The women own and control 87 per cent of all wealth and have direct veto on the spending of 90 cents out of every dollar! I predict the women will soon hold all of the top responsible positions in law, banking, government, communication, education and transportation! We men will be at the mercy of stern hands! . . . Our boxers, wrestlers, football, baseball and all sports heroes will be women and the sports heroes of the past will be conveniently forgotten and written out of the records! . . . Any women can win any argument over a man simply by asking, *Why not give women a chance, you men have made a mess of it so far, haven't you?*

October 27:

I predict that the next craze in foreign flights will be the so-called "Sex Flights" where you may come as a single and end up in an orgy high above the clouds! Some Oriental flights of this nature were most popular but now they will soon be scheduled from Europe and Asia as home bases!

In 1972, Criswell's third and final book, *Criswell's Forbidden Predictions Based on Nostradamus and the Tarot*, was published by Droke House/Hallux, Inc. Robert Himmel designed the jacket.

The jacket flap reads:
Criswell meets Nostradamus! Using the Tarot cards for divination, Criswell has evoked the spirit of the famed 16th Century French seer and interviewed him.

The predictions that result are more dire, more sensational than those in his two previous books—two books that are known coast to coast.

This is Criswell's first book in three years, and by far his most intriguing.

Within these pages are the original "forbidden predictions" of Nostradamus, with their true meaning interpreted by Nostradamus.

In the preface Criswell describes the impact of his mysterious meeting with Nostradamus.

To me, the incident with Nostradamus was no fantasy, no dream, no imaginary voyage into non-reality. Nostradamus was no paper cutout, but a living, breathing human. His solid-ity astounded me. His words were waxen and covered all with no questions asked.

Was there an inter-change of souls between this great Prophet and myself? I will admit that I lived, read, studied and absorbed the personality of Nostradamus for almost a year before I would dare to present his forbidden predictions. Almost as though I had a seventh sense, the pages of this volume became print; his instructions on the Druid Tarot implanted on my mind, where it will never be erased. I have tested this Druid Tarot on others, and I want to tell you that it really works! The forbidden predictions were also tested, one against the other, and they are a monument to future events.

Did I become entranced as did Bridey Murphy, the traveler between two worlds, or an H.G. Wells, Lewis Carroll or Jules Verne? Was I possessed by the over-powering strength of Nostradamus, or was it merely wishful thinking? I can deny wishful thinking as I have always been most impersonal!

As Trismigistus philosophized, "As the desired thing is accomplished, the steps leading up to it are also accomplished." Here are "The Forbidden Predictions of Nostradamus" as a living proof that some contact was made!"

Always in your future,

Criswell

On the next page Criswell describes his meeting Nostradamus in, PART ONE: THE ENCOUNTER.

303

Some call it "Hallowmass," some "All Saints' Day" but most call it "Halloween." No one, but no one, is superstitious; for coincidence is the language of fools. Strange things happen on Halloween, but the strangest thing was my scientific encounter with Nostradamus!

My telecast had gone extremely well that night. We openly invited the disembodied to visit everyone, for they would be welcomed, as the door to the twilight zone was left ajar. Halloween had been declared visiting day for those of the nether realms by the Gods that be. We were little prepared for what happened. But it did, and there were witnesses.

The audience had departed, the lights were turned off, and a pleasant half-darkness permeated the studio.

I entered my dressing room, flipped on the lights, and removed my make-up and costume.

An ominous silence seemed to fill the air, almost like the breaking point of a coming storm.

There was a sharp tap on the door as it swung open, and like an echo thru a long corridor came a voice clearly, but most powerful, saying "I am Nostradamus."

I looked at the reflected image in the dressing room mirror, and there he stood. His image caused me no fright, as he seemed so kind and so natural. Most famous people carry a glow with them to proclaim their greatness, as did Nostradamus.

Criswell then describes the great prophet's appearance and says he "could have passed as a hippy of our generation."

And then Nostradamus started to speak in his well modulated, educated voice. Although in French, it was understandable in English. You could hear time marching ahead. Suddenly the scene started to change around me and we were in a huge grotto, almost cathedral in size, with lighted tapers on the wall. I was suddenly removed to another time, another place. The voidness of space.

Nostradamus walked to a table of oaken boards, seated himself in a huge chair, and

motioned for me to take the other chair opposite him. The walls were transparent and

enclosed by the canopy of a star-filled sky.

My mind became relaxed and attentive and my powers of retention became multiplied.

I soon was not conscious of his voice and the entire scene was a mental exchange of words.

Nostradamus then recited his biography and some of his more famous predictions that had come to pass in the last 400 years including his, and Criswell's, final date of this earth, August 18, 1999. "A date in which terror strikes the hearts of all those unfortunate enough to be alive. Many of you will witness this supreme destruction."

Part two of the book is titled "The French" and lists Nostradamus' predictions in his native language. Part three is "Nostradamus' Forbidden Predictions Translated."

As Nostradamus and I looked into each other's eyes across the table, I somehow felt that I, too, was seeing the next twenty-five years into the future. He carefully explained that he was editing his predictions so they would only include our next quarter of a century. His low key but dramatic voice unfolded the years to come and here are his direct quotes: "When the polar ice caps melt the world will be in for a shock! Many monsters, frozen for thousands of years in the ice will suddenly revive and again walk the earth . . . The world will turn to the worship of women for they will be exhalted (sic) to a new high respect, love and adoration . . . Five hundred and eighty plus seven hundred and three days after the eightieth year of the Twentieth Century, there will be established life beyond in other planets. This will displease the many students and scholars who wish to keep things as they are . . . In the year of 1987, all books will be censored and the offending ones destroyed . . . There will no longer be secret studies for all secrets will be bared . . . The first woman president will rule with a eunuch at her side. She will hold forth for seven years and be both hated and loved . . . A huge population of women from the Aegean area will unite and go against the liberation of women by being much more radical and greater tyrants. They will have nothing to do with man except to enslave him, buying and selling him like cattle. Normal sex will be outlawed and they will propagate only through artificial insemination. Huge sperm banks will be set up throughout their domain and men will be forced to make a weekly deposit . . . A lost space ship will return in triumph amid much rejoicing. Considered lost for over three years, they miraculously weathered the dangers of outer space bringing back with them the first child born on another planet! Outer space suddenly becomes nearby space . . . The combined Russian and Chinese Red empires will give the kiss of death to the rest of the world as we sleep in ignorance.

After many more of Nostradamus' predictions along these same lines comes "Part Four: The Tarot As Used In The Divination Of Nostradamus" in which he explains to Criswell the history and power of the "Tarot" which is the Druid word for "Truth." Nostradamus then demonstrates how to place the cards in the seven manners of reading, which are illustrated and described on the next few pages that are then followed by illustrations, descriptions, and meanings of all the cards in the Tarot deck.

NOSTRADAMUS' FINAL WORDS

Each card and symbol of the Tarot can be matched to any person. Living, dead, or yet to be! This also can stand for nations, politics, customs and any other condition!

When the 20th century closes on August 18th, 1999. When it corrodes like a rotten apple, and men are busily at war, they will stop their pillage, murdering and raping for a brief moment to know that "The Portuguese are not pleased!" for Portugal at that time will be the central power of the Latin World, and will control the Papacy!

May God protect all in the coming days ahead!

The lights returned to normal in the dressing room, and I was again confined backstage at the television theater.

Nostradamus was gone . . . but he left behind the heritage which I now leave to you.

I pass this burning torch to you to carry on in our Olympics of Life.

The last chapter of the book is "Our Final Century! One Hundred Events in Your Future."

SOMEWHERE OUT THERE IN THE FUTURE . . . are events awaiting to take place . . . events so brazen . . . so shocking . . . so terrible and so unexpected, that I scarce tell you about them! . . . So let me pull back the curtain which divides us from the future!

I forecast a time of dread, alarm, fright and horror. Apalling (sic), fearful, dismaying, perilous, apprehensive, astounding events!

EVENT SEVEN: A peculiar madness will take place in the brain of each and every one of the animal kingdom and they will overpower every human in sight!

EVENT SIXTEEN: Planets will explode and the sun, a living physical being with psychic energy will astound all, and shower the universe with electrons!

EVENT TWENTY NINE: Scorpio brings the influence of pollution where each drop of water is contaminated with a gross vileness. Bacteria will so grow in size that they will be seen with the naked eye. They will fill the air.

EVENT THIRTY TWO: The planet Mercury will swing close to planet Earth, and the air will become solid with electricity, with bolts of lightning in every nook and corner. This will nullify the bacteria threat.

EVENT SIXTY EIGHT: Mental powers become so vast that there is no sickness, no colds, no headaches, no toothaches and no stomach trouble as it will be cleared by the power of the unswerving mind. There is no meantime for pain, as it vanishes magically and everyone becomes a healer.

EVENT EIGHTY: The largest séance in the history of the world will be held at Prarie (sic) City, South Dakota and will draw one million ardent psychics from all over the world. Reports will be received that will make headlines. Actual visitations from the other side of life will be photographed and recorded in conversation for those of disbelief or doubt.

EVENT NINETY NINE: The earth will be bombarded by exploding planets. Quakes, tidal waves, tornadoes! People will be tossed around like popping corn. Quakes, heavy violent quakes! And the Earth will corrode like a rotten apple, from the center it will bubble, break and lie helplessly open to the elements.

EVENT ONE HUNDRED: After the crises comes peace. Desolate peace. Not one thing moving. Not one thing growing. Not one thing living. Somewhere out there in the future waiting for you and for everyone, a better world . . . a much better world! We have danced and now we pay the piper! You will not be permitted to go through all this trouble without reward, and I prophecy that it will come to pass.

And thus it shall be, this final century. Finality predicted by Nostradamus and hidden these many years in the symbolism of his forbidden predictions, Now predicted again—by Nostradamus—and by Criswell.

Always In Your Future!

Criswell

Criswell appeared in front of about eighty people attending a meeting of the Tuesday Club of Newport Harbor at the Newporter Inn in Newport Beach on January 25, 1972. He predicted that Richard Nixon would serve a third term after the Constitution was changed, permitting him to serve a succeeding term. Amid a few gasps of surprise, some oohs and aahs, and a sprinkling of laughter he predicted that in the coming year women's fashions would look just as they did in 1907, his birth year, except the modern woman's dress would be almost transparent and slit up the side and that fat would be beautiful. "So you full-figured girls have nothing to worry about." He also predicted that within three years all nine members of the Supreme Court would be women and that in America, "We will all be carrying guns again like the days of the Old West." In a newspaper article covering the meeting, he claimed he had just completed a sixty-city tour and was preparing for a junket to Anchorage, Alaska. "Where my seven performances there are already sold-out."

On February 5, 1972, Kenne Duncan, Dr. Acula in *Revenge of the Dead,* died from an intentional overdose of barbiturates. Kenne had also appeared in four other Wood productions but began his career as mainly a Western villain in serials, films, and television from the late 1920s to 1950s, with around 250 on-screen appearances. His funeral and wake was well attended by Criswell, Paul Marco, Ed and Kathy Wood, Buddy Hyde, David Ward, and others. Kenne was sixty-eight-years-old and buried at Grand View Memorial Park Cemetery in Glendale, California.

On April 14, Criswell attended a gathering of silent movie stars to honor Claire Windsor, who was in attendance. A home movie was presented showing her with Randolph Hearst, Charlie Chaplin, Fay Webb, and Adolphe Menjou, cavorting at the Hearst Ranch. A photo from an article reporting the event showed Criswell with his cohorts Vivian Duncan, Cass Daley, and unnamed Paul Marco. In September, Criswell appeared on a live radio broadcasts on KFI radio from the Tour Center of Universal Studios with Yvonne DeCarlo, Werner Klemperer, Sybil Leek, Patricia Morrison, and George Shearing.

An October 5 article in *The Daily Mail,* Hagerstown, Maryland, hometown newspaper of Criswell's former television show producer Buddy Hyde, detailed Buddy's visit back home and recounted his four decade career. "He left this city in the early '30s, answering the call of vaudeville, then variously involving himself as a master of ceremonies, a movie actor, a radio producer and performer, night club owner, host of a TV talk show, and now a producer of documentary films." The article tells of his award winning life-saving documentaries, public service filming of municipal projects, and some of Los Angeles Mayor Sam Yorty's TV releases, some with Audie Murphy as a collaborator. It then tells of other big names in Buddy's past like Judy Canova, Christine Jorgensen, and Jeron King Criswell, "predictor of futures, has engaged Buddy Hyde Productions to make the specials that have been used by talk shows hosted by Johnny Carson, Mike Douglas and Virginia Graham. 'Criswell Predicts' may be remembered as a series on Channel 13 sometime ago. This modern prophet has recently published some of his predictions in a book titled, 'Nostradamus', from the Latin name of the sixteenth century French astrologer and seer."

On October 19, "the 20th Century Nostradamus" would make one of his last appearances on network television on the *Mike Douglas Show* with co-host Lou Rawls and guests Sandy Baron, Freda Payne, and Bill Dee Williams.

An article in the Saturday, October 21 edition of the *St. Petersburg Times,* reported on Criswell's visit to St. Petersburg to promote his *Forbidden Predictions* book, quoted here.

There's so much death about the affable, chubby man. He smiles, dark eyes piercing from a face molded after W.C. Fields and Alfred Hitchcock, predicting the end of the world. Slaughter. Horrible bloody holocaust. Catastrophe after calamity will sweep this old world before the century turns, he says. We have until August 18, 1999. He doesn't claim to be a mystic, seer or clairvoyant. "I don't think I'm a medium," he says, puffing a cigar, "I don't even know if I am psychic. But I've always been very intuitive and I never ignore a hunch. I see things as cause and effect. Jeane Dixon says she talks to God, but I certainly don't."

The article then tells of how he became a prognosticator and that he relies on his "photographic memory" to guide his predictions. He then relates how Nostradamus appeared to him on Halloween saying "I don't know why he chose me. He wanted me to pass on the information." When asked why we would want to know, he replied. "So we can prepare. We can store up for the famines or store up Black Plague serum. It is no more preposterous than Bridey Murphy, or the visions of the saints or Fatima. They (predictions) come more spontaneously now, I think, since I've built up a background of research." He gave a few spontaneous predictions. For St. Petersburg he saw a "huge new hospital here, one of the finest in the South. You should hear of it next year." and "I predict cancer will be cured through diet alone; the basis of the diet will be a portion, the root, of the cactus plant." He said his favorite hobby is travel and his constant companion is a bedraggled, sawdust-leaking teddy bear "given to me by Grandmother Criswell on my first Christmas, 1917 (sic). I always have him with me, I don't know why. He's a talisman. I don't know what would happen if I didn't keep him with me; I'd be afraid to try." He then packed teddy into his briefcase next to slick photos of him and Mae West and him in the movies. There was also a copy of the new book and when asked if he thought it would sell. "I hope so. Teddy Bear will bring me through.

Criswell finished 1972 with book signings at department stores in Los Angeles then headed east for the start of the new year. On January 8, 1973, Criswell was the speaker at the Indiana Auctioneers Association convention banquet and "kept the large audience entertained with his ten predictions for the coming year which were made public last summer." The following week he was back in California and predicting for 1973, at Southwestern College's Mayan Hall in Chula Vista and on January 23 he appeared in Newport Beach at the meeting of the Tuesday Club of Newport Harbor held in the Empire Room of the Newporter Inn. An article in the *LA Times* reported on the appearance telling of his predictions and saying he "spends much of his time traveling about the country telling audiences what he 'knows' about their future. He has just completed a 60-city tour and is preparing for a junket to Anchorage, Alaska, 'where my seven performances there are already sold out.' he said. Although members of the audience listened to him with amusement and some disbelief, most of them were obviously interested in what he had to say." February 14, saw Criswell at the Cerritos College's Burnight Center Theatre with the subject being "Your Next Ten Years." Tickets cost one dollar for general admission and fifty cents for students.

The premier issue of *Mystique: Adventure Into the Occult* magazine hit the newsstands in April 1973. Along with Jeane Dixon, David Dubar, and Nostradamus, Criswell was included in a section called "Predictions for 1973 and Beyond." The bio before his predictions has his name mistaken as Jerome and tells of his prediction twenty-five years previously of man landing on the moon before 1970. "All those present told him to go back to Hollywood and become a fiction writer." A 1960s style line drawing cartoon illustrates one of his predictions.

CRISWELL PREDICTS . . . Roumania will become the first nation to hold a public sex lottery for taxation. This will happen in 1982.

In August, the Pasadena *Star-News* ran a piece by Virginia Kay titled "Friend Sends Urgent Plea For Help."

It was perhaps two years ago, give or take a little, when I sat with friends in a Pasadena theater. After the feature film there was a "personal appearance" by the man whom many had come expressly to see, hear, and perhaps to meet. The man whom almost everyone will remember from his countless television and radio appearances was Mr. Criswell of the "Criswell Predicts" hour. Today we have an appeal from that Mr. Criswell, so urgent, that he sends word we may print his telephone number. But it is for use only, as you will understand, if you can answer his troubled request. He asked Diana Deimel (Mrs. Jack Watts) to write a letter for him to this column. Dear Virginia: I'm writing today because someone needs help fast, and the someone is the famous Mr. Criswell of "Criswell Predicts." A few weeks ago Mr. Criswell almost died when a splinter in his foot turned into blood poisoning. He was rushed to the hospital where he would have died in two hours if they had not caught him right then. As it is, the surgery the doctors had to perform means that he will be in a wheelchair for months. His problem is that he has two quiet, lovely dogs that he now cannot care for. They must be put to sleep if we cannot find a home for them. He has had them for three years and will not separate them. Can you help in your wonderful column? Your readers are so kind in helping out in so many ways. Mr. Criswell's number is—463-3841. Time is running out for those two poor animals. I will pick them up and deliver them to anyone who can give BOTH of them the right kind of home. Hopefully, DIANA, Sierra Madre.

The sixty-six-year-old Criswell finished off the year of 1973 making personal appearances at fundraisers and benefits.

Death the Proud Brother

We are all lighted candles in a darkened world, weary travelers on the highway of life, plodding on to our endless existence! For once we exist, we continue to exist! Our span of life compared to the billions of years of time, is but a fast twinkle in the eye of God! We are all ten seconds from Eternity and the limitless time thereafter! Surely the things we have today pass with us into this pleasurable void!

Criswell

Myrtle legally separated from her husband of some thirty-four years in 1974, most likely to prevent Criswell from obtaining any of her property or her inheritance from her father if she happened to pass away before him.

VERNE LANGDON: We saw him out there one day. In later years, TV building one and TV building two started to look pretty ratty. The awnings had holes in them, and they sort of sloped as awnings of that are kind of breaking down and the paint was peeling horribly on the buildings and there was a cyclone fence up now as protection from the neighborhood I guess, or protecting the neighborhood from Criswell, whichever. And the beautiful green lawn that used to be there was all dead and brown. It was really rather seedy and one day as we went by, checking up on Criswell, he was out in a rocking chair or an Adirondack chair I guess, on the porch in just like a t-shirt looking very much like Brando would look if he did

316

Streetcar today with the suspenders. It was a tank top type t-shirt. And the hair was all messed up. He really looked like he had come off a three-day bender. Which might be entirely possible. I don't know. If I was Criswell I think I would tip.

Former Tulsa, Oklahoma Mayor Terry Young:

I was the producer of Generation Rap, the topical show done by Judy Hagedorn and Jan Kizziar. I booked all the guests. My favorite was an almost washed up Criswell (of Criswell Predicts). Never have seen anyone wear as much make-up in my life.

In 1974, Criswell appeared on the Canadian game show Front Page Challenge as the mystery guest. In May a newspaper article ran that checked back on Criswell's predictions made the previous year on the Mayan Hall stage at Southwestern University in Chula Vista. Titled "Criswell predicts...wrong," the article declares "...sounded like a seer, even if he did not forecast like one. His voice was sonorous and meticulously modulated ... dressed in a black frock coat with a gold medallion dangling over his cummerbund, telling some 200 unenlightened souls what to expect in the future; 'I am very fantastic in my predictions. I am the only predictor who places his predictions in print and I want you to check my accuracy.' That was in January 1973. Since then, events have given him an almost perfect record—Of failure." The article then details how all the predictions he had made for 1973 had been flops then "Criswell, who lives in Los Angeles, could not be reached for an explanation of his failure to accurately predict the future. Two booking agencies which have handled him report they have not arranged an appearance for a year. One thing is for certain, though. He did receive his speakers fee which Southwestern College Dean of Student Activities Wayne Allen said was between $500 and $700." The day after this article, another paper ran a story of the opening of the new Martin Derek Hair Design salon and its offer to donate fifty dollars to the Leukemia Society of America for each celebrity who showed up at the opening. Criswell was there along with Bill Macy who played Maude's husband on the TV show, one member of the rock group Chicago, five members of the picture "Harrad Summer," and Judy Canova. In June, Criswell was the featured speaker at the, "Mid Summer Night's Eve with Stars of the Psychic World" at the home of Mrs. Wade Lamming. The event was to benefit the City of Hope Medical Center and also featured Countess Maria Graciette discussing "Astrology and Your Sex Life," as well as "Dorothy Valles, Rozanne, psychics and clairvoyants, tarot card readers, palmists, Tahitian dancers, and special guest Liz Renay."

A December 30 newspaper article reported on Criswell as being one of the key speakers at the first annual convention of Predictors, Forecasters and Psychics Association held at the Hilton Hotel

Criswell and Paul Marco at unknown gathering. Courtesy of Jason Insalaco.

in Fullerton held the previous weekend. The theme of the conclave was "What's Ahead for 1975." Criswell predicted that the U.S. economy would improve in 1975 and that President Ford would stepdown by April 1 and Nelson Rockefeller would take over the office with Ronald Reagan appointed Vice-President. He also predicted that former President Nixon would recover and be appointed to a high government position, that it would be a poor year for doctors and undertakers as people were becoming healthier, the Yellow Cab Co. would only hire women drivers because they are not picked up so often for drunk driving, Las Vegas would offer free marriages and divorces, Mae West's *Pleasure Man* would be a best seller and television would go third dimensional.

1975 was a relatively quiet year for Criswell. In March, it was reported that he predicted to a realty firm that his property on Cassil Place would sell within thirty days at close to the asking price of $115,000. On September 11, the Long Beach *Press-Telegram* ran a piece on Criswell for his upcoming address to the Shipbuilders Council at the Queensway Hilton. He was quoted in the article as saying that Nixon was still big in the Midwest and would again attain high office because of his continuing popularity in the nation's heartland. Two photos accompanied the article and showed a still lively Mr. Criswell, but with a puffy and aging appearance similar to W.C. Fields. The article gave his typical biography and recounted some of his predictions concluding with, "Future fashion will see American women blossoming out next spring in swishing gowns, circa 1907, their heads adorned with large, floppy garden hats—in plastic. The lengthy skirts of that modest era will feature slits to the thigh, however. And the frocks are likely to be see-through, Criswell said, his baby blue eyes twinkling in anticipation."

On January 3, 1976, the *Syracuse Post-Standard* ran a piece titled "The Crystal Balls" by Jenkin Lloyd Jones. It began with "MAN'S HUNGER TO LEARN his future is as old as his brain, and those psychics,

Criswell, Paul Marco, and Maria Graciette. Courtesy of Jason Insalaco.

seers, soothsayers and clairvoyants who claim to peer through the dark curtain of the unhappened are especially vocal and popular as each New Year comes around." Calling Criswell "one of the most fearless of the breed," it recounts his prediction for the world to end on August 18, 1999, then relates some of Jeane Dixon's prognostications which continue into the year 2000 with China emerging as the dominant industrial power and conquering all of Asia until the United States and its allies counterattack with "nuclear blasts, radiation, firestorms followed by pestilence." Criswell's predictions for the new year were that the government would give practically all of New Mexico back to the Indians, nearly all the dairy cattle in Wisconsin would die of a new disease, it wouldn't rain anywhere for ten months, and people will rush to the Arctic and Antarctic to get snow and ice, but the good news was that a woman in Pratt, Kansas, would become a national heroine for some reason. The article ended with the authors own predictions. "As to my own predictions for 1976: Detente pole will collapse, leaving us struggling beneath the canvas. Exactly 86 stars of stage, screen and TV will describe their informal cohabitations as a 'deeper, more meaningful relationship than marriage' the week before they move in with someone else. Many prominent people will die. There will be widespread discontent as citizens everywhere cuss the unusual weather. A total of 172,384,222 Americans will eagerly read every available New Year prediction by the syndicated mystics. Twelve will keep files."

March 18, 1976:

SPECIAL PREDICTIONS:
MARIA GRACIETTE, the noted Latin psychic famous for her uncanny predictions foresees for the next two years "the legalization of latrile for the control of cancer called B 17." . . . The second gun which killed SEN. ROBERT KENNEDY will be found through the true killer (not Sirhan-Sirhan) . . . Ponchos from South America will be the fashion for men. Bright, daring colors, worn next to the skin . . . Three top stars like BURT REYNOLDS, ROBERT REDFORD and PAUL NEWMAN will become enemies over the filming of a super pornographic movie being produced this year by a major studio . . . PATRICIA HEARST will be found innocent of all charges, predicts Maria Graciette.

September 12, 1976:

I predict that our public schools will become so crime infested with drugs, theft and murder and that all schools will be operated in a military manner. Very strict laws of obedience will be enforced. On some school premises there will be a jail. Many students will vote for a firing squad. Impossible? Just wait and see.

I predict by the end of two years, we will have three women on the Supreme Court. Three judges are failing rapidly and cannot live out this year. Congress will balk, but the women will win out.

I predict that California will soon give the death penalty for all narcotic users, including marijuana. Above the roar of the Ultra Liberals this will be accomplished and put into effect.

I predict that all babies at birth will be given a serial number tattooed under the right ear. This will outlaw babies being used as pawns by the parents and collected on two or three times for welfare and death benefits each year.

I predict that King Charles III will soon occupy the throne of England. The ensuing tragedy will strike the heart of the world.

December 26, 1976:

I predict that a suicide club in Hollywood will be uncovered and a scandal will sweep the world. The members would leave their property and money to the club and in some cases it will be proved members were pressured.

CITIZEN'S BAND—I predict that citizen's band radios will soon be equipped with microwaves, which are shorter than the regular radio wavelength. The Federal Communications Commission will turn a sour eye on jokesters who go "blue" with their conversations and broadcasts. Some of the greatest offenders, it will be discovered, are women who delight in reading off—color joke books over the air. I further predict that the question of copyrights will also enter the case next year . . . I predict that graverobbing will become popular with some teenage groups, and that many memorial parks will install electrical warning systems to prevent this action. The resting place of a famed director was disturbed, and the body thrown crudely in front of his home a week later. This band of young atheists, who hunt trouble, have gone their limit, and will be prosecuted!

WILLS—I predict that the final will of Adolf Hitler and Eva Braun will be on probate and that the 8,960 acres of valuable land in Colorado will be on the market. . . .

On January 16, 1977, a photo of an older, spit-curl-less Criswell ran in the "Tele-Vues" section of the paper with the caption: "Criswell didn't predict the end of his show in 1962, but his predictions on many subjects entertained viewers during his nine-year TV career on Chs. 5, 9 and 13. A film clip of his 'Criswell Predicts' will be shown on ch. 5's 30th anniversary special at 8 p.m. Saturday."

July 21, 1978, kicked off a weekend of unusual events when the nation's most renowned psychics, UFO and Holistic Health experts converged on the Western Exhibit Center in Commerce, California for the "Encounters UFO & Psychic Show." Over 400 members of the UFO and psychic communities were expected to attend and "mystify, amaze and entertain the entire family." Criswell appeared with other experts such as Dr. J.K. Jamieson, Gary Wayne, Gene Marvin, Dr. Don Torres, Dixie Yeterian, Maria Graciette, and Dr. Frank Stranges.

On August 29, 1978, Halo's local paper ran an article titled "Sells Her Home in Hollywood" It states that Myrtle Louise Stonesifer King had lived in Hollywood for more than twenty years and had sold her home to Mickey Haggert former, Mr. America and husband of Jayne Mansfield. The home was to become a tourist Sport for Health Shrine, with a plaque to honor Mickey Haggert and the late Hollywood Star Jayne Mansfield and Hollywood Honorary Mayor Criswell. The article listed the address of the property and noted its location next to the Blessed Sacrament Church and the International Village of Howard Hughes. It then claimed that Criswell had a mobile home with two alternative drivers and was scheduled with bookings for the next five years and he would guest on TV with his 87 percent accurate predictions. The article concludes telling of Halo's appearance on the Groucho Marx show and that her play "Hotel for Women" starring Linda Darnell was often on the late movies.

Shortly after the property was sold, one of the units became a world famous punk rock flophouse called "Disgraceland." It was a

notorious crash pad and party place for the next decade for the bur-
geoning Los Angles underground punk music scene with tenants
including members of The Gun Club, The Go-Gos, and Germs. Touring bands that partied and crashed there included REM, Poison 13,
Big Boys, Hickoids, Dicks, Blondie, and The Cramps. Party goers included members of the Red Hot Chili Peppers, X, The Vandals, TSOL,
The Mentors, The Dickies, Tex and the Horseheads, Fishbone, The
Runaways, and Guns 'n Roses. After the police would shut down a
party, the partygoers would climb down into the bomb shelter built
by Criswell and continue to "get bombed."

At the request of Ed Wood in 1978, Pendulum/Eros released
an LP record of the soundtrack from *Plan 9 From Outer Space*
(previously quoted). Wood was working as a sleaze/hack writer
for Pendulum at the time, as well at Gallery and Calga, and the
release of a "straight" film soundtrack would have been very un-
characteristic for the company. This very special, rare, and never
released again edition features a special note to the fans of the
film written by Ed Wood himself. It was written within two weeks
of his death and is his last known public writing. The following
are the final excerpts:

A SPECIAL NOTE FROM EDWARD D. WOOD, JR. Writer-Producer-Director of *Plan 9 From Outer Space:*

> When the producers of this record album asked me to write
> some notes for the jacket, I was delighted. Needless to say,
> when I made "Plan 9 From Outer Space" in 1959, I never
> dreamed that it would still be playing on television to millions
> of loyal fans some twenty years later.
>
> Of course, I always knew "Plan 9" was my finest work, but
> that doesn't always guarantee a movie's place in film history.
> So while big budget turkeys like "Cleopatra" and "Dr. Dolit-
> tle" quickly fade from the public's memory, "Plan 9" endures.

(Indeed, if I had guessed that "Plan 9" would hold up so well, I would have asked for more money up front.)

But time has proved the fans right. Not only is "Plan 9" a hit on late night television, but now it has been permanently preserved on this phonographic record, which contains nearly all of the film's dialogue and music. I would be lax if I did not mention the wonderful music by Gordon Zahler. I think it is his finest work, surpassing even his superb scores for "Mutiny in Outer Space" and "Women of the Prehistoric Planet."

Finally, a special note to all of my special friends. I am retired now, and living comfortably in the home of a good friend. I still keep a watchful eye on the Hollywood scene, and I still dream of the day when my sequel to "Plan 9," "The Night of the Ghouls," will be rescued from the Pathé Laboratory and released for all my fans to see and enjoy. Until that time, I manage to occupy myself by puttering in the garden and watching football on television.

So here is the record of "Plan 9 From Outer Space." I hope you enjoy listening to it as much as I enjoyed creating it. Edward D. Wood, Jr., December, 1978.

Edward Davis Wood, Jr. went to the Great Beyond on December 10, 1978, at the age of fifty-three after he suffered an alcohol-induced heart attack while watching a football game. In February 1979, Paul Marco, Ed's widow Kathy, Criswell, and minister David DeMering called friends together at the home of actor Peter Coe where Eddie had passed away. Reverend David delivered the eulogy, which referenced several of Eddie's films and the actors who appeared in them, ending with "Now with keeping with what I am sure would be Ed's wishes, let us all drink a toast to his memory and wish him the very best in his life to come." Buddy Hyde, David Ward, and a few others were also in attendance.

Criswell, Kathy Wood, and Rev. David DeMering. Ed Wood's Wake. Courtesy of Jason Insalaco.

PAUL MARCO: I felt it was my duty to have a memorial service as Kathy was in no shape to do it. Criswell spoke, I spoke, Kathy spoke very little and naturally, David did the sermon. If you ask me, Wood was way ahead of his time as a filmmaker. He made very good bad movies. His films are the greatest worst movies and they're so bad they're entertaining. Wood's pictures were funny to people even when they first came out but that wasn't his intention because he always meant them to be dramatic and suspenseful. That's all Ed Wood lived for. He wanted to make movies and that's what he did.

Eddie was cremated at Utter-McKinley funeral home and his ashes were scattered at sea. There is no memorial marker anywhere to honor or pay respect to him. He would never know the relative fame and notoriety he had always craved, but would eventually come to his name and his films in a few short years.

After Myrtle sold the apartment buildings, Criswell began residing with his friend, employee, and partner Robert Harrison in a West Hollywood apartment. They would send co-signed Christmas cards, attend events together, and were traveling companions.

Postcard to Paul Marco from Honolulu, Hawaii, 1979:

Hi! Having a wonderful time & the air is fresh & the weather is warm & delightful!

Flying to the Island of Kauai tomorrow & home Thursday!
Best Regards, Criswell & Robert

Cris and Robert would remain living companions until the end of Criswell's life.

In May 1979, Myrtle presented the original manuscript of her play *Evasive Joy* to the Littlestown High School Alumni Association.

JUDY SCOBEE: I recall, in the 1980s, I think it was, while I was walking east on Hollywood Boulevard in the late afternoon, I saw Criswell walking west—and passed right by me—I noticed him, but didn't stop him to say hello, even though I thought he did see me, but may not have remembered me and keep on walking . . . I turned around to watch him continue strolling on (probably to his apt.), and thought, *Wow! There's Criswell!!! How cool to have seen him again!*

Verne Langdon met Mae West for the first time when he was fourteen-and-a-half-years-old in San Francisco. His father took him to see her *Diamond Lil* show the night that General MacArthur returned from the war. During the performance as sirens sounded escorting the general from the airport, Miss West stopped the show and said, "That must be Mac waiting to come in." She brought the house down. Verne's father was a huge Mae West fan and took his son backstage to meet her. Verne was impressed by her remarkable kindness. He later met Mae again during the late 1960s in Hollywood after getting her number from Marty Krofft. He wanted to produce a record album of her doing bedtime fairytales for adults. She agreed to meet him on the project and invited him up to see her.

The album was never produced but Verne developed a close friendship with her that lasted until she passed away.

VERNE LANGDON: Mae West made it known to me that she was into spiritualism and had a couple of favorite spiritualists and seers and her good friend was Criswell. And I knew that already 'cause I had the Decca album, and she does the song "Criswell Predicts" which she wrote. So, one day I went up to see her and who was sitting there, smoking a cigar yet, but Criswell. She introduced me to him, and I was stunned that he had the audacity to smoke in her apartment, in front of her, because she just detested cigarette smoke and I presumed cigar smoke although she revealed in her autobiography that her father smoked a cigar, and her brother smoked a cigar so maybe it brought back pleasant fragrant memories to her. I never really figured that one out. Be that as it may, there was Criswell sitting in his shirt and suspenders, as I recall, and looking very much like a used car salesman, with all apologies to the profession. He was a very showbiz kind of guy with a George Putnam sort of delivery. He did not give me a cold reading, thank you, fortunately. I couldn't have taken that because I've been in and out of that racket most of my life. I know most of those people and I know what they do and how they do it. I am personally a firm believer in the Great Beyond, but I know that we don't need channelers like those guys to do it. But Criswell was more of a predictor than a channeler. She had a couple of channelers that she was fascinated with. I met him a couple of times up there and usually she'd schedule you, "Well you wanna come up, you can come up at two o'clock." Well she had somebody up there that she was seeing at one and they'd be leaving as you'd be arriving and that was the way you usually met everybody she knew. "This is so and so, and this is Verne, blah, blah, blah." I met a lot of interesting people that way. George Raft used to go up and see her often. She gave Cary Grant his start in pictures, and he always credited her with that too. He did two films with her. She always said, "He was so good I had him twice." She'd wait for the laugh and of course you'd give it. The great thing about her was when you went to visit her, you didn't have to do anything, you just sat there and listened to her for an hour. She'd tell you the stories and she had them down pat. That's where I met Criswell, at Mae's and apparently she was very entertained by him. I guess the last time I saw him was at Mae's service in Forest Lawn. I think at the Wee Kirk of the Heather or something like that chapel and Criswell was very, very thin and very wan and he was wheeled in in a wheelchair and he did not look good, and I think he passed away within a year or so of her.

Criswell's good friend Mae West went to the Great Beyond on November 22, 1980. According to Paul Marco, Criswell convinced Mae's boyfriend Paul Novak to have an open casket service at her funeral.

VERNE LANGDON: Originally, Paul (Novak) had planned on a closed casket and when he went to the mortuary and saw what a beautiful job that they had done on her remains, he said, "No, by all means let's have an open casket." She was wearing one of the gowns that Edith Head had designed for her for *Sextette* (1978). It was a gorgeous gown, all bugle beads and rhinestones. In the chapel there were two beautiful tall rectangular stained glass windows and it had rained that morning, but the rain had cleared up and the sun had come out. And as the funeral service progressed, the sun came up outside and shone through those windows on her in state in the casket and glistened off the bugle beads. The mourners gasped audibly almost as one. It looked like she was breathing because the light was glistening on these beads. It was the eeriest thing I have ever seen in my life. We were stunned, the entire chapel, there were about a hundred people there, by invitation only. It was just a breath taking incident.

In 1980 the book *The Golden Turkey Awards* by film critics Michael and Harry Medved was published. It was a follow-up to their first book *The Fifty Worst Films of All Time (and How They Got That Way)* (1978), celebrating "so bad it's good" cinema and asking the readers for a vote for the best of the worst films of all time in various categories. The results were presented in the 1980 book which describes 200 "turkeys" nominated and honored. Of the 3,000 votes tallied, *Plan Nine From Outer Space* won the Grand Turkey award with 393 votes. An awards ceremony was held at the Nuart Theater in West Los Angeles in March 1982. The book is credited with giving *Plan 9 From Outer Space* the dubious distinction as "the worst film of all time" and Ed Wood as "the worst director of all time." The book has been criticized by film scholars and film buffs who argue that the Medved's opinions are biased and unfair. Nonetheless, the book helped spawn an Ed Wood mania with a resurgence of interest in his films with late-night showings and festival screenings. Criswell attended one such screening in a wheelchair.

The *Gettysburg Times* ran a column called "Glimpses" on July 12, 1982, that was a portrait of Myrtles life.

Excerpts:

Victorian furniture in the grand salon of the grand home at 14 S. Queen St. Littlestown is shrouded by plastic. A grand piano holding scores of classical music by Debussy, Mendelssohn; a six by eight-foot gilded mirror; a chandelier with three lamps each dripping 10 strands of crystal: pictures of a willowy woman in misty settings, all hint a grandeur that has long past.

The mistress of this manse on S. Queen St. is Myrtle Louise Stonesifer King. Myrtle Louise will do. Everyone in Littlestown knows Myrtle Louise.

The elegant furniture is cloaked in plastic. The hard wood floor is bare. The entryway walls are lined with her sketches of people and flowers; the kind her namesake, Aunt Myrtle Newman did. Aunt Myrtle's heavy oil paintings of flowers hang in the parlor among other pictures of Myrtle Louise as a young girl, adolescent, young woman and her later years. Sheet music of works with pictures of Louise Howard and Halo Meadows, "Hollywood personality," on the front; a well-thumbed hard copy of her book, "How to Have Everything You Want," cover the top of the grand piano in the corner. She says she has written 14 plays, numerous poems and three books. As she sat on the folding campstool in the middle of the grand salon reflecting on her life, Aunt Myrtle's huge mirror threw back a three-foot by five-foot oil portrait of a stunning young woman. Raymond S. Pease, a New York artist, gave her the painting he had done in 1937, when Louise Howard was the "hottest thing on Broadway."

She's Myrtle Louise now, still the spirited daughter of the man who gave the town its swimming pool: home against his wishes. Her life in Littlestown is not quite victory: not quite perfection; but, she's "taking it" well.

On August 30, 1982, Criswell was admitted to St. Joseph's Medical center in Burbank for the treatment of several illnesses. He had suffered a number of strokes over the previous year. In the early morning of October 4 he suffered a cardiac arrest and passed away at the hospital. He was cremated October 7 and interred at Pierce Brothers Valhalla Memorial Park, North Hollywood, in the Niches of Remembrance, F-10, Space 2. His death certificate has the address of 1760 W El Cerrito Place, Apt #20, Los Angeles, as his residence. His occupation is listed as Psychic for forty years. Kind of industry or business is of course listed as Entertainment. Robert G. Harrison was listed as Executor also residing at the same listed address.

Obituaries appeared in *Variety, Los Angeles Times, Los Angeles Herald-Examiner, The Evansville Courier, Princeton Clarion,* and the *Gettysburg Times.* Some were inaccurate and contained erroneous information. One stated that he died in his Hollywood home, while others listed his first name as Jerome or Jared. Some said he had only been in the hospital for about a week. Some said he died of a stroke, but his death certificate states, "cardiac arrest." One would say he began predicting as a child while another would say he started prognosticating during his radio news-casting days. Even in death, the "facts" about Criswell did not jive. The most lengthy and detailed, but still containing some inaccuracies was in his hometown paper the *Princeton Clarion*, where they had his name as Jerome.

Excerpts:

Charlie King, as he was known growing up, never gave any indication during his childhood and adolescence that he was special in any way, according to those who knew the young Criswell. Former classmates' comments ranged from "he was quite a character" to "he was nothing out of the ordinary." An old family friend described Criswell as an "all-around guy, nothing too outstanding."

The self-styled psychic allegedly claimed he first realized he could predict the future when he would tell his mortician-parents who their next customer would be.

However, according to a family member, Criswell's father never ran a mortuary.

Charlie King Sr. sold insurance in Princeton and died long before his son became a world-recognized figure, said the family member.

October 8, 1982, *The Gettysburg Times*, Obituaries:

Charles C. King
Charles Criswell King, 75, long-time syndicated columnist and television personality, died in his home in Hollywood,

Calif., Monday night. He had suffered a series of cerebral apoplexies in recent months. King was the husband of Myrtle Louise Stonesifer King of Littlestown. Born in Princeton, Ind., Aug.18, 1907, he went to Cincinnati University then on to the New York theatre scene in the mid-30s. He met and married the former Miss Stonesifer in 1940. A noted soothsayer and prediction artist, his books—"To the Year 2000," "Criswell Predicts Your Next Ten Years," and "Criswell's Forbidden Predictions"—caused sensations when they were released. He was a talk show host in the 1960's and lectured with Jeane Dixon on occasion. Besides his wife, from whom he was legally separated in 1974, he has no known survivors.

An October 24, 1982 commentary article by Tom Shales claims that "In a 1976 interview, Johnny Carson denounced the writers of 'Saturday Night Live' for hanging a joke on the death of a comedian known as 'Professor Backwards.' The joke was that the Professor had perished because people ignored his cries of 'pleh, pleh.' That's 'help' spelled backwards. Carson thought this tasteless, he said then. But he is nothing if not adaptable. Recently, after the death of an entertainer and pop psychic known as 'Criswell' of 'Criswell Predicts' fame, Carson joked about it on the air. He said the sad thing about Criswell's death was that Criswell hadn't predicted it."

From *The Picture of Dorian Gray* by Oscar Wilde:

When they entered, they found hanging upon the wall a splendid portrait of their master as they had last seen him, in all the wonder of his exquisite youth and beauty.

Lying on the floor was a dead man, in evening dress, with a knife in his heart. He was withered, wrinkled, and loathsome of visage. It was not till they had examined the rings that they recognized who it was.

The Long Arm of God

Who knows but what future generations from some other planet will dig down through seven layers of rubble and find us some 2,000 years hence, crowd around a museum glass containing a broken fragment of a Coca Cola bottle, a bent hairpin and a parched copy of our Bible which managed to escape the terrifying destruction of our civilization!

They will wonder what on earth was meant by the words "Henry Ford" or "Hollywood" and what in heaven's name was a Criswell?

Criswell

In 1983, the *Adams County Illustrated Press* ran what they called an "Exclusive."

MIND GUIDE By M.L.S. King (Wife of the late columnist "Criswell Predicts")

Marriage vows with words like "sickness" and "death" end dream of Prince and Princess.

Not many would think "love" if they considered the other bringing life of pain, lower-level, nagging, aggravation, frustration and insults.

Communication is now main problem; but how many communicate before marriage, except for flattery.

Find oneself by being true to another; admit wanting sex habit, drink, smoke or gambling. Admit wanting another to work for your interest and forget theirs.

If both truly want to slave for propagation and education of young, then marriage is definitely for them.

If you want self improvement, consider two can climb in society scheme, but which one will be in front waving and who pulls the oars in that boat?

Maybe frankness can't exist as it would kill the game; if so, why complain about our Fate?

Even the front person will get a Judgment Day even while living, so who wins?

1983 saw *Revenge of the Dead* finally released as *Night of the Ghouls* after Wade Williams paid the twenty-five-year-old lab fees and rescued Criswell's second film appearance from obscurity, and increasing the cult following of Ed Wood. After the film's long await-ed release, writer Ken Hollings observed:

> In a curious tale of ghosts, man-made monsters and haunted houses filled with mysterious corridors, Kenne Duncan, look-ing about as psychic as a set of brass knucks, plays turbaned swami Dr. Acula, bilking the rich, the gullible and the recently bereaved of their money with the aid of his phony seances. Unfortunately, the special effects budget for Ed Wood's movie was so low that even the rigged spirit communications seem fake. They were good enough for Criswell, however. Under their influence, he crosses over from his usual role as the film's narrator to appear in its closing moments, revealing himself to be a creature from beyond the grave, conjured up from "the everlasting pit of darkness" by Dr. Acula's hocus pocus.

The Skeptical Inquirer; The Magazine for Science and Reason is the journal for the Committee for the Scientific Investigation of Claims of the Paranormal (CSICOP for short). The Fall 1983 issue featured a column in the editors News and Comment section called "Criswell Predicts: A Quick Look Back."

> Few people knowledgeable about such matters took the 'psychic' Criswell seriously, but much of the public did. A good guide to the accuracy of his predictions comes from the article 'Criswell Predicts Your Next Ten Years,' published in the November 1969 *Saga*. Reader Richard L. Tierney recently dug it out of his files. Since the ten-year period it foresaw has now long passed, it is illuminating to recall the predictions. As Tierney says, 'They are hilarious in their glaring inaccuracy.'

Criswell is then debunked by quoting six of his predictions including this one. "On a quiet Sunday afternoon, the sulphuric gases from outerspace will sweep the world . . . This gas will strangle and choke to death millions of people . . . This time Man will perish! Date: 1978."

On Sunday, May 12, 1985, Myrtle passed away at her home in Littlestown. She had just turned eighty years old. Her body was laid to rest next to her parents at Mount Carmel Cemetery, which was founded by her maternal grandfather William F. Crouse in 1861. The *Gettysburg Times* ran an article June 13, about a committee picked to distribute the Stonesifer trust. The trust, of which the community of Littlestown was the major beneficiary upon the death of Myrtle, was estimated to be in excess of $500,000. They then ran an editorial on July 6, 1986, on the development of the Littlestown Community Park. Plans included expansion of the park to include a lake, boat dock, pavilion, more lighting and roads, a parking lot, restroom facilities, and landscaping. One intent was to increase the appeal of the area to families with children and retirees, a place for contemplation and recreation, a place away from noise, and concrete, and bustle. "To those who knew her, that is the kind of place that the late Myrtle Louise Stonesifer King, heiress to the trust, would have liked. She was a free spirit—an author, playwright, actress—who was always probing the sights and sounds around her."

Excerpts from:

ATOMIC LIFE OR 4th DIMENSIONAL PERSPECTIVE
By Halo Meadows

If two people go too far out in thought the world is lost, as they are lost from each other, and when two who connect in thought are lost from each other the lines of thought separate for all.

Two people can be brought back in line through love or hate. Hate makes people sick and produces sick line. Love makes people happy and successful and is the only good line. If two people ever really love enough to go through heaven and hell to get together after a separation there would be no more heaven or hell on earth or the other side of life, and we would have the millinenium (sic) when all would be true to himself and take joy and pride in his own choices. All would recognize the need of each other and that each should feel quality of satisfaction in himself.

If you make design you are in experimentation and that holds energy together, and energy makes matter.

The one who follows no design blows away and the world will disintegrate and blow away into evolutionary dust that will blow away, and after an evolutionary time span of planets for re-forming, the dust will integrate for another planet.

Myrtle Louise Stonesifer Howard Criswell King Halo Meadows, is fondly remembered in her hometown with a "Littlestown Walk of

Fame" star in her honor placed in the sidewalk outside the front door of her former home and at the Stonesifer Memorial Garden located at the family plot in the cemetery.

Rudolph Grey became interested in Ed Wood and his "so bad they're good" movies when he saw a four page photo-illustrated article on the "Allied Artists release" *Night of the Ghouls* in the April 1959 issue of *Famous Monsters*. It seemed to him to be unlike anything else around at the time and it stuck in his mind. But the film would not be released for some time. Then in 1961 the independent New York television station WPIX-11 began telecasting *Bride of the Monster* and *Plan 9 From Outer Space* about every seven weeks for over five years. Rudolph would watch each telecast religiously to see Bela Lugosi in his last speaking role as Dr. Varnoff in *Bride of the Monster* and Criswell's unsettling introduction to *Plan 9*. During the 1960s, he learned of other Ed Wood movies but was only able to see the Wood-scripted *The Bride and the Beast* (1958), when it turned up on television. Then in the fateful month of December 1978, Rudolph saw *Glen or Glenda* for the first time during a Friday midnight screening. It was a revelation for him, and he would return each weekend with friends to share the experience. Soon after he began working with a colleague on a series of interviews and Ed Wood was high on the list for future interviews, but it was too late. Rudolph then began researching Wood's life and would do so for the next ten years, conducting hundreds of interviews and rescuing many one-of-a-kind photos from certain oblivion. The result of this obsession and perseverance came in the form of the book *Nightmare of Ecstasy; The Life and Art of Edward D. Wood, Jr.* published by Feral House in 1992. The book is an oral history presented by the people that knew Wood the best such as his parents, his wife Kathy, his previous wives and lovers, and people that worked on or in his films like Maila Nurmi, Conrad Brooks, and Harry Thomas. Through this method Wood is presented in his full glory exposing his obsessions, fetishes, loves, and unrelenting passion for filmmaking in whatever form it took. The book also includes an excellent chronology of Wood's life, a detailed bibliography of Wood's "adult" books and a complete filmography.

DR. MYSTERIAN: I was even more interested in Criswell upon reading about him in the Ed Wood biography. It sounds as though Criswell was the only one of the group ever to have made money on *Plan 9*. I don't remember the details, except that he was responsible for a showing in New York that became something of a cult success. If this doesn't show some sort of supernatural insight, I don't know what does. I am tickled by the fact that Criswell and Vampira were friends—she seems such a character that it is impossible not to assume that there must have been something pretty special about Criswell for her to want to spend time with him.

In 1994, Tim Burton's biopic *Ed Wood* was released exposing a new generation to the cult movie legend. The script was based on Rudolph Grey's book and was written by Scott Alexander and Larry Karazewski. The film focuses on the time in Ed's life that he made his best-known films and his friendship with Bela Lugosi. Ed Wood regulars, Conrad Brooks, Paul Marco, and Gregory Walcott made cameo appearances along with the previously mentioned appearance by Korla Pandit. Ed Wood was convincingly portrayed by Johnny Depp earning him a Golden Globe nomination. Criswell is also well portrayed by veteran actor Jeffrey Jones. He opens the film rising from a coffin a la *Night of the Ghouls* and introducing the film a la *Plan 9 From Outer Space.*

> Greetings, my friend. You are interested in the unknown, the mysterious, the unexplainable . . . that is why you are here. So now, for the first time, we are bringing you the full story of what happened. . . .
>
> We are giving you all the evidence, based only on the secret testimony of the miserable souls who survived this terrifying ordeal. The incidents, the places, my friend, we cannot keep this a secret any longer. Can your hearts stand the shocking facts of the true story of Edward D. Wood, Junior!?!?

VERNE LANGDON: I think I drove Jeffrey Jones by there (Criswell's apartments) when he was preparing for his Criswell role. He did a marvelous job. He was Criswell. We went to lunch with George Putnam. I love George, and he's a very dear friend of mine. Jeffrey asked what Criswell was like and I said, "I'll take you to lunch with George Putnam and you'll think you're sitting with Criswell." Not that George looked like Criswell, perish the thought, but George has a beautiful radio voice and tremendous radio presence and so did Criswell. That was how Jeffrey prepped for that role.

VERNON KOENIG: He was portrayed quite accurately in the movie *Ed Wood.* In fact, he was portrayed so well that I had some flashbacks to the mid-1950s, when I first met him.

Jeffrey Jones played Criswell to a T. He had Criswell's mannerisms, voice and gesturing perfect—complete with the sequin tuxedo.

Eddie and Cris' friend Bela Lugosi was so well portrayed by Martin Landau that it earned him an Oscar and Golden Globe for Best Actor in a Supporting Role for 1995. Rick Baker and crew were also awarded an Oscar for Best Makeup. Some said Eddie would have loved the "realism" of the film.

CLAUDIA POLIFRONIO: When I saw that movie *Ed Wood*, I said, "Ed Wood? Ed Wood? It couldn't possibly be the same person." I said, "Oh, not THAT Ed Wood." I can't figure out why they showed he was interested in Bela Lugosi; he was more interested in Criswell. That's what he told me; those are the three men I admire. But Criswell. . . . but I don't think Criswell gave him that much. He was very wise that way.

I was surprised they made a movie about Ed Wood instead of Criswell.

Some people who actually knew Bela Lugosi, Ed Wood, and Criswell say that the portrayals are not genuine to who the men actually were and some of the incidents portrayed in the film are not accurate and were fabricated. Certainly that is true since the film was made for entertainment purposes and not as a completely factual documentation of the events portrayed.

VERNE LANGDON: Tim Burton and everybody in *Ed Wood*, from Johnny Depp to Jeffrey to the gal that played Vampira (Lisa Marie) and Jim Meyer, George the Animal Steele who played Tor, just exquisitely captured the flavor of that period. Honestly, I could smell the Hollywood they were depicting in that film. They really brought that period to life. One of the finest movies I've ever seen. Just awesome. It speaks so highly of everybody involved. Especially Jeffrey, especially Tim Burton, especially Landau and the rest of them were just marvelous. That's what Hollywood looked like and smelled like. He really did a fine job with Criswell. Criswell would have been delighted. He was CRISWELL!

VERNON KOENIG: In the *Ed Wood* movie, there were lots of inferences to the Brown Derby. That is very true. We went there with Criswell, his wife, and several others. As soon as he walked in the door, people would stand up and want to talk with him. He was NEVER out of character. He was always CRISWELL!

Earl Kemp wrote that he views his VHS copy of the film on dark winter evenings to get back that old-time thrill. "They are all still there, whenever I want them or need them, just waiting to be watched. Watching them brings back all those wonderful feelings of yesterday. If I close my eyes and breathe deeply, I can see Bela Lugosi lurking just at the fringes of my imagination awaiting his cue to slink onstage ominously, and I can pick up the heady aroma of Criswell's Max Factor No. 5 pancake makeup and Wood's even headier dedication. With people like Dracula, Bela Lugosi, Ed Wood, and Criswell around, you don't need much more to get you through the night."

Sept. 6, 1999, The *New Yorker*, The Talk of the Town, POSTCARD FROM L.A. by John Whalen.

Excerpts:

"The world as we know it will cease to exist . . . on August 18, 1999," he forecast in his 1968, book *Criswell Predicts from Now to the Year 2000*. He went on, "And if you and I meet each other on the street that fateful day . . . we will open our mouths to speak and no words will come out, for we have no future—you and I will suddenly run out of time!"

Though Criswell departed the world as we know it in 1982, his friends and admirers hadn't yet been stricken mute by the evening of August 18th. On that Wednesday night, an as-

From left: Jeffery Jones as Criswell, Sarah Jessica Parker as Dolores Fuller, Martin Landau as Bela Lugosi, Johnny Depp as Ed Wood, George "the Animal" Steele as Tor Johnson, Max Casella as Paul Marco, and Brent Hinkley as Conrad Brooks. *Ed Wood* promotional photo.

sortment of them congregated at the congenially moldering Boardners, an old-time Hollywood watering hole and former Criswell haunt. They came to toast the Criswellian apocalypse, and to raise a Martini glass to one of Hollywood's first celebrity psychics.

As the clock neared midnight, Coulombe, dressed in tails for the occasion, donned a white wig and commemorated the planet's final moments by channeling Criswell.

Reading aloud the psychic's vision of doomsday, Coulombe intoned, "Future generations from some other planet will dig down through seven layers of rubble and find us some two thousand years hence. They will wonder what on earth was meant by the words 'Henry Ford' or 'Hollywood,' and what in heaven's name was a Criswell?

Alas, when the last revelers left, at 2 A.M., Boardners was still standing, thus dealing the Criswell legacy yet another harsh statistical blow. But on a much more important level, Hollywood's greatest seer had vindicated himself: he had posthumously conjured an enthusiastic party in his honor. The significance of August 18th? It's Criswell's birthday.

On August 18, 1999, the world could have been easily destroyed due to an event that very few people were aware of. NASA's Cassini spacecraft swooped past our planet at more than 42,000 miles per hour and used the Earth's gravity as a slingshot to accelerate on its way to Saturn. The Cassini contained over seventy-two pounds of plutonium fuel. If the Cassini had inadvertently entered the Earth's atmosphere, the electrical power system would have disintegrated, dispersing the plutonium so widely that 5 billion of the world population would have received ninety-nine percent or more of the radiation exposure. It would have given everyone on Earth lung cancer. NASA claimed that there was only a one-in-a-million chance that this could have occurred due to any number of malfunctions, including electrical short-circuits, meteors or space debris striking the space probe and erroneous ground commands. If the craft had veered even slightly from its course, it would have plunged into the Earth's atmosphere and burned up like a meteorite or like Criswell's "Vision of the End" from *CPY2K*.

There is a vision, which repeats and repeats and repeats. It is a black rainbow in the sky. And this black rainbow will herald the coming of the end of the world as you and I know it now. This black rainbow will encircle the planet Earth and it will be seen from every vantage point on the face of the earth for at night it will glow with an iridescent light and at night (sic) (during the day?) it will be a black streak across our sky; a rainbow, a jet black rainbow; an ebony rainbow; a black rainbow, which will signify the coming suffocation of our world. This black rainbow will seemingly bring about, through some mysterious force beyond our comprehension, a lack of oxygen. It is through this that we will be so weakened that when the final end arrives, we will go gasping for breath, and then there will only be silence on the earth. Every tick of the clock brings us nearer and nearer to this destiny.

Dr. Mysterian was a brilliant divinity student until a freak accident caused him to become beset with visions of the future, including one showing him the EXACT DATE OF HIS OWN DEATH— January 26, 2010! His prophecies for the future have independently been proven to be 98% correct, and he continued to write them until the irreversible date of his quietus.

DR. MYSTERIAN: Criswell is, of course, my greatest influence, although I will never be able to achieve the sort of delirious sense of a future where anything is possible that he regularly produced. My first encounter with Criswell was through *Plan 9,* as I imagine is true of most people my age (late 30s). Later, I found copies of his books in used bookstores, much to my delight. Although he was quite wrong about the future (thankfully, or the world would be ended by now), I found his predictions nonetheless fascinating. When he wasn't predicting some sort of lunatic tragedy, such as rioting cannibals in North America or rays from space destroying Denver, there was a sort of utopian quality to his view of the future. I presume he was some sort of closet nudist, as he seemed to have a taste for predictions in which inhabitants of the future throw off their clothes in favor of their naked bodies. And anyone who sees a future in which Mae West is president is doing something right, as far as Dr. Mysterian is concerned, even if he was wrong. His predictions seemed to be an odd mix of sexual libertinism, which I expect was the result of his reputed homosexuality, and cranky, the world is going to hell in a hand basket conservatism. The details of his home life intrigue me as well. I am responsible for adding many of the details about Criswell to his entry on Wikipedia, based on information gleaned from his various fan pages, and how is it possible not to like someone who threw regular weekend picnics and cocktail parties at the Brown Derby with the likes of Ed Wood and Tor Johnson! I have a copy of Ed Wood's "Necrophenia" [Necromania], or whatever it is called, and it is impossible for me to watch without thinking about the fact that the coffin in the film was on loan from Criswell.

I did have a shrine to Criswell, by the way, and may still, presuming it is not underwater in New Orleans. It was coffin-shaped, fit into the palms of both hands, and opened to reveal a photo of Criswell, plastic flowers, a key and a clock. I made the shrine myself and painted it to resemble a Mexican folk shrine. Whenever I prognosticated, I lit candles at Criswell's shrine. I hope to do this again soon, although I may have to make another shrine to do so.

The internet is a great resource for all manner of things Criswellian. On eBay you can find copies of his books, CDs of his record album (occasionally actual copies of the LP), VHS and DVDs of the films he in which he appeared, t-shirts, badges, a Ouija board, among other oddball items. The Internet Archive has audio files of the "Criswell Predicts" song by Mae West and his record album of predictions as well as the video of Criswell's 1966 appearance on the Johnny Carson show. There are a number of fan websites along with biographical listings on sites such as the Internet Movie Database and Wikipedia, as well as a listing for his grave on the Roadside America website and findagrave.com.

Ctheory, an online "international journal of theory, technology and culture" published two essays in the late 1990s, by Ken Hollings called "Criswell Predicts: Lost Voices from a Forgotten Future, 1956–59" and "We are All Depraved: Criswell Predicts Your Next Ten Years." They propose interesting analogies and strange connections between Criswell's life, film and TV appearances and his predictions, with events occurring in the twilight areas of the late 1950s on to the end of the 20th century. Hollings "reconfigures reality" in his writings. "And once more we see him, at the end of his story: Blond Criswell, Amazing Criswell, sitting under the studio lights in fantastic L.A., capital city of the Space Age. Its concrete and steel towers hold their breath in fear and admiration, waiting in the dark for their moment to come."

Reverend Steve Galindo founded the Church of the Heavenly Wood in 1996. The internet church practices the pop-culture based religion called Woodism, looking to Ed Wood as their savior. "We at The Church of Ed Wood use Ed and his films to inject spirituality into those who get little fulfillment from more mainstream religions like Christianity. By looking at his films and his life, we learn to lead happy, positive lives. We strive for acceptance of others and of the self. You might think that it's silly or stupid, but Woodism currently boasts over 3,000 legally baptized followers worldwide! That's over 3,000 who have joined Reverend Steve Galindo in keeping Ed Wood's spirit and message alive! You might think we're silly or stupid. And that's fine with us. After all, we don't expect you to believe in Woodism. We expect you to respect OUR belief in Woodism." Criswell is seen as a saint in the Church of Ed Wood. "The importance of Criswell in relation to Ed Wood's life is very strong. In the spiritual world of Ed Wood, Criswell seems to be seated next to our savior, sitting next to him as the man who occasionally Ed seeks guidance from. He was a very strong, eclectic man in life, and he remains so even in death." On October 17, 2004, the Church of Ed

Wood along with Cinema Insomnia hosted the first *EdWoodstock* in Sacramento, California, at the historic Crest Theatre. The event was advertised as "a freaky love-fest of music, B-movies and Edward D. Wood Jr." and featured a trio of bands, followed by a screening of *Bride of the Monster*. More than seventy people attended with forty baptized into the church by Reverend Steve.

In December of 2005, Legend Films released a colorized version of *Plan 9* on DVD with a number of bonus features including never-before-seen home movies of Wood and rare television commercials he directed.

In May of 2006, I traveled to Los Angeles for business and to conduct research and interview Criswell acquaintances, associates, and friends. Paul Marco was to be one such interview. Shortly after I arrived I received an email from film historian and actor Al Doshna containing a press release informing me that Paul had sadly passed away the previous day. Needless to say, I was saddened by Paul's demise and disappointed that a lot of tales about, and information on Criswell from his close friend was now lost. He had been recovering from complications of a broken hip he had suffered the previous year, but in recent months his health and career had begun to pick up momentum. He was interviewed the day before his death by a Lugosi biographer who said he seemed healthy and was in good spirits, telling stories of yesteryear with clarity. He had recently reprised his Kelton the Cop role for the DVD *Kelton's Dark Corner* directed by Vasily Shumov. The project is a series of short films in a noir style starring an older, more world-wise and hardened Kelton. The day of his death he was scheduled to shoot scenes for the second installment but when the production's driver called for him, the housekeeper said. "I think Mr. Marco is dead."

VASILY SHUMOV: Paul was a great person to have fun with and liked to make jokes during our production meetings and shooting.

I felt that we had a good chemistry and I saw how Paul enjoyed the "new" Kelton character, I used a technique of animated stills for this film and a green screen. I don't think Paul had ever been in a green screen session before and had never recorded his voice into a computer. Surprisingly Paul took all these new filmmaking technologies very well and was very comfortable during production. He was calling me often to talk about ideas and suggestions about characters and actors for future consideration. Actually it was Paul's idea to make five or six *Kelton's Dark Corner* episodes so it could be presented as a feature film. We were in the middle of shooting the second episode when Paul passed away, just a few hours before our crew was going to pick him up for the scheduled shooting session. I was on my way to the location when I got the news about his death.

In definite Ed Wood style, Vasily decide to continue production on the project and finish it using a body double and previously unused shots from the first episode. The next weekend I was invited to participate in the production with a small part as a street thug harassing a vendor selling oranges on my block. During the day's production, Al Doshna body-doubled for Paul covered by a blanket and lying in the trunk of a vintage Cadillac. A DVD was released in October 2007, by Center Productions and the series can be viewed on YouTube.

August 18, 2007 was the 100th anniversary of Criswell's birth and a celebration was held called "Cristennial." It was conducted at The Piano Bar on Selma Boulevard in Hollywood just a couple of blocks from Criswell's apartments. The event was co-hosted by Charles and Andre Coulombe and myself. Charles had arranged for the "Hottest new act in Vaudeville," Evans and Rogers to provide entertainment for the event and they did a wonderful job with timeless songs that transported everyone to another time and place.

As the evening progressed, there were sing-alongs, dancing, lots of drinking, and loads of fun. A number of Criswell friends and acquaintances were in attendance along with Criswell fans know as "Criswellians." Guests included Tequila Mockingbird, Judy Scobee, Patrick Langdon, Joel Talbot, Scott Michaels, Lance Barton, and Claudia Polifronio. About thirty of the attendees made a candlelight procession to the Criswell apartments. After arriving at the apartments, Charles spoke fondly of Criswell, his place in history, and his effect on our lives. Happy Birthday was sung for Criswell, the candles were blown out, and the party headed back to the bar for more drinking and fun. One of the partygoers described the event as "haut boheme."

WARREN BEATH: I love Criswell. An effete Jerry Lee Lewis or a mentholated Gorgeous George, he was a pompous and pompadoured flatulence—an albino raven perched on the main nerve of the collective unconscious in the nineteen-sixties. And he was a delight—there is something about his delicious posturing that skewered authority and the scientific deity of rationality that reigned supreme in the fifties and sixties. He was a personality—there was no apparent line between his screen persona and his real self (whatever that was) and he lived in a bizarre screen world of Ed Wood and was also one of the fascinating denizens of the Hollywood fringe demimonde peopled by such as Vampira, Bela Lugosi, and Tor Johnson. He was ridiculous, but he was also an antidote and a tonic for everything that ailed the times—and the present time.

VALDA HANSEN: Everyone listened to Criswell. Whether you made fun of it or not, he had a following that wouldn't stop.

VERNON KOENIG: He once told me, in so many words, that he wasn't a psychic, that his predictions were based on history repeating itself. Criswell was considered "schlock" Hollywood, but he did have a following though.

MAILA NURMI: He claimed he was not psychic. I know he was. John believed it too. But the prophecy was intended to shock. And he said, "No, I'm not. I'm not psychic." It was for the money was understood, it was inferred, but he didn't say it.

ROBERT HANKS: My grandmother explained that Criswell was born and raised in Indiana, and recognized (as did others) that he had a special psychic gift early in his life. She told me that Criswell told her that when he began to profit from his gift (which I believe was real) he lost his ability and descended into the campy "I Predict" schtick, which, while often seeming insincere, was nevertheless very successful. He had real charisma and could take a room by storm. His campy, exaggerated act hid a high intelligence.

FORREST ACKERMAN: I don't know where in the world he got his reputation because I don't recall a single prediction ever coming true.

CLAUDIA POLIFRONIO: Well, he didn't really like show business that much. He called it "Wormwood" or whatever. He didn't like it. He was just kind of pushed into it because of his presence. So he would always say, "Ah, the price I pay for this fame." Which I thought was funny. Almost every other day, "Ah, the price of fame."

I don't think he really liked it that much. He put on a good show. But he could put on a good show lecturing about vitamins or political things. I just had the feeling he was very politically inclined. But they were more metaphysicians. And that's the part I was more aligned to, mind science, occult things, psychic things. And so we connected on that.

His hair was not white, it was platinum blonde. Pure blonde. That's why I thought I was standing in front of Dorian Gray. And when I got to know him, I found out that's why he came out here, to [try out for the role in the Dorian Gray movie.]

. . . when they wanted to make the movie in Hollywood, he was up for the part. Which he was sure he was going to get. And that was the biggest heartbreak of his life. He didn't get it. Hurd Hatfield got it. So that's the whole story. Not the details.

LITA BOWMAN: My son, Christian, was influenced by Criswell, sat in with the elders who discussed philosophy, science, history, religion, truths, etc. . . He relished "deep thoughts." When he noticed he too had psychic powers, he studied metaphysics and related subjects and went onto get a Ph.D. in Comparative Religion.

Lita's son posted on Criswell's virtual grave web page. "I met you when I was about 6 years old and you were very kind to me. My sister and I used to play in your backyard because we lived in an apartment building and had no yard of our own . . . and it was okay with you since you knew 'we were very quiet and well-mannered children'. Thanks for your kindness. God bless you.—Christian"

CONRAD BROOKS: I was hoping when he did predict about the *Graverobbers from Outer Space*, I was hoping that would be true. Which, that's about the only one I knew that finally turned out to be the right one.

JOHN GILMORE: He had a following in Hollywood, a specific group on the fringes of the industry. Many gay people were puzzled by him because he had, much earlier, been involved in the gay scene himself (according to those who knew him), and then, they felt, he had turned against them. It was rather clear that he would exploit all he could for whatever he could get out of it. Many people read his writings to be amused, like watching the TV stuff, not to be taken seriously (except by the "fringe" followers, tarot cards, crystal balls, etc.) Many people in the industry thought of Criswell as a "cheap fraud", a "wholly disagreeable person", and a "fraud" . . . a "fake" who desperately wanted to be in the same place as a Manley Hall or a kind of "revered mystic" but would never rise above the Ed Wood and Vampira league. He would love to have had the support granted to Manley Hall, but while Hall believed in what he did, it is said that Criswell only cared about how many bucks whatever he did could draw. A frustrated actor/star, it has been said he adopted the role of "mystic" and "psychic" in order to "sucker in" the sheep to be fleeced. That's one side of it. I found him to be a fascinating character, like that of an ultra-smooth con man.

WARREN BEATH: I have several signed copies of Criswell "texts" and to touch that which he touched is a religious experience for someone who elevates to godhood those inimitable figures who lived courageously counter to science, good-sense, and good taste. His sexual ambiguity—well, maybe he was hardly ambiguous sexually—was emblematic of the big question mark he posed and that made him something of an enigma and mystery. He was a Christ-like figure of reconciliation between the rational and the forces of darkness, making augury palatable when it was tuxedo-ed and immaculately coiffed. He was the Hanged Man of the Tarot—the man who lived contrary to the world and to whom uncommon sense was common sense. A wonderful guy to share a Beefeater martini with—I regret I never met him.

CLAUDIA POLIFRONIO: Ed Wood told me once, he would come downstairs every so often, he wasn't a very talkative person. He was kind of shy, but he said. "There's three people that I think are the greatest: Bela Lugosi, Vincent Price, and Criswell." But Criswell, he said he's the best. He really liked Criswell.

Criswell was always speaking. Very charismatic. Everyone would always be around him. A typical Leo. Very pompous and showy. Great sense of humor. Very nice disposition. You hardly ever saw Criswell bitter or grumpy. He had a benevolence about him.

MAILA NURMI (VAMPIRA): I think people took him seriously. Whenever you wear a good suit and a diamond ring, people tend to take you seriously.

In those days there were very few people who had one name.

THE AMAZING KRESKIN: Did I consider him in any way a legitimate prophet? Of course no, not even remotely. He was funny. And yet people I had met that knew him said that there were times when he took himself quite seriously, but they weren't sure. It was almost as if he was he pulling everyone's leg 'til the very end and if so, my God, more credit to him!

CHARLES COULOMBE: Yes, well, scoffers may scoff! But we true believers know that all of us on earth are simply dwellers in the Criswellian aftermath!

DR. MYSTERIAN: When I first became a prognosticator, it was directly based on Criswell's influence (with a little Dr. Strange thrown in, I suppose). I took a few specific lessons from Criswell. Firstly, claim a high percentage of your predictions are right. Secondly, predict boldly. Thirdly, be fun. In the long run, it is less important that a prognosticator be correct about the future than accurately reflect the possibilities for the future. Reading Criswell's predictions is less a look at how wrong he was than it is a fascinating look at a period in which the future could contain such things as a vending machine that dispenses pills that will cure any illness. And perhaps that future is still to come.

In a general way, a number of Criswell's predictions could be called accurate such as; shifting from paper money and coins to credit cards and other electronic forms of currency, electronic instant-delivery of mail, constantly updated news reports, increased government surveillance, bizarre weather and catastrophic storms, tragedy and scandal for the British royal family, private companies taking over duties of the postal service, a greatly increased reliance and dependence on technology that he called "automation," and the generation of "contented discontents" who only derive pleasure and satisfaction from complaining.

Epilogue: The End with Charles Coulombe

eron Charles Criswell King, in his own bizarre way, symbolized the nature of fame in twentieth century America. He tried unsuccessfully to break into and find fame on Broadway and Tin Pan Alley, but these failures did not prevent him from co-authoring three books on how to succeed in those fields. The story of Criswell, in both his triumphs and defeats, is the story of a typically American quest for fame, and one that could not have happened without television. He had his fifteen minutes of fame long before Andy Warhol made his famous, frequently quoted observation on modern culture that rings even more true now in the twenty-first century. Since Criswell's day, the tube has created an army of celebrities who are "famous for being famous." He has the dubious honor of being one of the first. His story sheds a great deal of light on the American dream and the aspirations that most of us share. His story also asks, explores, but can't answer the eternal question of "What is the true measure of success?"

Criswell's relative fame in the early stages of the mass-media era was an innocent, harmless symptom of the beginning and continuation of the blurring of the razor-thin line between News with factual information and Entertainment fiction disguised as News in the late-twentieth century. That line (re: Fairness Doctrine) has now been all but obliterated in the twenty-first century. His willingness to merely "make things up" and pass them off as the truth and also proclaim himself a success, even after continuous relative failures, shows some of the original, seemingly innocuous roots of the current societal climate of harmful and unrestrained fake news, alternative facts, and conspiracy theories. The spread of unintentional and intentional misinformation and disinformation aided by the exponential growth of information and media access has led to the current sad state of affairs of an unquenchable thirst for infotainment. Not facts. The old and wise adage of, "Don't be so quick to believe what you hear because lies spread faster than the truth." and the often incorrectly attributed to Mark Twain quote, "A lie can travel around the world and back again while the truth is lacing up its boots." couldn't be more true now and shows no sign of slowing in the future.

And in closing I would like to say, oh my friend, when all else is lost, remember the wonderful future still remains. I'll be lonely without you and may all your shattered dreams be mended by morning and may success overtake you overnight. Goodnight my dearest friend and God bless you.

Cruswell

Biographies

FORREST ACKERMAN was a leading expert on science fiction, horror, and fantasy films, a founder of science fiction fandom, as well as a magazine editor, science fiction writer, and literary agent for Ed Wood.

WARREN BEATH has authored books on the death of James Dean due to his childhood born obsession with the rebel actor's demise after seeing a crash photo on the cover of a tabloid. He is also a horror fiction author and avid fan and follower of Criswell.

CONRAD BROOKS was an actor and appeared in a number of Ed Wood productions.

CHARLES COULOMBE lived with his family in Criswell's apartment building, knew him well, and threw a party in his honor on August 18th, 1999. He moved with his parents to Hollywood at age six and has been called "the youngest member of the Ed Wood set" because of his living under the Criswell roof and his recollections of that time. Coulombe is a now a historian, lecturer, and author.

JOHN GILMORE was an actor, screenwriter, director, author, and has been called "the quintessential L.A. noir writer." He claims to have met Criswell through Ed Wood at the time he was writing adult books.

VALDA HANSEN was an actress that appeared with Criswell in the Ed Wood film, *Revenge of the Dead* aka *Night of the Ghouls*.

THE AMAZING KRESKIN has had a six decade career as a bona fide Mentalist or thought reader. He has had a television series, his own board game by Milton Bradley, twenty published books, and a major motion picture inspired by his work.

VERNON KOENIG fell into Criswell's orbit as a youth when his father went to work for him selling Criswell Family Formula vitamins.

VERNE LANGDON was a musician, producer, composer, writer, legendary horror make-up and mask designer with Don Post studios, as well as a professional wrestler. He was introduced to Criswell by Mae West at her home.

PAUL MARCO was an actor that became acquainted with Criswell through working with Ed Wood. They became collaborators, traveling companions, and very close friends. He was also a lifelong friend to Criswell's wife, Halo Meadows.

DR. MYSTERIAN was a brilliant divinity student heavily influenced by Criswell when a freak accident caused him to become beset with visions of the future, including one showing him the exact date of his own death.

MAILA NURMI (VAMPIRA) met Criswell while she was at the height of her TV career hosting late-night movies thus becoming the first glamour ghoul and horror movie host. She appeared in *Plan 9 From Outer Space* with Cris and they were lifelong friends.

CLAUDIA POLIFRONIO met Criswell at the height of his fame and lived in the Criswell apartments with her mother and brother. She was the art director for his TV show and became a close friend and confidant of Cris and Halo.

Bibliography

Brinkman, Tom. "Criswell Predicts: Fate & Spaceway." *The Digest Enthusiast Book Four.* Larque Press, 2016.

——. *Bad Mags Volume One.* Headpress, 2008.

——. *On the Rack Issue #1*, Badmags, Winter/Spring 2009.

Brooks, Conrad. "Criswell Predicts." *Cult Movies*, Issue #11.

Coulombe, Charles A. *The Muse in the Bottle.* Citadel Press Books, 2002.

——. *Vicars of Christ.* Citadel Press Books, 2003.

Criswell, Jeron King. "Criswell Predicts" *Fate.* Clark Publishing Company, July 1949.

——. "Criswell Predicts for 1949" *Fate.* Winter 1949.

——. "Criswell Predicts" *Fate.* March 1951.

——. "Prophecies I Have Heard" *Fate.* April 1953.

——. "Criswell Predicts on Outer Space." *Spaceway.* Fantasy Publishing Company Inc., February 1955.

——. "Criswell Predicts: The Dying Planet." *Spaceway.* April 1955.

——. "Criswell Predicts on First Moon Flight." *Spaceway.* June 1955.

——. "Criswell Predicts Bottomless." *Hippies.* Seven Seventy Publishers, July 1967.

——. *Criswell Predicts from Now to the Year 2000!* Droke House Distributed by Grosset & Dunlap, 1968.

——. "Criswell Predicts Your Next Ten Years." *Saga: The Magazine for Men.* Gambi Publications Inc., November 1969.

——. *Your Next Ten Years; Criswell Predicts.* Droke House, 1969.

——. *I Predict.* Peacock Press, 1971.

——. *Criswell's Forbidden Predictions; Based on Nostradamus and the Tarot.* Droke House/Hallux, 1972.

———. "Predictions for 1973 and Beyond." *Mystique Magazine.* Picture Books Inc., 1973.

Edwards, Frank. *Strange World.* Lyle Stuart Inc., 1964.

Frazier, Kendrick. "Criswell Predicts: A Quick Look Back" *The Skeptical Inquirer.* Committee for Scientific Investigation of Claims of the Paranormal, Fall 1983.

Fuller, Curtis. "I See by the Papers." *Fate.* February 1983.

Grey, Rudolph. *Nightmare of Ecstasy: The Life and Art of Edward D. Wood, Jr.* Feral House Press, 1992.

Hayes, David C. *Muddled Mind: The Complete Works of Edward D. Wood, Jr.* Ramble House, 2001.

Howard, Louise and Criswell, Jeron. *How to Crash Broadway; The Authoritative Handbook for a Successful Theatrical Career.* Howard & Criswell, 1939.

———. *How Your Play Can Crash Broadway; The Authoritative Handbook for a Successful Play-Writing Career.* Howard & Criswell, 1939.

Jones, Arthur. *How to Crash Tin-Pan Alley; The Authoritative Handbook for a Successful Songwriting Career, as told by Arthur Jones to Louise Howard and Jeron Criswell.* Howard & Criswell, 1939.

Kemp, Earl. "The Bela Tolls for You" *el12.* February 2004.

Lennig, Arthur. *The Immortal Count; The Life and Films of Bela Lugosi.* The University Press of Kentucky, 2003.

Philbin, Regis. *I'm Only One Man.* Hyperion, 1995.

Slatzer, Robert F. *The Life and Curious Death of Marilyn Monroe.* Pinnacle Books, 1974.

Stormont, Gil R. *History of Gibson County Indiana; Her People, Industries and Institutions.* B.F. Bowen & Co., Inc., 1914.

Talbot, Margaret. *The Entertainer: Movies, Magic, and My Father's Twentieth Century.* Riverhead Books, 2012.

Teutsch, Matthew. "Holloway House and the Black Literary
   Underground" *Black Perspectives* Blog, 2019.
Webster, Robert N. "Editorial" *Fate.* Winter 1949.
Wilde, Oscar. *The Picture of Dorian Gray.* 1890.
Wireman, Charles F. "Panic on Celluloid" *Spaceway.* February 1955.
——. "Jeron King Criswell" *Spaceway.* April 1955.
Wood Jr., Ed. *Hollywood Rat Race.* Four Walls Eight Windows, 1998.

Filmography

2004

Ed Wood	Touchstone/New Line; Jeffery Jones as Criswell, Audio from *Plan 9* introduction; Special Edition DVD
Orgy of the Dead	Rhino Home Video; The Emperor, Narrator; Special Edition DVD

2005

Plan 9 From Outer Space	Legend Films; Himself, Narrator; Special Edition DVD, Colorized

2009

The Weird World of Weird	Something Weird Video; Himself; Special Edition DVD-R Original television air date 1970

Sound Recordings

1955

"What's in the Future? Criswell Predicts 1955"
Philco; 12" 78 rpm one-sided LP

1963

"Final Curtain" read by Criswell & "The Day the Mummies Danced" read by Tor Johnson
Written, Directed, & Produced by Edward D. Wood, Jr. Unreleased

1969

The Legendary Criswell Predicts! (Your Incredible Future)
Horoscope Records; 12" 33 1/3 rpm LP

1978

Plan 9 From Outer Space
Pendulum-Eros; Soundtrack LP

1989

Plan 9 From Outer Space
Performance Records; Soundtrack LP & CD

1992

Orgy of the Dead
Strangelove; Soundtrack release on CD

1995

"Someone Walked Over My Grave" by Criswell & "Home on the Strange" by Paul Marco
Dionysus Records; 7" 45 rpm single

Acknowledgements

Special thanks to Al Doshna, Charles Coulombe, and Warren Beath for all of their indispensable help, research, sharing of knowledge, and encouragement.

I'm much obliged to David Kerekes at Headpress for invaluable input, guidance, and taking a chance on a first time hack writer and thanks for the spot-on proofreading of Gareth Wilson.

Thanks for information, assistance, time, and use of valuable materials: Jason Insalaco, Judith Scobee, John Whalen, The Amazing Kreskin, John Gilmore, Tom Brinkmann, Verne Langdon, Tom Hatten, Carol Nachtwey Shook, Maila Nurmi, Dana Gould, Paul Marco, Vernon Koenig, Scott Seely, Gregory "Lance" Barton, Conrad Brooks, Jeffrey Jones, June Wilkinson, Bob Blackburn, Greg Dwizer, Steve Apostolof, Jordon Todorov, Joe Blevins, Leslie Morris, Terri Sadler, Claudia Polifronio, John and Susan Polifronio, Ewing "Lucky" Brown, Lita Bowman, R. Christian Anderson PhD, Bela G. Lugosi, Anthony Cardoza, David Ward, Monte Wolverton, Basil Wolverton, Sam Kopetsky, Ted V. Mikels, Brett Thompson, Ron Borst, Mark Flatman, Mark Kratzman, Shawn Monday, Jake Royal, Michael Copner, Buddy Barnett, Jon Doucette, Shane Wilson, Don Hoke, Liam Kemp, Mark Kratzner, Steven Kiviat, The Gibson County Historical Society, Dr. Mysterian, Mister Lobo, Owen Leitsch, Earl Kemp, Bob Hanks, Ken Hollings, James J. J. Wilson, *Filmfax* magazine, Corey Recko, Patrick Langdon, Scott Michaels, Aaron Rosenberg, Vasily Shumov, Tor Hershman, The South Carolina Room at the Anderson County Library, Andrew Honigman-*FATE* magazine, Bill Hamilton, Suzanne Mueller, Gary Rhodes, Max Sparber, Rylan Bachman, Joseph A. Ziemba, Ben Ohmart, Jim Clatterbaugh, Michael and Steven Kronenberg, Tequila Mockingbird, Andre Coulombe, Curtis Harrington, Mary Jo Newman, Roy Harris, Nieal Grewal, Justin Case, Doyle Wildersin, Dave DelVal, Pedro de Marco, Moose Holmes, Mike Bates, David "the Rock" Nelson, John Whisler, Daniel McVey, Stacya Silverman, and Justin Time.

This project was informed, improved, and inspired by the works of many writers:

Charles Coulombe, Warren Beath, K. W. Jeter, David C. Hayes, Rudolph Grey, Charles F. Wireman, John Whalen, J. K. Criswell, Louise Howard, Adam Parfrey, Billy Childish, John Mosburg, Michael Copner, Buddy Barnett, Patrick Smith, David Wentink, Gary Rhodes, Bob Blackburn, Greg Dwizer, Joe Blevins, David Huggins, David Kerekes, Gregory "Lance" Barton, John Gilmore, Alan Doshna, Tom Brinkmann, Anna Merlan, Gil R. Stormont, Jenkin Lloyd Jones, David de Clue, Verne Langdon, Judith Scobee, Edward D. Wood, Jr., Earl Kemp, Mark Travis, Jeff Lee, Robert F. Slatzer, Ken Hollings, Max Sparber, Stacya Silverman, Margaret Talbot, Frank Edwards, Titus Moede, Matthew Teutsch, Arthur Lennig, Frank Slatzer, and Leo Guild.

Special thanks to my parents, Edwin Keith and Donna Canfield for teaching me to enrich my knowledge and understanding of life and the world through reading.

Forbidden Predictions is an "internet" book. A great deal of the information in it was found on the world-wide-web by searching various databases, genealogies, library listings, newspaper archives, fan sites, blogs, wikis, online auctions, and social media. I also sent and responded to hundreds of emails contacting anyone I could that had known Criswell or had any information about him. My laptop computer was an important tool in the composition of the manuscript and book. I traveled quite extensively and being able to have the manuscript, research materials, photos, etc. . . on my laptop and in my backpack was a tremendous help and a wonder of our times.

Criswell didn't predict the personal computer, the smart phone, or the internet. As like most people living in the mid-to-late twentieth century, Criswell saw the future of computers as the massive "Super Computer" that would control everything in a benevolent and extremely efficient manner, making humankind destined for a life of leisure that was pleasant and fulfilling. Certainly, another inaccurate prediction.

January 1959, Criswell, Halo, Buttercup, and Paul Marco in front of the Criswell's Apartments. Courtesy of Jason Insalaco.

December 1966, Unknown persons, Paul Marco & Criswell. Courtesy of Jason Insalaco.

August 1968, Unknown persons with Criswell center and Halo behind him with Maria Graciette to her right and Judy Canova in blue. Courtesy of Jason Insalaco.

Stephen C. Apostolof aka A.C. Stevens, Unknown and Criswell. Stephen C. Apostolof Estate.

April 1969, Criswell, Judy Canova, and unknown persons. Courtesy of Jason Insalaco.

April 1969, Criswell, Judy Canova, and unknown man
with Paul Marco. Courtesy of Jason Insalaco.

April 1969, Criswell, unknown man, and Judy Canova. Courtesy of Jason Insalaco.

May 1969, Criswell and Judy Scobee. Courtesy of Judith Scobee.

May 1969, Criswell in yard of Criswell's Apartments.
Courtesy of Judith Scobee.

October 1969, Criswell and unknown young
men. Courtesy of Jason Insalaco.

October 1969,
Criswell, child,
Judy Canova, and
unknown persons.
Courtesy of
Jason Insalaco.

February 1972, Kenne Duncan's funeral. Paul Marco,
Kathy Wood, Criswell, Ed Wood, Buddy Hyde.

February 1972, Kenne Duncan's funeral. Criswell and Paul Marco with Mae West's Cadillac Limo she gifted to Criswell. Courtesy of Jason Insalaco.

1972, Ed Wood, David De Merring, Criswell, unknown woman, and Stephen C. Apostolof aka A.C. Stevens. Stephen C. Apostolof Estate.

Paul Marco, unknown young man and Criswell. Courtesy of Jason Insalaco.

February 1979, Ed Wood's wake. Criswell, unknown persons, Kathy Wood, Minister David De Merring, unknown, Paul Marco. Courtesy of Estate of Kathy Wood.

February 1979, Ed Wood's wake. Criswell, Kathy Wood, Minister
David De Merring, Courtesy of Estate of Kathy Wood.

February 1955, *Spaceway
Science Fiction* pulp cover.

June 1955, *Spaceway
Science Fiction* pulp cover.

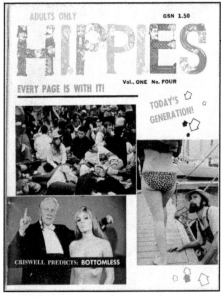

July 1967, *Hippies* magazine
cover. Titus Moody with beard.

Index

Linn, Roberta, 205
Lipkind, Dr. O., 34
Live Again (stageplay), 34, 57, 59, 285, 295
Lloyd, Harold Jr., 164
London, Jack (producer), 195
Long Beach Press-Telegram (newspaper), 102, 104, 107, 109, 319
Long Gray Line, The (film), 135, 136
Look to Heaven (stageplay), 59
Lopez, Trini, 263
Lopez, Vincent, 160
Lord, William, 35
Louis, Joe, 212
Love Life of Dorian Gray (stageplay), 53, 58, 59
Loves of Liberace, The (book), 88
Lowell, Linda, 286
Lowery, Nancy, 232
Lowery, Robert, 232
Lugosi, Bela, 66, 91, 117, 126, 131, 142, 145, 146, 163, 178, 182, 186, 187, 191, 224, 338, 339, 341–343, 348, 350, 354,
Lynch, Tony, 267

Macombo (night club), 130
Macy, Bill, 318
Mama Black Widow (book), 90
Manlove, Dudley, 183, 191
Mann, May, 217
Mansfield, Jane, 241, 246, 263, 264, 323
Marco, Paul, 5, 118, 131, 142, 178, 183, 186–191, 194, 205, 206, 240, 241, 285, 288, 295, 299–301, 310, 318, 320, 325, 326,

329, 339, 343, 348, 359, 365
Marie, Lisa, 341
Marilyn (book), 130
Marilyn Files, The (book), 130
Martin, Derek, 318
Martin, Dewan, 205
Martin, Mary, 115
Martin, Paul, 49
Marvin, Gene, 323
Marx, Groucho, 87, 164, 179, 323
Marx, Harpo, 29
Marx, Melinda, 229
Mason, Tom, 182, 183, 186, 192
Maxwell, Elsa, 33, 61, 62
McCarthy, Andrew, 120
McKinnon, Mona, 183, 194
McMahon, Ed, 229
Medved, Harry, 329, 330
Medved, Michael, 329, 330
Menjou, Adolphe, 310
Merman, Ethyl, 267, 284
Merrill, Bob, 35
Merrill, Buddy, 153
Merring, Minister David De, 192
Meyer, Jim, 341
Michaels, Scott, 350
Mickey Mouse (television), 195, 258
Mikels, Ted V., 225, 366
Miller, Henry, 119
Miller, Max, 99
Mind Cosmology (book), 75
Minugh, Carl, 83
Moede, Titus (Moody), 299, 300
Mockingbird, Tequila, 2, 350
Mondo Cane (film), 153
Monich, Jo, 210
Monroe, Marilyn,

127–130
Montagu, Mercia, 77
Moore, Duke, 183, 189, 191
Moore, Terry, 287
Moorehead, Agnes, 298
Morris, Bentley, 89, 90
Morrison, Patricia, 310
Morse, Robert, 289
Mosby, Aline, 95
Mother Shipton, 85, 260, 270
Murder in the Old Red Barn (stageplay), 30, 31
Murphy, Audie, 311
Murphy, Bridey, 303, 312
Murray, Ken, 218
Murray, Mae, 222
Musso and Frank's (restaurant), 130, 251
Mussolini, Benito, 94
Mysterian, Dr., 158, 339, 345, 354, 359

Nader, Ralph, 299
Napoleon, 156
National Enquirer (tabloid), 172, 291
Necromania: A Tale of Weird Love (film), 294, 346
Navarro, Ramon, 222
New York's World Fair, 50
Newhart, Bob, 216
Newman, Paul, 261, 321
Niagara (film), 128
Nicholson, Jack, 206
Night of the Ghouls (film), 193, 194, 325, 335, 338, 340, 358
Night Tide (film), 58
Nightmare of Ecstasy; The Life and Art of Edward D. Wood, Jr. (book), 339
Nixon, Richard, 279, 289, 309, 319
Noble, Ann, 285, 286
Norvell, Anthony (Trupo,

CPSIA information can be obtained
at www.ICGtesting.com
Printed in the USA
JSHW071355220123
36478JS00003B/3